Paths to God

"Ram Dass makes the Bhagavad Gita . . . easily accessible and practical in how we can touch the deep mystery and live a good life in modern times."

—Angeles Arrien, Ph.D., author of *The Four-Fold Way* and *Signs of Life*

"What a blessing: Ram Dass on the Bhagavad Gita. Who better to lead the Western mind into the profound depths of this spiritual classic. With wisdom, humor, and great compassion, *Paths to God* illuminates the liberating power of the Gita—a rare gift in these unsettled times."

—Joseph Goldstein, author of *One Dharma: The Emerging Western Buddhism*

"Ram Dass is the perfect person to relate the timeless wisdom of the Bhagavad Gita to the real challenges, joys, and sorrows of our present time. Through offering a wide variety of approaches to spiritual happiness, *Paths to God* is one of the most inclusive and inviting books available to us."

—Sharon Salzberg, author of *Faith: Trusting Your Own Deepest Experience*

Books by Ram Dass

Identification and Child Rearing (Richard Alpert) with R. Sears
and L. Rau (Stanford University Press, early 1960s)
The Psychedelic Experience (Richard Alpert) with Timothy Leary
and Ralph Metzner (University Books, 1964)
LSD (Richard Alpert) with S. Cohen and L. Shiller (New American
Library, 1966)
Be Here Now (Lama Foundation; Crown Books, 1971)
The Only Dance There Is (Anchor Books, 1974)
Grist for the Mill with Stephen Levine (Unity Press, 1976;
new edition by Celestial Arts, 1987)
Journey of Awakening (Bantam Books, 1978)
Miracle of Love (Dutton, 1979; new edition by Hanuman Foundation,
1996)
How Can I Help? with Paul Gorman (Alfred Knopf, 1985)
Compassion in Action with Mirabai Bush (Bell Tower, 1992)
Still Here: Embracing Aging, Changing and Dying (Riverhead Books, 2000)
One-Liners: A Mini-Manual for a Spiritual Life (Bell Tower, 2002)
Paths to God: Living the Bhagavad Gita (Harmony, 2004)

LIVING THE BHAGAVAD GIT

Ram Dass

Three Rivers Press ⚓ New York

Paths to God

LIVING THE BHAGAVAD GIT

Copyright © 2004 by Ram Dass

Foreword by Marlene Roeder
"Buddhist Mealtime" by Joseph Goldstein
"Mindfulness Meditation on Food" by Jack Kornfield

Originally published in hardcover in the United States
by Harmony Books, an imprint of the Crown Publishing Group,
a division of Random House, Inc., New York, in 2004.

Library of Congress Cataloging-in-Publication Data

Ram Dass.
  Paths to god : living the Bhagavad Gita / Ram Dass.—1st ed.
  1. Bhagavadgåitåa—Criticism, interpretation, etc. 2. Yoga. I. Title.
BL1138.66.R345 2004
294.5'436—dc22   2004015183

ISBN-13: 978-1-4000-5403-9
ISBN-10: 1-4000-5403-6

Printed in the United States of America

Design by Lauren Dong

20

First Paperback Edition

To my gurus . . .

Acknowledgments

There are three women whose contributions have made this book possible—the Three Graces: Jo Anne Baughan, Gita (Lee) Brady, and Parvati (Betty) O'Neill. Without the gifts of each of them, this book could not have happened.

At many gatherings nowadays, there is what is called a "Keeper of the Heart"—someone whose task it is to hold an open, loving space, no matter what is going on around her. Jo Anne has been the Keeper of the Heart for this book. In a thousand unsung ways, she has literally loved this book into being.

Gita created both the glossary and the resources guide for this book, starting from a shoe box full of random clippings and scribblings. Out of her deep familiarity with spiritual literature, she has spun straw into gold and created a spiritual storehouse full of all sorts of rich and tasty treats.

Parvati, who was one of the students at Ram Dass's Naropa workshop, phoned to offer her help at a crucial moment, when the transcription of the lectures was hopelessly stalled. Not only did she transcribe some of the tapes, but she sent along a treasure of Naropa memorabilia, including some personal photos of the event and a copy of the original syllabus, which we'd given up hope of finding. Parvati died of cancer in 2001. Her gift lives on in this book.

In addition to Jo Anne, Gita, and Parvati, we also want to extend thanks to the staff members of Naropa University for their encouragement and cooperation, and special thanks to Richard Chamberlain of Naropa's Development Office for somehow managing to lay his hands on a copy of the original 1974 summer schedule, which provided a wealth of information about the event. Our thanks to Joseph Goldstein and to Jack Kornfield for generously allowing us to use their food meditations in this book; their practices added a fresh dimension to the workshop, and now to this book as well. And thanks to Rameshwar Das for being our "eyes" at the workshop, and for sharing some of the photographs he took there.

When, at the last moment, we found we needed to track down sources for the many quotes that had been included in the Naropa lectures, a number of volunteers stepped forward to help with the task. Our thanks to all of those who joined the treasure hunt: James Beane, Carolyn Behnke, Caroline Bloomfield, Denise Coates, Stefani Cohen, Robin Collins, Aaron Crawford, Nonda Gaylord, Deborah Hopping, Linda Kleckner, Dale Martin, Bobbie Mims, Ralf Mrutzek, Kathleen Murphy, Linda Nicholas, Sharon and Larry Roll, George T. Stergiou Jr., and Paul Wilson.

And, of course, most of all, thanks to Neem Karoli Baba, for gracing us all with parts in this dance. *Ki jay!*

Contents

BACKWARD AND FOREWORD
Or . . .
Where This Book Came from, and How It
Might Be Used

This book has a curious history. It grew out of a workshop called "The Yogas of the Bhagavad Gita" that Ram Dass taught in the summer of 1974. He presented the workshop as part of the curriculum for a summer session at the newly established Naropa Institute (now Naropa University) in Boulder, Colorado.

Naropa was founded by Chögyam Trungpa Rinpoche, a Tibetan Tulku and Vajrayana master. Trungpa was trained in the philosophical and meditative traditions of two branches of Tibetan Buddhism—the Kargyu and Nyingma sects—and he was one of the first teachers to begin introducing Tibetan practices to the West.

Naropa's aim was to explore the teachings of Eastern religious traditions within a rigorous, Western academic environment. The program for the summer session announced, "The purpose of Naropa Institute is to provide an environment in which the Eastern and Western intellectual traditions can interact and in which these disciplines can be grounded in the personal experience and practice of staff and students. All of the staff members are involved in the practice of some discipline related to psychological and spiritual growth. It is this direct experience which can form the sound basis for integrating the complementary intellectual and sensory-intuitive approaches to living in the world."

In other words, Naropa set out to meet the Western academic establishment on its own terms, to become an accredited, degree-granting institution of higher learning, but one that would offer degrees in fields like "Buddhist Studies, Exploration of Self and Society, and a cross-cultural, inter-disciplinary combination of the two." Courses included "not only the more intellectual disciplines—the humanities and the social and physical sciences—but also meditation, sensory awareness, dance, t'ai ch'i chuan, theater, art, and music." You could get credit toward a B.A. from Naropa for taking Ram Dass's workshop.

Ram Dass supported the establishment of Naropa because he was interested in the experiment that such an institution represented. But more than that, Ram Dass honored the teachings and traditions of Trungpa Rinpoche, and wanted to help them take root in the West. And so, in June and July of 1974, he joined the faculty for the summer session that would inaugurate Naropa.

That summer at Naropa brought together an outstanding cast of teachers. Besides Ram Dass and Trungpa Rinpoche, the faculty included Allen Ginsberg, Gregory Bateson, José Arguelles, Jack Kornfield, Ben Weaver, and some two dozen others. Ram Dass's own staff of teaching assistants included Krishna Das, Joseph Goldstein, Rameshwar Das, Mirabai Bush, Paul Gorman, and Ram Dev. Mirabai called that summer at Naropa "the seedpod" for the teachings that would shape the growing presence of Eastern spirituality in the West. There were courses in Tibetan and Theravadan Buddhism, in the Sanskrit and Mongolian languages, in Tantric literature and Japanese art—even in artificial intelligence (which was distinctly cutting edge in 1974!). One of the participants called that summer at Naropa "the Hindu-Buddhist Woodstock."

And in the program for the summer session, under the heading "Modes of Self-Exploration," was listed Ram Dass's course, "The Yogas of the Bhagavad Gita." The course description read: "The Bhagavad Gita (The Song of God) is both one of the most sacred books in India and also one of the most profound statements of yoga. In the West many of us find that karma yoga is the most suitable practice, and the Bhagavad Gita is unparalleled as a statement of this form, i.e., the yoga of conscious service. Through reflection on the text and the many commentaries (Krishna Prem, Gandhi, etc.), we can evolve a perceptual framework which allows us to transmute daily life experience into a vehicle for liberation."

Ram Dass's workshop was held in a building on Pearl Street in downtown Boulder. Photos and videos show a plain, whitewashed, cement-block building. There was a big stage, Ram Dass recalls, to accommodate the many musicians who took part in the program at one time or another (including K. K. Sah,* an extraordinary kirtan singer, who came from India for the workshop).

Naropa essentially offered Ram Dass free rein as to the topic for his workshop; so why did he choose to teach about the Gita? Ram Dass says, "Maharajji was always giving away copies of two books: The Ramayana and the Bhagavad Gita. Since those were the books he seemed to think were most important, I felt it behooved me to learn as much as I could about them. Through being around Maharajji and spending so much time at his temples, I felt I had absorbed at least some understanding of the Ramayana. Teaching this course at Naropa seemed like an opportunity to plumb more deeply into the other book, the Gita."

Ram Dass had a second motive for focusing on the Gita, as the course description suggests, and that was his appreciation for its unique appropriateness to our own cultural circumstances. The philosophy of the Gita is one that turns out to be especially suitable for us in the West, because instead of encouraging us to turn away from the world, it turns our lives *in* the world into our spiritual work. We don't have much room in our society for wandering mendicant monks, or many caves where sadhus can hang out. We're a culture of "doers," and so, as the course description pointed out, "Many of us find that karma yoga is the most suitable practice."

---

* K. K. was a lifelong devotee of Neem Karoli Baba, and he was present when Ram Dass first met Maharajji. It was to K. K.'s home in Nainital that Ram Dass was taken following that first meeting.

Ram Dass prepared intensively for the seminar. He had an old school bus, which he'd outfitted as a camper,* and he spent the two months before the workshop living alone, out in the desert, immersing himself in the Gita. He spent his time reading the Gita, meditating on the Gita, studying commentaries on the Gita. He had with him some half dozen or so different translations of the Gita, and he read and reread them all. He typed out the text of the Gita, with big spaces between each of the verses, where he wrote comments about the slokas. He stayed at Organ Pipe Cactus National Monument in Arizona for a while, and then at Joshua Tree National Park in California; he said, "I gave the first version of the Gita lectures to the jackrabbits that were hanging around the bus."

At Naropa, Ram Dass's class alternated evenings with a class called "The Tibetan Buddhist Path," taught by Trungpa Rinpoche. Although Ram Dass and Rinpoche deeply respected one another, their teachings were widely divergent in style and approach. Trungpa's teachings were rooted in his lineage, and they followed a traditional Buddhist intellectual approach, with exact categories and precise definitions. Ram Dass's teachings were devotional, rooted in the intuitive and less tightly structured. Ram Dass said, "Trungpa was teaching about meditation and emptiness, and I was teaching about devotion and the guru. The students felt like they were at a tennis match!"

There were over a thousand registered students in Ram Dass's workshop. Although students were supposed to register for one course or the other, there were many "crossover" students who came to Ram Dass's workshop and vice versa; and while most of them came simply to hear what Ram Dass had to say, some were Trungpa parti-

---

* Ultimately, the school bus wound up parked at the Lama Foundation, a spiritual community in the mountains outside of Taos, New Mexico, where it housed the community's sole telephone and was used as office space for the Lama staff. In a fierce forest fire which swept through Lama in 1996, the bus was one of the few structures that was not totally destroyed; however, the side of the bus that had faced the fire was burned black, while the other side was unscorched—an interesting symbolic close to its story.

sans who came to needle Ram Dass. Ram Dass remarked at one point that he had received "lots of letters from you, with many qualitative judgments about me."

There were no ill feelings between the two teachers; in fact, at the end of the summer Trungpa offered Ram Dass a place on the Naropa faculty. Trungpa said that that kind of diversity was good for the students. But the students themselves were more factional in their feelings; the conflicts came to be known around Naropa as "the Holy Wars."

In an interesting way, those circumstances turned out to be uniquely fortunate for Ram Dass's workshop. Rameshwar Das wrote, "The confluence of Buddhism, Hinduism and America in Boulder that summer was chaotic but profoundly unifying. Trungpa and Ram Dass teasing each other on stage provided great humor and lightness, and the contrast between Buddhist clarity of intellect and the Bhakti heart has never been better illumined." The situation imposed a more rigorous standard of expression on Ram Dass's teaching. If preparing for the workshop deepened Ram Dass's *understanding* of the Gita, teaching the workshop honed his *formulation* of that understanding.

In teaching about the Gita, Ram Dass was exploring one of the most significant and influential books in Indian culture. Mahatma Gandhi wrote of the Gita, "When doubts haunt me, when disappointments stare me in the face and I see no ray of hope on the horizon, I turn to the Bhagavad Gita and find a verse to comfort me, and I immediately begin to smile in the midst of overwhelming sorrow. Those who meditate on the Gita will derive fresh joy and new meaning from it every day."

The influence of the Gita has not been limited to India; it has touched the West as well. Henry David Thoreau said that in comparison with the Gita, "our modern world and its literature seem puny and trivial." Ralph Waldo Emerson called it "the first of books . . . the voice of an old intelligence."

It is believed that the Bhagavad Gita was written sometime during the first millennium B.C., and later inserted into a much vaster and probably much older work, the Mahabharata. The Mahabharata is not, strictly speaking, Hindu *scripture* (as are the Vedas and the Upani-shads), but one of some twenty Indian epics, called the Puranas. The Puranas contain the stories of the lives of the various incarnations or living manifestations of God: there is the Brahma Purana, and the Garuda Purana, and the Linga Purana, and so on. And among those are the two so-called *Maha*puranas, or *Great* Puranas: they are the Mahabharata and the Ramayana. The two Mahapuranas are woven so deeply into the culture, life, and thought of India that one pundit said, "The Mahabharata and the Ramayana *are* India."

In the middle of that great tale of the Mahabharata we find the Bha-gavad Gita, said to contain "the essence of Hinduism." Historically speaking, the Gita did, in fact, represent Hinduism's response to cer-tain Buddhist ideas that were exerting increasing influence on Indian thought at the time. The Gita specifically addressed the Buddhist emphasis on disengagement from the world as the primary path to God. In place of that, the Gita offered a practice of *action* in the world as a method for coming into unity.

The Gita is at once an instruction manual for living a spiritual life and a profound, ecstatic vision of the ultimate nature of God. There are many beautiful English versions of the Gita, but the one chosen for the Naropa workshop was the translation by Juan Mascaro. Ram Dass said, "I picked the Mascaro text because it's delightfully easy to work with. It is, in some ways, wanting in its profundity of interpre-tation, its sophistication from a Sanskrit point of view; but it doesn't seem to have as many axes to grind as some of the other translations do. And I confess: I also chose it because it was the one that happened to be available in the temple where I lived in India in 1969, and so it was my first introduction to the Bhagavad Gita. And you know how you always get hooked on your first love!"

Although Ram Dass's lectures at Naropa (and by extension, this book) were *based* on the Gita, it would be a mistake to think that they were *about* the Gita in the usual sense. What Ram Dass offered at Naropa was not a scholarly exegesis on the Gita, or an analysis of its text, but a series of riffs on the Gita's major topics. The themes of the Gita were the launching pad for what turned out to be Ram Dass's quintessential teaching on applied Hinduism. His premise is that the Gita outlines a series of practices that taken together comprise a complete yoga for living our lives as a spiritual act. Ram Dass's accomplishment in the workshop was to shape those practices into a form that we as Westerners could understand and adopt.

This book is derived from transcriptions of the lectures Ram Dass gave at Naropa. It is both historical document and perennial philosophy. The workshop was a unique blend of metaphysics and methods, and so this book is also a rich weave of philosophy and practice. Ram Dass presents a vision of where we're going, and he also teaches us about the path for getting there.

Ram Dass's lectures were only part of the participants' experience of the workshop. Each student received a copy of a syllabus (see pages 247–281), which presented a series of experiential exercises, through which the participants could begin "bringing the Gita back home," so to speak. The introduction to the syllabus stated, "In addition to the lectures, this course includes a number of exercises designed to provide experiences which can evolve into a complete sadhana (a program of spiritual practices), based on the *Gita*." Participants set up puja tables in their rooms; they made their own malas and chanted with them. They took silent meditative walks, and they practiced hatha yoga asanas. There were eating meditations, and journal-writing exercises, and all-night chants. And every afternoon there were discussion circles, led by Ram Dass's staff of teaching assistants. In short, what the workshop provided was the opportunity and the encouragement to focus intensively for a time on cultivating the spiritual side of things; it provided a space to plunge deeply into spiritual practice.

Emerging as it did from the workshop, which was a participatory experience, this book presents you with a choice. The first possibility is to take it simply as a book to read. Great!—you'll find it's a wonderful book. It's Ram Dass's most profound teaching on the nature and practice of Hinduism, and his insights and observations will deepen your understanding of the Gita and its message.

But you'll find there is another option available. You can engage with this book in a way that makes it personal. You can take it to be a kind of do-it-yourself workshop; it can be a *path* to enter, a way of coming into a new relationship with your life. Taken that way, you'll discover that the book presents you with a delicious array of opportunities, with descriptions of practices, and little samplers of various techniques. Should you find yourself drawn to one or another of the methods, there is a wealth of resources to help you get started. The syllabus from the workshop is one such resource. There is also a supplementary syllabus (pages 283–305), comprised of some instructions and examples of practices presented during the workshop. The resources guide (page 319) will lead you to books, CDs, tapes, videos, and websites. It's a rich offering.

So what started life as a series of lectures given to a family of jackrabbits in the California desert has morphed into the book that you are holding in your hands. It's a book that represents Ram Dass's deepest wisdom about one of India's most profound spiritual texts. It shows us the way those of us here, in this contemporary Western culture, can translate the yogas taught by the Bhagavad Gita into a living spiritual practice of our own.

Marlene Roeder, editor

Offer in thy heart all thy works to me,
and see me as the End of thy love,
take refuge in the Yoga of reason,
and ever rest thy soul in me.

Bhagavad Gita, ch. 18, verse 57

Paths to God

LIVING THE BHAGAVAD GITA

Intro

...ston.

1. conflict of motives that beset human action
   clinging fetters of selfishness which check us on the path

2. subtle evasions of the lurking whispering of the heart.

3. every stage of Indian Philos. – & Gita shows they all lead to single goal.

4. practical suggestions

~~Royal Race~~
...put Race transmission (R̄ām̄ & K. avatars (later Gotama) –
is war led to Brahmans taking over.
...fratricide

as we awak. in
royal race
like ancient Egyptic
& Chaldeans.

Red ...puts	Brahmans,	Vaishyas,	Shudras	– each 'dharma' – do your own
...wth & liberation	wh. eternal immortality ancestor offering worship to ancestor inheritance rice & water or anc. goes to hell first planes	yellow same plus priests medumistic	bl. fierce gods. evil eye mesmerism	intermarriage barrier – mulatto – mule-I missed pure transmission each diff. spiritual insight & relig. id
...nishads				
...oth		mid	south	
...ture sink to soul ...piration ...th				
↓				
...danta of the Veda.				

4 gt methods
intuition
intellect
work
feeling

1. Intuition (Rajputs)

...danta – two destinies. – vos. rebirth via heaven dream rewards – death dom
until liberation dawned.

then he sees guiding hand on cycles, he is guarded, watched, provided for. &
that guardian is own Self.

~~at x roads – much conflict~~

...y 2.) Reason (Brahman) – Sankhya (Number)
using mind not soul.
piercing insight to One Being. – first cause. → differentiation
then into time & spa then space, (all divos occuring simult
cause, time & space = three great tendencies - all mirages
Only One & multiplicity is illusion.
so intellect used to disentangle us from mind –

Ram Dass's Lecture Notes: A portion of Ram Dass's handwritten notes, with an overview of some of the themes of the course.

Introduction

*T*his is a book that is based on a course about an ancient Hindu text, which was taught at a Buddhist university, by a Jew who has a great love for Christ and Muhammad—so you can imagine what you're in for!

When I say this is "about an ancient Hindu text," I don't want to mislead you. This isn't really a book "about" the Bhagavad Gita. It isn't an analysis of the Gita, or a commentary on the Gita, or anything like that. Rather, it's a series of reflections about the major themes of the Gita—themes that touch on the various yogas, or paths for coming to union with God, that the Gita investigates. It's an attempt to look at how those yogas might be relevant to our own lives, in this day and age.

The Buddhist part of the equation, Naropa, was an institution founded by Trungpa Rinpoche, a tulku of a Tibetan Buddhist lineage. But it was an institution concerned as much with the development of the intellect as with its Buddhist lineage, with scholarship as much as with tradition. And that presented me with a number of interesting challenges, because my course on the Gita was primarily concerned with issues of the heart—with the devotional and karmic-yogic aspects of life. Mine was not "the thinking man's" course.

I should point out that I'm not anti-intellectual. I think the intellect is a beautiful instrument that can be used very productively, when one isn't attached to the idea that *thinking* is what it's all about. But we are coming out of a kind of sickness here in the West, a sickness in the way in which we have *over*thought, the way in which we have been intellectually way ahead of our hearts' and our bodies' wisdom. We're just now learning how to quiet down a bit, and get it all together, which means that people who are trying to work with the intellect as their primary yoga are dealing with a very hot fire. I honor them, but it isn't my own major path.

❖

Besides feeling a little intellectually out of place, I had some other qualms about my plans for the course. In talking with Swami Muktananda (a very beautiful holy man from India) just before I went to Naropa to teach that summer, I expressed to him my feeling of presumptuousness at attempting to teach about the Gita. What could I possibly have to say about it? Most people in India probably know more about it than I do. In India, many ordinary people are great scholars, really, who have made extensive studies of the Gita. Often in India I've gotten into long, philosophical discussions about the Gita with a railway conductor, or a sweeper—people who, when they've finished with whatever job they do for a living each day, do their important work, which is studying spiritual books like the Gita or the Ramayana.

So I was telling Swami Muktananda that I thought I was being a little presumptuous in imagining that I had anything to teach about the Gita, and in response, he told me this story.

Krishna, at one stage of his incarnation as an avatar, was a beautiful, young boy (something you'll need to know to understand this tale). Now there was a great student of the Gita, an old man. He was so intent on studying the Gita that he had stopped doing all of his work; he wouldn't do anything but read the Gita all day long. Soon he and his wife were without food. His wife was very harsh with him, saying, "You have a duty to go out and bring food home for the family." She kept pressing him, making his life very difficult, but he'd just go off into the woods and study the Gita every day.

One day, as he sat in the woods studying the Gita, the old man came across a line in the book in which Krishna said, "If you offer all of your devotion to me, you need worry about nothing in the world. It will all be taken care of." And the man thought, "Well isn't that a peculiar line? I mean, here I am, totally devoted to the Gita, to Krishna, but my wife and I have no food, and she's all upset with me. It says right here that if I am devoted to the Gita, everything will be taken care of. Why isn't everything being taken care of? *Could there possibly be something wrong with the Gita?*" At that point he took his pen and drew a line through that sentence, because he wasn't sure about it.

Now at that moment, back at his house, there was a knock at the door. The wife went to the door and there stood a handsome young man, with bags of rice and of lentils and of flour—huge bags, a supply to last for many months.

The wife said, "Who are you? What is all this?"

The young man said, "This is for the family of somebody who studies the Gita."

As the young man started to carry the bags of food into the house, the wife noticed that his shirt was open, and that there was a wound on his chest, with blood oozing out of the wound. She said to him, "What happened? Who did this to you?"

He said, "This was done to me by a man studying the Gita out in the woods." He said no more, put down the bags of food, and left.

When the husband came back home and saw all the food, he asked his wife about it. She said, "You know, the most peculiar thing happened." She proceeded to tell him about the young man's visit, and she said, "When I looked at him, I saw there was blood coming out of a wound on his chest. And when I asked him how it had happened, he said it had been done by a man studying the Gita out in the woods."

At that point, Swami Muktananda told me, the old man realized what had happened, and he fainted. Because he saw that when he had underlined the book out of his sense of doubt, he had wounded the body of Krishna. Swami Muktananda said, "You see, you have to understand: The Gita isn't a book *about* Krishna—the Gita *is* Krishna." And then he said to me, "You don't have to worry about teaching the Gita—that's none of your business. The Gita will teach itself. Krishna will do it in spite of you." So I felt I was taken off the hook by Swami Muktananda.

One important reason why I agreed to teach at Naropa that summer was because I wanted to honor its founder, Chögyam Trungpa Rinpoche, and the lineage he represented. Once we here in the West began to turn our attention to consciousness and the spirit, we discovered that there were traditions that had been concerning themselves with those questions for a long, long time. Trungpa represented one of those exquisitely pure traditions or lineages.

Ram Dass and Chögyam Trungpa: Chögyam, the Tibetan founder of Naropa and a graduate of Oxford, and Ram Dass, the Harvard social scientist, would hold colloquia in the afternoons and debate the fine points of bhakti, or devotional practice, versus Tibetan Mahayana Buddhism. It was a very playful exchange, but behind the laughter both shared a deep understanding of dharma and an appreciation for one another's spiritual paths.

We in the West seem to have become very reactive toward traditional religious forms, which I think comes from the way we've seen rituals and ceremonies used as ends in themselves—as a mechanical, ritualistic priestcraft, with the living spirit gone out of it. That has certainly happened in the East, and it's happened in Western religions as well.

A lot of us now have come through a time of throwing over one tradition after another. In this culture, we've thrown over sexual traditions; we've thrown over traditional social relations concerning marriage and the family; we've thrown over traditions about economics and working conditions; we've overthrown all kinds of political traditions. In most cases, that's come out of a healthy awakening to the deadness of the existing structures. But somehow we've gotten a little lost in thinking that traditions per se are bad, when maybe what's needed is not to throw them away, but to reawaken them. I think that one of our challenges now is to become sophisticated enough not to throw out the baby with the bathwater.

I have gone to a lot of traditional religious ceremonies in both the East and the West. You go into a church or a temple, and often what you see is that everybody's going through the motions: they go through the ritual as if they were checking off their shopping lists at the supermarket. They may be singing wonderful songs about resurrection and rebirth, but nothing's happening. The ceremony and the ritual originally came out of living spirit, but that's gotten lost in the shuffle, and what's left is just the mechanical stuff.

But now if I come back to it with eyes that are tuned to other planes of consciousness, and if I can center and not get lost in my old reactions to the situation, suddenly there it all is: Living Spirit again. I think that we are all being prepared—*all* of us—to serve in that capacity of reinvesting our society with Living Spirit. And that happens through our *becoming* Living Spirit—because the only thing you really transmit to another person is your Being. The fancy words don't mean a thing.

In that awakening process we're all going through, there are various stages, levels in the evolution of consciousness, and some of those stages are characterized in the Gita, as we trace Arjuna's awakening through the eighteen chapters of the book. First there's despair, then there's possibility, then there's the beginning of awakening. Then comes the opening of the mystic vision, and the deepening of the direct experience—that's in chapters 7 through 12. Then comes the last part, which happens when the faith is strong: there's an opening to the deeper wisdom. That's the way the phases of the journey are spelled out in the Gita.

We represent among us many different levels of consciousness. It's not a matter of better or worse, we're just at various stages of the trip. Some of us are just beginning to feel the first touch of unease, a little discomfort with the way the game's been going. And at the other end of the scale, some of us are so drunk with the bliss of mystic visions that it's all we can do to stay here and not go running off to a cave!

As we move through levels of consciousness, we find that our understanding about the nature of our lives changes. Just to get the flavor of the transformation, let's listen to the statements of some of the beings who have gone the whole journey. For example, this is Jakob Böhme, the Christian mystic, speaking: "The external world, or the external life, is not a valley of suffering for those who enjoy it, but only for those who know of a higher life. The animal enjoys animal life, the intellect the intellectual realm. But he who has entered into regeneration recognizes his terrestrial existence as a burden and a prison."[1]

Kabir said: "Dancing is not for me any more. The mind no longer plays the tune. The vessel of desire is broken, the gown of desire has become frayed. Parts enough have I played; I can act no more. Friends and companions have all forsaken me. God's name alone I now have."[2]

And Thomas Merton: "The lightning flashes from east to west, illuminating the whole horizon and striking where it pleases, and at the same instant, the instant liberty of God flashes in the depths of a man's soul, and he is illumined. At that moment he sees that, though he seems to be in the middle of his journey, he has already arrived at the end. Although he is a traveler in time, he has opened his eyes for a moment in eternity."[3]

Each of those is a statement of the *possibility* inherent in human consciousness. And while some of them may be spoken in ways that are difficult for us to hear just now, perhaps in the course of exploring the Gita we will start to have a new perspective on things. We may notice that our primary identification is no longer with the plane of reality that we started out with; we may notice that we are already participants in *another* realm or plane of consciousness, which has become more real to us than the one we left behind. (This new realm, too, will turn out to be an illusion, of course . . . but that will come in its own due time.)

As we start to reperceive the nature of our lives through a book like the Gita, it gets harder to play out some of our old social roles. I remember when that began to happen for me: It was back at Harvard in the early sixties. Tim Leary and I were doing research on psychedelics under the umbrella of the university, and Harvard was getting a little concerned, because we had just ordered half a million dollars' worth of LSD from Switzerland. So the university set up a "watchdog committee." It was unheard of for faculty members to watch over each other, but Harvard was getting pretty desperate. I was on that committee, actually, and we couldn't agree on anything; finally, some of the members took things in their own hands, and arranged a public meeting to put down our work. The thrust of the meeting was that we were not being "scientific"—mainly, they said, because we were ingesting the chemicals ourselves, and how could you be a "scientist" when you were changing your perceptual viewpoint in the midst of your observations?

Now there is, in fact, a very rich tradition in psychology called "introspectionism," which deals with inner experience, but it was held in very low repute in those days because of the takeover of psychology by the behaviorists. Behaviorism had embraced physics as its model for the study of the human mind, and so it rejected anything that could not be seen from the outside. Our interest in presenting the things that were happening *inside* of us as the data in our experiments flew in the face of all that behaviorist theory.

At the meeting, Timothy took the stand and said, "You're wrong— I *am* a scientist. You people just don't understand what real science is." He argued that they were persecuting scientific inquiry because of their own preconceptions.

Now, Timothy happens to have been a darned good philosopher of science, and I think he had a very good argument, but it wasn't quite the same as mine. The most powerful things that had ever happened to me were happening to me through our Saturday night sessions with psychedelics, and somehow that was more real to me than what I was teaching on Monday, Wednesday, and Friday. I was not sure, though, that I could make the point about our scientific methodology, so I took a stance very different from Timothy's. I said, "Ladies and gentlemen, you're absolutely right. I am no longer a scientist. I'm turning in my badge. From now on, I should be considered a 'datum.' I'm the data, and you may study me, to see what happened to him who 'did that in the sixties.' You can be the scientists; you can have that role. I give it up. I really don't want it anymore."

Why didn't I want it? Because I'd discovered it's a drag. If I adopt that role, I've got to sit in intellectual judgment on everything that comes to me. I've got to say, "Will I accept this? What is its statistical likelihood? What is the probability of its recurrence?" I've got to live inside a probabilistic model, and sit with a skeptical stance of doubt.

I had realized I didn't want to do that anymore. I wanted to be at the place where, later on, when I sat in a village in India, and heard people tell me miracle stories that would set off the doubt alarms in all my Western scientific friends, I could say, "Yeah! Of course! Far out!"—and mean it! I had realized I'd rather cultivate faith than skepticism. It was a new definition of who I am.

Now, we have been talking about this whole process as a transformation, as an *evolution* of consciousness. But maybe it's less a matter of evolving or changing, than of simply acknowledging who we already are. The way I see it is that there are states of consciousness that are always available to us if we have not veiled ourselves from them through our attachment to our own thoughts. *All* of it is *always* available to *all* of us—but whether we *know* that or not (or, better, the degree to which we know it) depends on who we *think* we are. What the Gita does, then, is to present us with a template for *expanding* our definitions of who we are, and therefore for appreciating our lives in a whole new context.

P. D. Ouspensky said an interesting thing—he said: "I found that the chief difficulty for most people was to realize they really heard *new things*—that is, things that they had never heard before. They kept translating what they heard into their habitual language. They had ceased to hope and believe that there might be anything new."[4] He's reminding us of how hard it is to open to something new without immediately labeling it in terms of our old formulas, our old attachments.

I'd like to encourage you to come to our exploration of the Gita being open to the possibility of hearing something *new*—that is, being open to a new perspective, to a new understanding of how we might perceive and live our lives. The Gita *is* Krishna, remember, and Krishna is a manifestation of our own inner being, so opening to the study of the Gita will open us, in a profound way, to our own deeper selves.

◈

In what I'm going to be saying now, I'll have to assume that you're familiar with the Bhagavad Gita, at least in a general way. If you haven't read it yet, I encourage you to do so; it will only take you about three or four hours. I would suggest that you read it through that first time just as a very interesting story: Who is Krishna? Who is Arjuna? And how do they find themselves in this peculiar predicament, sitting in a chariot, out on a battlefield?

I would further suggest that you plan to read the Gita twice more. I would suggest that you read it again after we have finished our discussion in chapter 1 about the basic conflict in which Arjuna finds himself, and after you have personalized that conflict sufficiently so as to understand what his predicament is. I suggest you read it that time identifying with Arjuna; that is, once you have figured out what your own conflict is, your own spiritual struggle, then use that as the framework, and listen to Krishna telling you how it all is regarding your own battleground.

Then, when you are ready, may I suggest a third reading of the Gita, in which you read it identifying with Krishna. Because that, in fact, is *also* who you truly are.

Now, that last reading may raise some interesting problems for you. If you are Krishna, then you are the Gita. Maybe you'll be reading along, and you'll come to a line and you'll think to yourself, "I would never say that!" But the fact is, the Gita *does* say that, and we're supposed to be taking Krishna's perspective. What to do?

This is where your spiritual exercises come in, like the ones we'll be talking about or the ones in the syllabus. For instance, you might work with your perplexities through a practice like contemplation: You sit down in front of your puja table or in any quiet space; you take both the line as it's written and the line as you think it ought to be, and you sit with both those thoughts. The process will show you exactly where you're hanging on. You'll think, "I never would have said that!" Ah!— there it is. That's the one! *Who* is the "I" who would never have said that? Where is the clinging? Those are the lines that will turn out to be the richest ones for you, because they will show you where you're holding on, where your secret stash of attachment lies.

Implicit in the suggestion that you use an exercise like contemplation to go deeper with your third reading of the Gita is a more general thought about the way you might want to approach this exploration. Since this book emerged within the context of a workshop, it includes suggestions for practices, like the contemplation exercise we just talked about. The practices offer an opportunity to expand your experience outside the covers of a book, and to engage with the material in a deeper way. The practices can profoundly enrich your appreciation of the way the Gita's teachings work.

Here's another example: journal keeping. Since going through this experience will, in a way, be like going on a journey of exploration, you might want to consider keeping a journal as you make your way through this book. When you travel, don't you keep little journals of all the far-out things that happen to you? Writing about those things can be useful, in showing you transformations that might otherwise slide by or be forgotten. Something that puzzles you this week may seem crystal clear a few weeks from now, and that's interesting to notice. Or something that happens through your reading disconfirms some cherished belief system; if you don't write it down, you might selectively forget it, in order to keep your ego-sense consistent. That's why journals and diaries can be very useful devices.

(Maharajji, my guru, always kept a diary. Every day he would close himself up in his room and write two pages in his diary. Now, you might wonder, "What would a guru's diary be like? What would he write in it?" Would it be "I saw this many people today. . . . I gave them 'the touch.' . . . I spent the afternoon with Krishna and Rama and Christ. . . . Christ is looking much better these days"? What would he put in a diary? After Maharajji had left his body, we were finally shown the diaries. For each day, there would be the date, and the name of the place where Maharajji was staying; and then there would be two pages where the major events of the day were written: "Ram, Ram, Ram, Ram, Ram, Ram, Ram, Ram, Ram, Ram, Ram, Ram, Ram, Ram . . ."—on and on, for two pages. The name of God was all that seemed to have been relevant that day. And the next day. And the next.)

If you decide to keep a journal, please start right away; you'll find it's much more useful if you do it continuously, right from the outset. You can use it to record your reflections about lines in the Gita, or examples of the ways you personalize the teachings of the Gita through your own experience. You can add quotes or pictures. Some of the journals I've seen over the years are incredibly beautiful, filled with artwork, with wonderful poetry, with all the stuff of our ruminating minds.

So keeping a journal is one more way you might consider deepening your participation in this journey. There will be more suggestions as we go along, so you can jump into the whole process at whatever level of involvement feels right for you. You can simply read this book, and maybe find in it some thoughtful perspectives about the Gita and about Hinduism. Or you can personalize it, you can use it in a different way: you can dive into it as a spiritual exercise, with journals and puja tables and contemplation practices and all the meshuga stuff.

Those are all like the side trips on a tour, and you can take as many or as few of the excursions as you'd like. It's up to you to decide what feels right for you at this moment.

❖

As we read the Gita, we'll notice that it is designed in a very interesting way. Everything that really needs to be said is pretty much said in the first two chapters. After that, it's said over and over again, but with more and more exquisiteness and with more and more detail. The whole book becomes like a spiral, and we find that we see the themes of the Gita from many different vantage points as it unfolds, and as our engagement with it deepens.

This book will unfold in the same way, with ideas appearing again and again in new contexts, and with methods and practices that complement and build on one another. That whole process will keep presenting us with new perspectives and new possibilities as we go along, and each one will be an invitation to go a little deeper, something coaxing us to awaken a little more.

And if this book *really* works, it will turn out that who you are at the end of it won't be quite the same you as the one who's reading these words right now.

Context and Conflict

*B*efore we approach the Bhagavad Gita, we need to have a contextual framework for the way it fits into the Mahabharata, of which it's a part. The Mahabharata is one of the two great Indian epics (the Ramayana being the other). The Mahabharata is a *huge* book—a typical edition runs to nearly six thousand pages. It is said to be the longest literary work in the world; it is seven times the length of *The Iliad* and *The Odyssey* combined, and the only unabridged English edition runs to twelve volumes. It's thought to have been written somewhere between 500 and 200 B.C., and it covers a distant period of Indian history: tradition places the battle of Kurukshetra in 3102 B.C., although historians say it was probably more like 1400 B.C. when the events that inspired the Mahabharata took place.

At one level, the Mahabharata is an historical study of a kingdom; but at another level, it is an extraordinary *symbological* study of all human interactions, of all human emotions and motivations. It's like an incredible psychology book cast in the form of a drama, and it's written from a very conscious point of view, which means that although it can be read just for its romantic, melodramatic story line, it can also be read to uncover its deeper symbolism. And right in the middle of the Mahabharata, on the eve of the climactic battle between the kingdom's two warring families, comes the dialogue between Krishna and Arjuna that's called the Bhagavad Gita, or "the Song of God."

The story of the Mahabharata concerns the kingdom of Bharat, in northern India. The king of Bharat had two sons, Dhritarashtra and Pandu. Dhritarashtra was the elder brother, and ordinarily would have been next in line to inherit the throne after their father died; but he had been born blind, and the traditions of the time didn't allow for a blind king, so Pandu became the king instead, and ruled the kingdom.

Now, what it is that Dhritarashtra's blindness represents in the story is something that has been expounded upon with great relish by countless Hindu pundits over the centuries. Some say his blindness represents his attachment to his son, Duryodhana, which makes him blind to the dharma, blind to truth or to higher wisdom. Some say the blindness represents the nature of the human condition, which is blind because it lacks the higher intellect. The symbolism is very rich.

Pandu, the younger brother, the king, had two wives—Kunti and Madri—and he had five children by them. Of these five children (and these turn out to be the good guys, by the way—the Pandavas), Yuddhisthira was the eldest. Yuddhisthira was virtually the embodiment of dharma, although he did have one minor failing, which was that he gambled—he liked to play dice—and that, we will see, is what ultimately leads us to the predicament we find ourselves in at Kurukshetra. Bhima, Pandu's second son, was very strong and rather reckless. Arjuna, the third, was pure, noble, chivalrous, and heroic; he turns out to be our hero in the Gita. And there were two younger sons, twins by Madri.

Dhritarashtra—the elder, blind brother—had a hundred children, all by one wife. (I know—a hundred children—but we're just going to have to allow for these strange things in the Mahabharata. We make room for them in the Old Testament, with 120-year-old men having scores of children. So let's just assume that things are different in different times.) Dhritarashtra's wife, Gandhari, was incredibly devoted to him. She was so devoted that since he couldn't see, she kept her own eyes bandaged throughout her entire married life, because she said that it would be unseemly for her to see when her husband was blind. That's *devoted!*

Well, a few years into his reign, Pandu accidentally killed a Brahmin. Killing a Brahmin, even by accident, is a *very* bad thing to do, so

Ram Dass Blowing the
Conch Shell: The conch
shell is significant in
Hindu symbology; the
spiral form reflects the
upward journey of the
soul, and since the shell
is one of the articles
carried by Vishnu, the
preserver of creation,
its sound is considered
auspicious. The conch
shell is blown at the
start of rituals such as
arti to summon the
deities and to awaken the
power of Truth, which
the shell represents.

to atone for it, Pandu retired to the forest to do *tapasya* (penances),
leaving the kingdom in the care of Dhritarashtra. After some years,
while he was still away in the forest, Pandu died as the result of a
curse, and Dhritarashtra just went on ruling Bharat.

As the children grew up, Duryodhana, Dhritarashtra's eldest son,
grew more and more jealous of Yuddhisthira, the eldest son of Pandu.
You can see that the laws of succession would be a little hazy in this situation, but it looked as though Yuddhisthira, as the eldest Pandu son,
was going to be the one to inherit the kingdom whenever Dhritarashtra died—and Duryodhana wanted it for himself. He pulled every dirty
trick in the books to try to get it; the Mahabharata devotes hundreds of
pages to descriptions of all the ways Duryodhana went about scheming
to get rid of the Pandavas, so he could take over the kingdom. Finally,
Duryodhana held a huge celebration, and invited all the Pandavas to
attend. He had a magnificent palace built to house them, but he had it
made of some very flammable material, and during the night, when he

expected all the Pandavas to be asleep inside, he set the building afire. Luckily, the Pandavas had been forewarned by a loyal servant, and so they—the five boys and their mother—had escaped through an underground passage and gone off into the jungle, into hiding.

Now, just to give you a little more of the flavor of this story: While they were in hiding, living in a cave in the jungle, the Pandava boys heard that there was to be a *swayamvara,* a husband-selecting ceremony, for Draupadi, the beautiful daughter of a very high king, to find a suitable mate for her. All the princes would be there, of course, because they all wanted to marry this rich, beautiful lady.

At the gathering, a number of tasks were set for the would-be suitors: stringing a magical bow, shooting a target by looking at its reflection in a pool of water, feats like that. All the princes tried, and all the princes failed. Then this poor young Brahmin priest came along, and he easily accomplished all the tasks, one after the other. That was Arjuna in drag, of course. So Arjuna won Draupadi's hand, and he and his brothers took her and headed back to their cave in the jungle.

As they approached the cave where they were living, the boys yelled out to Kunti, their mother, Come out, Ma! See what we have brought today!

Kunti was in the cave and couldn't see her sons, but she called out, Whatever it be, share it equally among all of you. That's a good thing for a mother to say to her five children—usually! But this time it meant that all five brothers ended up being the husbands of Draupadi—she had five husbands by the mother's "boon."

Well, after some years in hiding, the Pandavas made their way back to the kingdom of Bharat, and Dhritarashtra (who wasn't a bad guy, really—it was his son who was out of control) insisted that Duryodhana give them a piece of land to rule. Duryodhana, as you'd expect, picked out the worst piece of land in the kingdom to give to the Pandavas; it had *nothing* going for it. But in spite of that, Yuddhisthira and his brothers made a go of it, and created a very good kingdom, prosperous and well ruled. That just made Duryodhana more jealous than ever, of course; he grew *insanely* jealous, and all he could think about was plotting against the Pandavas.

Duryodhana remembered that Yuddhishthira, the oldest Pandava brother, really liked playing dice, so he challenged Yuddhisthira to a dice game, and got a crooked dice player to play opposite him. The two of them played out their dice game, and in the course of it Yuddhishthira lost everything: He lost his kingdom, he forfeited his brothers into servitude, he sold Draupadi down the river—everything he had, went.

Duryodhana was ecstatic! He was so haughty about what he'd done that he had Draupadi brought in, planning to strip her naked in front of the court, to shame her. But when he went to pull off her sari, he found that no matter how many saris he pulled away, there was always one more underneath. He had piles of saris everywhere, but Draupadi was still clothed, because she was protected by the purity of the dharma. (And, of course, Krishna, whom the Pandavas had met while they were off in hiding, was helping secretly, on the side.)

When Dhritarashtra heard about the episode with Draupadi, he was so embarrassed by his son's behavior that he offered Draupadi three boons. She said, Well, for the first one, let my husbands go free, and for the second, give them back their weapons. And that's enough—I won't even need the third boon. They'll be able to take care of things from there."

Well, Dhritarashtra kept his promise and freed the Pandavas; but as soon as the brothers were free, Duryodhana sucked Yuddhisthira into another dice game. (Yuddhisthira just never seems to learn, does he?) In this dice game, the losers (who, of course, turned out to be Yuddhisthira and his four brothers) had to go off and live in the jungle for twelve years. And then, in the thirteenth year, it got even worse: They had to hide out for that whole year, because if they were found by Duryodhana during the thirteenth year, they'd have to do still *another* twelve years in the jungle. But if they made it through all that, Duryodhana promised that at the end of their exile they'd get their kingdom back.

So back they went to the jungle. They did their twelve years, and in the thirteenth year, in order to hide out, they became servants to a king in a neighboring kingdom. Duryodhana tried *everything* to find them, but he couldn't. At the end of the thirteenth year, they came back to Bharat and presented themselves before Duryodhana and said, "OK, we did it. Now we want our kingdom."

Duryodhana said, "Tough. I'm keeping it." He said, "I wouldn't even give you enough land to carry on the tip of a needle."

Now that is the background to the situation in which we find ourselves at the time when the events in the Bhagavad Gita are about to take place. That is, Duryodhana has finally pushed the Pandavas too far, and they have no choice now but to fight. Injustice has taken over their kingdom. Arjuna and his brothers have been cheated and lied to; truth has been trampled on. The dharma has to reassert itself—the good guys have to make a statement. War is their only recourse.

At this point in the story, an interesting event takes place: Arjuna and Duryodhana both go to Krishna, who happens to be God in an avataric form, and they both ask him for his help. In a kind of Solomon-like decision, Krishna says to them, "OK, here are your options: One of you can have *all* of my weapons and *all* of my armies . . . and the other one can have me, but without any armies or weapons." Arjuna immediately says, "Well, I want you—forget about the armies." His mind was turned toward God, and so he said, "All I want is God on my side."

Well, Duryodhana was *very* pleased with that! He, being the worldly, adharmic fellow, said, "That's perfect! I'm very happy. I get all the arms and all the might." So now the bad guys have this *huge* army, while the good guys have a *much* smaller force. And Krishna, although he's God, is only the *charioteer* for Arjuna—he's not even carrying a bow.

At this point, let me introduce you to a little more of Krishna's story, so we can see how he came to this moment on the battlefield. Krishna was the child of Vasudev and Devaki, and Devaki had a very mean brother named Kamsa. Kamsa was so mean that he put his own father in jail, just in order to take over the kingdom.

But mean though he was, Kamsa had a soft spot in his heart for his sister Devaki. So when she married Vasudev, Kamsa threw a big celebration for her, with a great feast, and afterward announced that he would drive the chariot himself to take the couple to their new home. While they were on their way there, however, a great voice suddenly spoke from the sky and said to Kamsa, "Beware! The eighth child of this couple will kill you."

Well, that, of course, freaked the brother completely! He was about to kill Devaki and Vasudev right on the spot, but they begged for their lives, and he finally relented. He said, OK, I won't kill you. But you'll have to agree to live in jail for the rest of your lives, and to give me all your children as soon as they're born.

What could they do? They agreed.

So Devaki and Vasudev were imprisoned, and their first seven children were taken away the minute they were born. The first six were killed by Kamsa; the seventh has a complicated story of his own, which we won't go into here.

When the time came for the eighth birth, Kamsa was especially wary. He put extra guards on duty at the prison, and he locked Vasudev and Devaki in chains. But as the time of the birth approached, the guards began to feel very sleepy, and they all dozed off. And then the baby was born. As he came out of the womb, the baby (who, of course, was Krishna) said, "Take me to Gokul, to Nanda's house, and there you will find a girl-child. Substitute me for that baby girl."

Vasudev said, "How can I take you to Gokul? The doors are locked, and I'm in chains." At that point, Vasudev's chains dropped away and the prison door flew open. Well, Vasudev felt that was a pretty clear message, so he took baby Krishna to Gokul and brought the baby girl back in his place. The guards woke up and saw the baby, and went to tell Kamsa. The wicked brother came to the cell, and thinking that the little girl was his sister's child, he grabbed the baby by her feet, planning to throw her to the floor. But as he touched her feet, she flew out of his hands and up into the sky. As she was going, she called back, "I would have killed you, but you touched my feet; and even though you did that intending to kill me, I will treat it as though you were honoring me and let you go this time." Then she disappeared up into heaven.

That left baby Govinda (which is what Krishna was called as a child) over at the other house in Gokul, where he was raised by a simple village woman—Yasoda, the wife of Nanda. As Govinda was growing up, all sorts of miracles kept happening around him, but everybody just treated them as if they were hallucinations. I mean, how could anybody believe that they had the avatar of the ages living right there, in their village!

For instance, at one point somebody came to Krishna's mother and said, "Yasoda, your little boy, Govinda, has been eating mud!"

Yasoda said, "That's terrible! Come here, Govinda—open your mouth and let me see." Govinda opened his mouth, and Yasoda looked in . . . and there inside his mouth she saw the entire universe: all the galaxies, and all the stars, and all the planets—even a little Earth, with her and Govinda on it. Yasoda freaked completely! And then, the Puranas say, "Govinda, out of the compassion of his heart, veiled her eyes again with mother love." Isn't that a beautiful image? So once again she saw only her child standing there, and she dismissed what she had seen. She said, "Why—I thought I saw . . . tsk, tsk! I'd better lie down, I think I'm feeling faint." You know how that goes.

When Govinda was still a tiny baby in the cradle, a demon was sent to kill him, and Govinda kicked the demon so hard that he went spinning into the air and was killed. The people of the village said, "Wasn't it lucky the way that hurricane came and carried the demon away, so the baby wasn't hurt?" When Krishna killed a huge poisonous snake that was living in the river, everyone said, "It's a good thing that snake drowned before it could bite Krishna." Nobody could accept what was really going on, so they found other explanations for what they were experiencing. (Sound familiar?)

But even though everybody in Gokul dismissed the *miracles,* they couldn't help being thoroughly charmed by Krishna. He was a cowherd as a boy, and he was very mischievous, very much the rascal, stealing butter, and teasing the village women. But he was hardly ever punished because he was so incredibly captivating. And, of course, he played a very good flute!

We have to understand that this is an aspect of God we're talking about here, in the same way that Jehovah is. Krishna is an expression of a certain *quality* of God. But whereas Jehovah is the righteous face of God, Krishna is the loving, playful, rascally aspect. It felt so good to be around him that wherever Krishna went, everyone wanted to hang out with him. The other cowherd boys loved him as a playmate, and all the Gopis—the milkmaids—were absolutely drunk with love for him, and followed him everywhere he went.

Krishna is perhaps the most joyful avatar we have. He was always laughing, playful, active, enthusiastic. He was like warm, radiant life itself, which is an incredible image to have of God.

Well, after a time, word of the miracles made its way to Kamsa, and he realized who this Krishna must be. So he came up with a plot. He planned a big festival, and he invited Krishna to attend. And at the festival there was a *huge* wrestler, who challenged little Krishna—little twelve-year-old Krishna—to a wrestling match. Krishna, of course, accepted the challenge, and killed the wrestler with no difficulty. Then he leaped up into the stands. He grabbed hold of his uncle and said, "Your time has come, too!" and he threw him down to the ground and killed him. He released Kamsa's father from prison, and made him king again.

But at that point Krishna had shown his hand. I mean, you just *couldn't* think of him any longer as "that little boy from down the street who causes all the mischief." So he didn't go back to Gokul after that—in fact, his whole manifestation changed at that point. He went off and built a city called Dwarka, and lived there; and from then on his role was that of a sort of kingmaker, a guide and helper to the leaders of the society. He advised on diplomacy and statecraft, but he lived as a perfect yogi, giving away everything he had, always helping everyone. And in the course of that, he befriended the Pandavas.

Now, that brings us to the point in the story where we find Krishna talking to Arjuna out on the battlefield. But just to finish Krishna's story: After this battle at Kurukshetra, when practically everybody on both sides has been killed and all one hundred of the Kurava sons have been wiped out, Gandhari, the mother of the hundred sons, is walking through the battlefield lamenting, and she meets Krishna. She says to him, "You stood by when all this was happening. You let this slaughter take place. Now there will be killing within your own family, and thirty-six years from now you yourself will be slain in the midst of warfare."

Krishna's response to that is interesting: He bows to her and says, "Thank you, Mother, for helping me to find the way out." In other words, Krishna sees that Gandhari's curse will give him the means for getting finished with his incarnation, and he takes that to be a blessing. (The Gita keeps forcing us to jump levels that way: "Oh, that's terrible!" "No, that's wonderful!" We'll see the way the book constantly flips levels on us like that, reminding us that all is not as it first seems.) Eventually, Gandhari's curse came true: As Krishna lay down to rest during a time of battle, he was killed by a hunter, who mistook him for a deer. But at the other level, that was just the ruse Krishna needed in order to drop his body; and so, as he died, Krishna thanked the hunter and blessed him, and the hunter immediately went to heaven.

So now we come back to the other main character in our cast: Arjuna. We've already seen quite a bit about him through his exploits with his brothers. Arjuna is a *kshatria* (a member of the warrior caste). He's a prince, and a pure, good son. He does his duty perfectly. He's very moral, very intelligent, but he's basically very practical and pragmatic. He's not a philosopher; he's definitely a man of action—and that makes Arjuna an appropriate mirror for our own society, because ours is that kind of active, rajasic culture.

In the situation of the battlefield, Arjuna and Duryodhana are a study in contrasts. Duryodhana is totally inflated with his own ego; all he does is to get more and more haughty—the rougher things get, the haughtier he grows. He ends up ordering the elders around, even commanding his guru what to look at, showing no respect for anyone. Arjuna, on the other hand, facing the very same crisis, takes an entirely different tack: He turns to God. And because Arjuna is very principled and because his karma is good, he's ready to go the next step: He's fit to receive higher knowledge.

Since it's our ability to empathize with Arjuna's predicament as it's laid out in the first chapter of the Gita that will decide how much significance the rest of the Gita has for us, it's worth taking the time to make sure we're clear about the various levels of meaning that the conflict represents. To begin with, here is the way the Gita lays out the scene.

> Krishna said, "See, Arjuna, the armies of the Kurus, gathered here on this field of battle." Then Arjuna saw, in both armies, fathers, grandfathers, sons, grandsons, fathers of wives, uncles, masters, brothers, companions, and friends. When Arjuna thus saw his kinsmen face to face in both lines of battle, he was overcome by grief and despair, and he spoke with a sinking heart: "When I see all my kinsmen, Krishna, who have come here on this field of battle, life goes from my limbs and they sink, and my mouth is sere and dry, a trembling overcomes my body, and my hair shudders in horror. I see forebodings of evil, Krishna."

At the first level, the predicament that that reflects is a social one: Arjuna has looked at the enemy, and he's seen that it's us. He has seen the human face of the enemy, seen that the people he's about to fight aren't some abstract evil, which he'd be happy to destroy; they're his friends and family. Here is somebody who is about to go to battle— to go to Vietnam, say, and fight the "holy war" for the United States. But then he takes a good look at the guys he's supposed to fight against, and when he looks at them he suddenly sees that they're not *them,* but *us.* All of a sudden, the whole identification with national interests is in conflict with a different identification—an identification with a moral sense of the brotherhood of man. That was really the whole issue we confronted with the Vietnam War: moral law versus social duty. At what point do people become "us" instead of "them"?

Who is "them"? I've told this story before, but it's worth repeating because it spells out the issue so beautifully. It concerns a discussion I once had with my father (this was back in the early 1970s), about a set of records I'd issued called *Love, Serve, Remember.*

My father said to me, "I saw those records you put out. They look great. But I can't understand: Why are you selling them so cheaply? You're selling six records for four and a half dollars? You could probably get fifteen dollars for those records—well, nine, anyway!"

I said, "Yeah, Dad, I know, but it only costs us four and a half dollars to produce them."

He asked, "How many have you sold?"

I said, "About ten thousand."

He said, "Would those same people have paid nine dollars for them?"

I said, "Yeah, probably they would have paid nine."

"You could have charged nine," he said, "and you only charged four-fifty? What are you, against capitalism or something?"

I tried to think how I could explain it to him. My father was a lawyer, so I said, "Dad, didn't you just try a case for Uncle Henry?"

He said, "Yeah."

I asked, "Was it a tough case?"

"Oh, you bet. Very tough," he said

"Did you win it?"

"Yeah," he said, "but I'll tell you, I had to spend a lot of time on that damn case. I was at the law library every night, I had to talk to the judge—a very difficult case."

I said, "Boy, I'll bet you charged him an arm and a leg for that one!" (My father used to charge pretty hefty fees.)

My father looked at me as if I'd gone crazy. He said, "What!—are you out of your mind?! Of course I didn't charge him—Uncle Henry is family."

I said, "Well, Dad, that's my predicament. If you show me anybody who isn't Uncle Henry, I'll happily rip him off."

Once it's all "us," it immediately changes the way we deal with other people. How can it not? And in Arjuna's case, it really *is* all family. The people he's supposed to face in battle are all relatives and teachers and friends. Arjuna might be a *kshatria,* but he doesn't want to go around killing the people he knows and loves.

There's also another side to Arjuna's reluctance about fighting against members of the family. Apart from his feelings of kinship and love for everybody on both sides of the battle, he also sees a social context to the situation: He sees the conflict as a potential breakdown of *family loyalties.* He's attached to his family not only by bonds of affection, but by binding social ties. In order to fulfill his dharma, he's being asked to set aside not only family *love* but family *loyalty,* and that flies in the face of some very powerful values in Arjuna's culture, things that were a deep part of who he saw himself to be. He's being asked to turn his back on all that, and to act out of a completely different set of motives. In other words, he's being asked to throw out the rule books and rely on what Krishna tells him to do.

The only thing that makes possible that level of transformation in our behavior is a deep inner change—a change so profound that it makes us willing to go up against things we would never have dreamed of questioning or opposing. It requires a change that shifts the very source from which our actions are determined.

After I took psilocybin for the first time, at Tim Leary's house one wintry night, I walked the few blocks to my parents' home, where I was spending the night. It was four o'clock in the morning. There had been a tremendous blizzard, and I decided to shovel the snow from my parents' walk. I felt healthy and alive, and there was all this snow, so . . . I'd shovel the walk. I started shoveling away—and suddenly my parents' faces appeared at the upstairs window. They flung open the window and they said, "Come in here, you silly idiot! Nobody shovels snow in the middle of the night!"

Now right there was the voice of authority, saying, "This is the rule. You do it this way." I had always listened to that voice. Up until then, I had been a really good boy all my life. That's how I got to be a professor at Harvard, after all—by always listening to what "they" said about things like when you should shovel the snow. But now, inside my heart, I felt this way: "You know what? It's OK to shovel snow anytime. Isn't that far out?" Buoyed up by the drug, yanked out of my cultural / social / adaptive / other-directed / Reissman-ized ways, I was connected to an inner place that was saying, "Right on, baby. Shovel snow!" So I looked at my parents, and I smiled and I waved, and I went back to shoveling the snow. And that was the beginning of the melo-drama of my life for the next few years, as I watched myself slowly moving further and further away from the culture's rites and rituals.

I think some experience like that is familiar to many of us. We found ourselves growing up within a set of traditions and cultural expectations: how you cut your hair, where you go to school, what kind of education you get, what you do with it, whom you marry, how you live after you're married, when you have children, when you don't, how much you save, how much you pay for your car, what kind of television set you have . . . on and on. Many of us found ourselves in conflict with some of those values, and we know how painful it was, and the inner wrenching we felt. That's the experience Arjuna is fac-ing at Kurukshetra, and it's significant for us when we uncover the parallel experiences in ourselves so we can empathize with him. He is hearing Christ's statement, "He who loves mother or brother more than me cannot follow me."

That's the first level of Arjuna's predicament.

But that's *only* the first level; that's just the beginning of it. The issue in the Gita isn't just a conflict between moral law and social duty, or the shedding of family ties, or a confrontation with cultural values. The game in the Gita is much bigger than that. At a deeper level, it's really about *all* of that versus higher consciousness. In other words, it's about the game of awakening, about the game of coming into Spirit. Shedding social roles is just the beginning; the changes Arjuna is going to confront will go much deeper than that.

You see, in a way all of Arjuna's arguments against fighting at Kuruk-shetra have been focused around what we might call "enlightened self-interest." He's a member of a caste, so he says, "I don't want to screw up the castes." He's a member of a family, so he says, "I want to pro-tect the family." In other words, Arjuna's arguments are based on his social roles, which means they are based on his models of himself from the outside looking in. That's the objective model, which is the model of the thinking mind. And what will be demanded of Arjuna is that he let go not only of some particular models of himself, but of his very reliance on the thinking mind out of which the models have come.

The way a culture socializes its children (and we are all products of the process) is by teaching them to rely primarily on judgments from outside themselves. To socialize a child, you need to instill in him only three basic principles: to accept his information from the outside; to look outside for his rewards; and to ignore his inner voice if it conflicts with what comes from outside authority. That's the way you train a child to be a member of a society—so that when Mother says, "Do this," you do it, even if in your heart it doesn't feel right. If you get good enough at doing that, you become a "success" in the society; if you don't, you're an outcast.

When we say, "Trust your intuition," when we start to encourage that, we're reversing the process. As we awaken, we begin to act from the inside out rather than from the outside in—and that's the transformation we're really looking for. It leads to behavior that is based not on enlightened self-interest, but on the workings of an awakened heart.

Awakening is like moving from one plane to another in the flow of consciousness, and at times it may seem that we're being forced to go against the current of the old plane in order to come into some deeper harmony with the new one. Arjuna finds himself in that kind of situation. He's still attached to all his old values, his old definitions of himself. They are in conflict with the new understanding that is beginning to unfold for him, but they're deeply ingrained, and he isn't free just to drop them at will.

That's the problem we all have with our egos. When we look closely at them, we see that our egos are just a gestalt, a constellation of thought-forms defining our universe—thoughts that tell us who we are, and who everybody else is, and how it all works. But those patterns of thought go very, very deep, and we can't just will them away. In order to move into the next level of perception of the universe, we have to extricate ourselves from that entire web of thought-forms. We have to slip out of it. The predicament is that the web of thought was designed precisely to keep us *in* it; it's not going to let us go so easily. And that's where the work of the spiritual journey comes in. We look for practices that will give us a foothold outside our thought-forms, or that will jolt us outside of our thinking minds, and set us free.

Meditation, for example, is a good practice for extricating ourselves from our thoughts. It lets us see clearly the way in which we keep re-creating the very network of thought-forms that's trapping us. Say, for example, that you're sitting in meditation: You're focusing on your breath and quieting your mind . . . quieting your mind . . . quieting your mind. And then suddenly something "happens" inside of you: You feel a sense of peace, or you notice some movement of energy. You think, "Wow! It's happening to me!" and you get a rush. That's the *ego* that's just rushed in. The ego was being pushed out by the meditation practice, by the "breathing in, breathing out, breathing in, breathing out." There's no room for much psychological stuff or much self-concept, when you're just "breathing in, breathing out." (Note that it's not even "I'm *good* at 'breathing in, breathing out' "— it's just "breathing in, breathing out.") But believe me, the ego is very tenacious, and right up to the very end, it'll be lurking there, waiting to jump back in.

My own primary spiritual practice is Gurukripa—the grace of the guru—and it works in its own way to break the limitations of thought-forms, to free me of them the way Arjuna had to be freed of his ideas about who he was. Maharajji was constantly doing things that would foil my rational mind and cut through the models I had of myself. Here's the kind of thing I'm talking about: At one point, he cast me in something like Arjuna's role—he made me "commander in chief." He said to me, "Ram Dass! You are the commander in chief. Take all these Westerners back to the place where they're living, and don't let them come here again until six o'clock." Well, now—I had clear instructions from my guru, right? Simple enough. I took everybody back to the hotel, and I said, "Don't go until six." I just did my duty.

But some of the people went at four, thinking, "Who the hell is

Ram Dass, to tell us what to do?" When they got to the ashram, Maharajji fed them, loved them, sat with them, laughed with them. At six, I arrived, leading the rest of the troops. Maharajji went into his room, closed the door, and wouldn't see anybody.

The next morning, Maharajji called me up to his tucket and he said, "Ram Dass, you're the commander in chief, remember? Yesterday you let people come at four. Today, don't let anybody come until six!"

So I took everybody back, and I said, "Now look, don't go until six!" Well, the same people who'd gone at four the previous day figured they'd go at four again, and some more figured they'd go, too . . . so now at least half the people went at four o'clock. Maharajji fed them, loved them, talked to them. I came at six, leading the diminished ranks. Maharajji shut himself in his room and wouldn't see anybody. He kept doing that to me, foiling me and frustrating me, and finally I couldn't stand it anymore. I said to his eldest Indian devotee, "Maharajji just isn't being fair!"

The devotee said, "Well, I think you'd better tell him that yourself."

I said, "I will!" You can hear that place in me, can't you—in me, and probably in yourself, you know? You've been pushed to your limit: "I just can't take any more of this."

So I went to Maharajji's room. He was sitting on his bed, with his blanket wrapped around him. He looked up at me and said, *"Kya?"*— that's like, "What is it? What's the trouble?"

I said to him, "Maharajji, you know my heart. You know what the trouble is."

He kept pressing me, saying, "What is it? What is it?", making me spell it out.

Finally I said, "Well, Maharajji, you're just not being fair." And I gave him my list of grievances.

I finished—and then, as I would do in a reasonable discourse with reasonable people, I sat back and waited for an explanation. Maharajji looked at me for a moment. Then he leaned forward, pulled on my beard, and said, "Ram Dass is angry!" And he *burst* out laughing— cackling away. Then, when he'd finished laughing, he sat back and he looked at me, as if to say, "OK, it's your move. You just had my explanation."

Now I was faced with a predicament: Either I had to give up my models, my ideas about "fairness," or I had to give up my guru. He'd put it right to me: Which way you gonna go, baby? Was I going to walk out and say, "Well, if you're not going to play my way, I'll find a guru who will. I'll find a guru who suits my model of how God is supposed to be." Because I was only asking for *reasonable* things—you understand that. *I* wasn't being unreasonable—*he* was being unreasonable. And he didn't even care!

So I thought about it for a moment. I saw what the issues were. And I stayed.

Like Arjuna, what I was facing in that moment was the disconfirming of a certain image of myself. In that situation with Maharajji, I had to give up the model I had of myself as "somebody who is pursuing a reasonable course of action." And when I did that, a part of my ego shattered. Arjuna is going to have to give up seeing himself as "somebody who doesn't go to war against family." He's going to have to give up the entire system on which he's been basing his actions; he's going to have to give up his models about protecting family and caste; he's going to have to change the entire way he defines himself. And doing that will crack open his ego and take him to the next stage.

When we start to examine the self-definitions that make up the structure of our egos, we see that there seem to be different intensities to them, and that some of the models feel much more deeply "us" than others do. So when it comes to letting go of them, some will be harder to work with than others. Maybe you'd find it easy to give up things like wealth and fame, for example. You might even find it possible to give up familial and social approval—the things that are confronting Arjuna.

But what if we take it a step further: How about giving up pleasure? Are you ready for that? *Pleasure?* I mean, isn't that what the whole game's been about—to get the maximum pleasure for yourself as a separate entity? But then you find that there are changes going on inside of you, changes that are leading you to identify yourself with something that sees pleasure as . . . just one more experience. That can be a scary moment.

The process of awakening brings you into a struggle with *every* habitual way you have of thinking about the universe, even the deepest ones, because every one of them has you locked into being some facet of who you think you are. "I'm somebody who's really getting on toward enlightenment, aren't I?" says the ego. Right up until the very last whisper, the ego is always lurking there, ready to play its next card. You've got to expect that the battle will never be over until the last vestige of self is gone.

What often happens when we face this stripping away of our models is that we will give up *this* and *that,* and instead grab onto *that* and *this.* It's too uncomfortable not to have *any*thing to cling to, and so we substitute a new set of attachments for the old ones. We give up family, we give up social forms—and we start clinging instead to spiritual leaders and spiritual forms. Uh-uh. It's *all* gotta go. Big clearance, everything must go.

That doesn't mean we have to give up everything at once; we can give things up as we come to not need them quite so badly anymore. And it doesn't mean we can't *use* spiritual forms; we just have to remember as we're using them that sooner or later they're going to have to go, too.

Knowing all that makes us feel very vulnerable: There's no authority we can turn to, nobody to tell us what to do. We can only keep turning to our hearts, listening for what feels like the right next move. We have nothing to hold on to.

It requires mental discipline to be in that place without flickering, and that's a kind of discipline Arjuna isn't used to. He's been used to the security of always knowing what's right, of having a fixed set of social rules to live by, rules that tell him how to behave and what to believe. He could always say, "I know what I ought to do, because I've got it written down right here." Now he's faced with the kind of discipline which Trungpa Rinpoche talked about in his book *Cutting*

Through Spiritual Materialism: the discipline of not being attached to any patterns whatsoever, the discipline of standing nowhere. That's a very scary discipline. It's terrifying to stand on the edge that way, to have no definitions you can cling to: no reference groups, no identifications, no self-concepts, no models. Will you dare do it? Will you dare to throw *everything* over?

It's only at the point where the conflict has become that real for you—where there is incredible confusion, and you don't know where to stand in order to judge what to do next—it's only at that point that you are open to the possibility of something new happening. It's only at that point that you are ready to hear something you never heard before.

That's why the message of the Gita has to begin with this crisis situation. Arjuna has to be shaken to his very roots before he can hear what Krishna has to say to him. Krishna and Arjuna have been hanging out together for a long time, remember—they've been good friends for years. But Arjuna wasn't ready before to hear what Krishna had to tell him. Not until they found themselves in the middle of a battlefield, not until that moment of crisis awakened Arjuna, was he ready to hear something new. And that something new will take Arjuna on a journey from giving up his attachment to things like family and caste to letting go of his attachment even to form itself.

Because that is the deepest level of the Gita's teaching. The final thing Arjuna faces is Shiva. He faces God in the form of chaos, God in the form of destruction—the destruction of all our illusions. Arjuna is facing the pain of having to ask, "If there is a God, if there is law, if there is *any* meaning to all of this, how can I be asked to make war on my own family? How can I be asked to do this horrible thing?" Arjuna is facing a terrifying fact: You cannot use reason to understand God's law.

In the Ramayana, Ram says over and over again, "Unless you honor Shiva, you cannot come to me." That is, until you have fully embraced the existence of chaos—*chaos!*—you cannot go through the door. If you want to be a preserver of love and beauty, you've got to be able to look at the destruction of love and beauty with wide-open eyes and say, "Yeah, right. And that, too." In nature there is creation, preservation, *and destruction*. Suffering and pain and catastrophe and death—all of those are as much a part of God's plan as delight and joy and renewal and birth.

At Kurukshetra, Arjuna comes face to face with Shiva. He's confronting a situation in which his rational mind can't help him, a situation in which his reasoning won't work, a situation in which surrender is the only way through. His image of himself as a good guy, his attachment to rational thought, his attachment to form itself—he has to say good-bye to all of them. He has to let go of every one of those attachments. The very basis of who he thinks he is will have to be torn apart in order to make room for something new.

So now the scene is set. We know who the armies are—the Kauravas and the Pandavas—and we also know what it is they represent for us. We've figured out what they're doing out there on the battlefield. We've understood Arjuna's predicament. And even more important, we have come to recognize that the choices facing Arjuna are the same choices facing us: How ripe are we to let go? How free of our egos are we ready to be? How willing are we to surrender to the mystery of God's plan? Those are the questions confronting Arjuna. That's the battle we face. That's what will be decided at Kurukshetra.

2

Karma and Reincarnation

*I*n the previous chapter, we examined the conflict that Arjuna is facing at Kurukshetra, looking at it in a way that brought it home for us and made it very immediate. We looked at the places in our own lives where, like Arjuna, we aren't quite ready to let go, the places where the roots of attachment still go a little too deep. We saw our dilemma as reflected in that quote from the Gospel of Matthew: "If anyone wishes to come after me," said Christ, "let him deny himself, and take up his cross daily and follow me. For he who would save his life will lose it, but he who loses his life for my sake will find it."

"He who would save his life will lose it, but he who loses his life for my sake will find it." That's a strong statement, but it isn't too melodramatic for the place in which Arjuna finds himself. Krishna is telling him to give up his relationships, to give up his values, in effect, to give up his life—that is, to turn his back on the entire life he has known so far. Arjuna is a warrior. Probably he's been prepared to give up his life on the battlefield. But nothing has quite prepared him for *this* kind of sacrifice. The Gita tells us, "When Arjuna, the great warrior, had thus unburdened his heart, he said, 'I will not fight, Krishna.' " Then he threw down his bow, and fell silent.

In other words, Arjuna still wasn't ready to surrender to his dharma; he was still too caught up in a pattern of thought that defined his version of reality. But he was prepared to listen; he "fell silent." He was ready to hear what Krishna had to say next.

Now, in the course of persuading Arjuna to fulfill his dharma and fight, Krishna presents several arguments, and we'll notice as we go along that they come from different levels. At one level they are the answer of an external teacher to his friend; at another level, they're the answer of God to the individual soul; and at still another level they are the answer of our Self to our self.

Krishna's first major argument to Arjuna is laid out in the early pages of the second chapter; in it he says: "We have all been, for all time—I, thou, and those kings and men—and we shall be for all time, we all, forever and ever. As the spirit of our mortal body wanders on in childhood and youth and old age, the spirit wanders on to a new body. Of this, the sage has no doubts."

Now, that statement hangs on a concept which we as Westerners need to stop and consider a bit more closely—the concept of reincarnation. In the East, it wouldn't be quite so necessary to justify the use of a reincarnational model, because reincarnation is pretty much taken for granted there. But here in the West we need to go a little more slowly and establish our ground; we aren't quite so confident about reincarnation, and yet it's central to the reasoning of the Gita.

When we talk about "understanding" something like reincarnation, we're not talking about an understanding that we can arrive at through the intellect, through knowledge. How could we "know" about something like reincarnation? "Knowing" comes from the rational mind, and that is part of *this* lifetime. To understand about something like reincarnation, we have to rely on a higher wisdom, on the "inner voice" we talked about.

It seems to me that there are two ways by which one might come to know about reincarnation via that inner wisdom. The first way is through direct experience: If you, personally, have experienced your previous incarnations, that's pretty convincing evidence, and there are people who report having done that. The other way is through meeting someone whose vision of things you totally trust, and having them tell you that that's the way it is.

For me, it was the second path that was the key. It was my relationship with another being—with Maharajji, my guru—that opened me to a sense of utter inner validity regarding reincarnation, so I no longer doubt the truth of it in any way.

My relationship to my guru is such that there is absolutely no place in me that doubts him; there is no place of mistrust left. It's the kind of trust that exists between a mother and a child. When a child is very young, there is a total openness to the mother, and to the mother's protectiveness. Only later does the ego develop, and with it the sense of separateness. Before the separateness, there is a kind of unlimited openness to another being, and in that space of utter openness, you trust implicitly whatever comes to you from the other. You don't sit around *wondering* whether you can trust it or not—you have complete, unshakable faith. Living in India, around my guru and other beings like him, I stopped asking, "Are they telling me the truth? Are they distorting the reports of their experiences?" I just opened to them: "Yeah. Right!"

Maharajji and other such beings whom I don't doubt have told me about reincarnation. They have told me how it is. Without exception,

Ram Dass Lecturing:
Rameshwar Das says, "You could hardly call these talks that Ram Dass gave 'lectures.' Ram Dass would weave these intricate stories, parables, and jokes that would go off on long tangents you'd think he would never be able to pull together, until suddenly there it was, some seemingly obvious fact of spiritual life, staring you in the face, punctuated by a deep, meditative silence, and a collective murmur of appreciation or acknowledgment."

all those beings accepted reincarnation with the same level of certainty that we in the West feel toward the laws of physics, and I could hear in them the truth of what they were telling me. So from my own point of view, that's been the primary route through which I've arrived at my understanding of reincarnation: Hanging around with Maharajji and with beings like him, I came to trust that that's just the way it is.

True, I've had lots of far-out experiences, mainly through psychedelics, where I flipped in and out of images of myself in other realms. Were those direct experiences of other lifetimes? Was I experiencing others of my incarnations? I don't know. But I do know that Maharajji took reincarnation for granted, and his truth communicated itself to me. Krishna said, "Of this [reincarnation], the sage has no doubts." That's good enough for me.

Let me read you a few quotes about reincarnation from some of those beings who, like my guru, are people I trust on this issue.

This is from Rumi, the Persian mystic: "I died as stone, and rose again as plant. I died as plant, and became an animal. I died as animal, and was born a man. Why should I fear? When was I less by dying? Yet once more shall I die as man, to soar with the angels. But even from angelhood, I must pass on. For all is change, except the face of God."[1]

Muhammad said. "Each person is only a mask, which the soul puts on for a season. It is worn for the proper time, and then is cast off, and another is worn in its stead."

This is a quote from Jack London, who writes of a character who was hanged:

> I did not begin when I was born, nor when I was conceived. I have been growing, developing, through incalculable myriads of millenniums . . . I am man born of woman. My days are few, but the stuff of me is indestructible. I have been woman born of woman, I have been a woman and borne my children, and I shall be born again. Oh, incalculable times again shall I be born. And yet the stupid dolts about me think that by stretching my neck with a rope they will make me cease.[2]

Now, Jack London was an American author, so we can conclude from his quote that there has been in the West a rich vein of belief in reincarnation, especially in literary circles. But our general cultural attitude toward reincarnation has been shaped less by that and much more by Western religious traditions, where we don't find so much acceptance of the idea. Reincarnation isn't part of the belief system in most of our synagogues and churches.

And yet if we read the Bible, we notice slipping into it quotations that seem to imply a belief in reincarnation. Christ said that John the Baptist was Elijah, previously. The Wisdom of Solomon says, "To be born in sound body with sound limbs is a reward of the virtues of past lives." The disciples ask Christ, "Was this man born blind because of something he did previously, or because of his parents, or what?" Without reincarnation, how could the man have done something *before* his birth to cause his blindness?

So what happened to those beliefs? In the early councils of the Christian Church, around A.D. 500 to 600, the question of reincarnation was actually hotly debated, and at first it was by no means clear in which direction church doctrine would go. But as the church fathers considered it, they realized that reincarnation wasn't such a functional philosophy for maintaining the church's control: after all, if this life was merely one step in a continuing dance, you couldn't be frightened about an eternity of hellfire and brimstone. So reincarnation was rejected as a tenet of faith, but back in the time of Christ it was a common belief.

Psychology in the West, like religion in the West, has traditionally dismissed the idea of reincarnation. Recently, though, psychologists have started to become interested in it, and now it's becoming a matter for "serious" study.

I was a psychologist, in one recent incarnation. I was a student of personality research. We tried to determine why children were the way they were, in light of their heredity and their environment, as we in psychology measured those factors. So we would measure everything that was measurable in the parents, and everything that was measurable in the environment—which was what we, in our sophisticated, theoretical way, understood to be the determinants of how you came out being who you are. We would score all the tests and feed all the data into our computers, and out would pop a prediction of who you were supposed to be. Then we would measure who you actually *were,* and we would see how closely our predictions matched the reality. In other words, we were building a body of scientific knowledge about cause and effect in personality, based on the assumption that you are totally the product of this lifetime, with its environment and its heredity.

Well, the best correlations we ever got with that kind of research—and we were probably about par for the course—were around 0.5, and a 0.5 correlation meant that we were accounting for about 25 percent of the total variability. That means that if I picked you and tried to predict who you were, based on knowing everything a psychologist could want to know about you in this lifetime, I would be able to predict about 25 percent of your characteristics; the other 75 percent would come out, essentially, at random.

In the face of that, I, as a social scientist, would then say, "Well, that's due to errors of measurement." Or I'd say, "It's due to the fact that we aren't complex enough in our systems." It would never enter my mind, as a psychologist, that my *theory* might be wrong—because we all get very wedded to our theories. It never occurred to me that heredity and environment might not be the only things that make you who you are. And yet we can see that that unaccounted-for 75 percent leaves ample space for reincarnational theory, so it's not necessary, really, to pit Western science against reincarnation. Reincarnation just gets lumped into the psychologist's "errors of measurement" category.

There is anecdotal evidence of reincarnation. Here in the West, we have the lives of people like Mozart. He created sonatas at four, gave public recitals at five, and composed his first opera at seven—did he really *learn* all that in such a short time?

In our midst at Naropa was the interesting phenomenon of Trungpa Rinpoche, who was what is called a Tulku—the acknowledged reincarnation of a high being. In the Tibetan tradition, when a high lama dies, a group of oracles sits in meditation until they share a vision of where his next incarnation has occurred. Then they send out a search party of monks, and they tell them, "Go to a house with a blue roof, by a lake two miles north of such-and-such village, and you will find a baby who at that point will be seven months old. That will be the Tulku."

The search party sets out. They find the house, and knock at the door, and say, "You have a son, seven months old?" The family, of course, says yes. The monks say, "Well, you didn't know it, but this is really lama so-and-so." And the mother says, "Oh, wow! And all this time I thought it was just my baby. I'm so honored that my baby turns out to be the reincarnation of lama so-and-so."

Then, just to be sure, the monks give the baby a number of tests: They test it with the dead lama's goblet and a new goblet, with the lama's old bell and a new bell, to see which one the baby chooses. If the tests are suitably passed, the monks take the baby back to the monastery and start to teach him. And for the next nineteen years (in Trungpa's case) there proceeds a system of intensive training to remind the new Tulku just who he really is.

Then there was the little girl I heard about in India: One day, when she was seven years old, she told her father, "You have to take me to . . . ," and she named a small village, miles and miles away, which neither she nor her family had ever visited before. She said, "I used to live in that village. I have two children there, and I must go and see them." She begged and begged her father, and finally she persuaded him to take her there. On the way, she told him all about the village, and how it had changed during the time she'd lived there—all of which, as the father found when they arrived there, was exactly the way it had happened. They located what the little girl said was her house, and, sure enough, there were two children of the appropriate ages. After her visit, the girl was taken back home, crying "No! No! You can't take me away from my children."

Or what about the experiences of what we call "déjà vu"? Haven't you ever met someone and felt, "Don't I know you from somewhere? Didn't we go through all this before?" A Western scientist will say, "Well, that's all just a similarity of cues." Maybe—but then again, maybe it's a glimpse of something further out than that.

Rodney Collin, in a book called *The Theory of Celestial Influences,* had an interesting slant on reincarnation. He said, it isn't like the *Bridey Murphy Story,* where you're born, and then you die, and then you're born again a few years later. It's really more like a fifth dimension: We've all been here—right *here,* in this very time and place—thousands of times. We've been running through the very same lifetime again and again and again. Don't you remember? I mean, I've told you a thousand times. . . . I've told you a thousand times. . . . I've told you a thousand times. . . . Collin's view of that experience of déjà vu is that it comes because the circuitry burns through occasionally, and we get a little flash of the last time we did all this.

People will argue, "But if reincarnation is true, why don't I remember who I was? Why don't I remember my past lives?" Lama Anagarika Govinda, the Tibetan teacher, answered: "Most people don't remember their births, and yet they don't doubt that they were recently born. They forget that active memory is only a small part of our normal consciousness, and that our subconscious memory registers and preserves every past impression and experience, which our waking mind fails to recall."[3]

Carl Jung, in his psychological work, kept wrestling with that issue of subconscious memory. He called it "the collective unconscious," which was a way that a Westerner could approach the idea of reincarnation, of information that was coming from outside this lifetime.

If, through whatever experiences, we allow for the possibility that reincarnation is true, then we immediately start to get curious about the mechanics of it all—how it works and why it works. There are dozens of systems to describe it; they all have their own structure of beliefs about where you go and how you get there. Sometimes they contradict one another; the Buddha told stories about people sinning and coming back as animals or insects, whereas teachers like Meher Baba claimed that each incarnation is a step forward, a progression, and that you can never backslide. There's no way to determine which one is right or wrong. Each system is just an *approximation* of the truth, created by a human mind.

Nor in considering a sequence of births can we assume that reincarnation happens only on the Earth plane. In the Gita, Krishna says to Arjuna, "Those who pray to the gods, go to the gods." That is, if you are devoted to the gods, then after you die you will go to a *heavenly* loka, a celestial land; that's where you'll be reincarnated. But that, too, will turn out to be just another plane of consciousness. You'll go there, and you'll stay there for some period of time—let's say for five hundred years from an earthly point of view, though time will undoubtedly mean something very different there; but then after those five hundred years, you'll come to realize that a heavenly loka is still a *place,* and that before you can get to no-place, there's more work you have to do—maybe work that can only be done on the human plane. And so maybe you will once again take a human birth in order to get on with it.

But that's just one more model. These are *all* just models, thought up by human minds for something that's beyond what the human mind can grasp. We have no way to know how it all really works! It seems we go around and around and around, but that each time around we're a little more conscious, until eventually we get to the level of yogic awareness, and we *remember.*

"Eventually" can mean a long, long time, however, when we're talking about reincarnation. We're talking about *vast* timescapes. Here is a beautiful image from the Southern Buddhist literature that gives us an idea of the kind of time spans we're talking about. The Buddha was trying to describe the length of time we've been playing this game of reincarnating. He said, "Imagine a mountain one mile wide, one mile long, and one mile high. Every hundred years a bird flies by with a silk scarf in its beak, and runs the scarf once over the face of the mountain. The time it would take for the silk scarf to wear away that mountain is what we would call a 'kalpa,' and we have been playing this game of reincarnation for kalpa upon kalpa, through innumerable ages."[4]

Apart from the mechanics of reincarnation, there's a deeper question: "Who exactly is this 'we' that's been playing this game?"

That is, what is it that continues on, and what is it that changes during all those kalpas? Obviously, the you and I we usually think of as ourselves won't be hanging around all that time, so what is it that will still be here?

Krishna says, "For beyond time he dwells in these bodies, though these bodies have an end in their time. But he remains, immeasurable, immortal." That's one way of describing the two aspects of our being: our bodies, which die, and that which dwells in our bodies, which doesn't. The trouble is that talking about reincarnation in that way—"*he* dwells in these bodies"; "*he* remains" (emphases added)—can make what stays around from incarnation to incarnation sound awfully solid, like there's a "somebody" who's passing through birth and death and birth and death. But if not a "somebody," what is it?

Personally, I'm comfortable with using the word "Soul" for what reincarnates. To the Buddhists, the word "Soul" carries too much connotation of solidity, and so they take me to task when I use the word. But I use it in a very specific way: The twist is that the Soul reincarnates—but at the same time the whole thing at every level, *including* the Soul, is an illusion. The Soul is an illusion, and the forms it incarnates in are illusions, but within the illusion is a subtle configuration, a continuity of traits, or values, or qualities, which persists despite the different forms, names, and egos it takes on, and that continuity is what I call the Soul.

The Buddha believed in reincarnation, which means he thought that *something* reincarnates. The Pali literature says: "There are no real ego entities hastening through the ocean of rebirth, but merely life waves, which, according to their nature and activities, manifest themselves here as men, there as animals, and elsewhere as invisible things." "Life waves"—that's a nice image. In Hinduism they're called vasanas, subtle thought-forms. Every act we do creates vasanas, life waves, based on the desires connected with the act. Those life waves go out and out. Even when we die, they continue; the physical body dies, and what remains are those subtle life waves, those mental tendencies that function like a kind of psychic DNA code to determine your next round. In Hinduism that's called karma. Karma is basically a pattern of life waves, or desire waves, that keep going and going, life after life, until they spend themselves. When they do, there's no more individual desire, no more separation, and therefore no more incarnation. The game is over.

If you experience your present life from that perspective—as one sequence in a long, unfolding pattern of karmic law—then the time and place you took birth, what your parents are like, who your brothers and sisters are, whom you marry, whether you have children, what experiences you have in life . . . you will see *all* of that as part of a predetermined karmic package. The universe and you in it are just an ongoing expression of karmic law. You and everything you see around you, alive and otherwise, are perfect law unfolding. There is no chance in the system, because there is no part of the universe that is exempt from the laws of karma.

You say, "What do you mean, it's all law? Don't I make choices? What about free will? In the Gita, isn't Arjuna being asked to *decide* whether or not to fight?"

Well, it's a stretch for us to come to grips with the relationship between free will and determinism, because we're so used to thinking in either / or terms. But on this issue, we have to deal with the paradox that both of those opposite realities exist simultaneously: free will, and total determinism. Things get a little clearer, though, when we see that although they exist simultaneously, they exist on different planes. That is, there is a plane of reality on which you think you are a free agent. You think you decided what to wear today, you think you decided what to eat for breakfast this morning, you think you decided whether to pick up this book and read it. On that plane, it's necessary for you to behave as if in fact you *are* a free agent—to make choices wisely, to decide to do your dharma. However, there is another plane, a different perceptual vantage point, from which you begin to see that all those thought-forms that said to you, "I think I'll have some granola this morning," didn't come out of the void. Well, actually, they *did* come out of the void—but they came *conditioned* out of the void. The choices arose out of a long chain of prior events that absolutely predetermined your decisions. I say, "I have free will"—that's my karma talking!

Whenever I think I'm making a decision about something, I remember an incident that happened with Maharajji. I had gone back to India for the second time in 1971, and I had gone looking for Maharajji, but he was nowhere to be found. No one knew where he was. So I decided to join up with some other Westerners at a meditation retreat in Bodh Gaya; that's where the Buddha got enlightened, and I figured if it worked for him, maybe it would work for me. But after a couple of weeks of meditating, I was ready to resume my search for Maharajji. One of the women in our group had come to India over land, in a big Mercedes bus, complete with a driver. She offered us the bus to take us from Bodh Gaya to Delhi, where we could celebrate Shiva Ratri, and then go looking for Maharajji from there. So thirty-five of us—thirty-four meditators and the bus driver—all set out for Delhi. After weeks in a meditation retreat, we were all looking forward to hotels with real beds and hot water, and to restaurant meals and ice cream cones.

The road to Delhi took us near the city of Allahabad, which is where, once every twelve years, a huge celebration is held, called the Kumbha Mela. Millions of people come there at an astrologically ideal moment to bathe in the confluence of three sacred rivers; it is the largest spiritual gathering held anywhere in the world. The Mela had taken place just a few weeks before our bus trip, and one of the people on the bus, who had been at the Mela, insisted that we should make a detour to visit the Mela grounds. On the one hand, it seemed like a reasonable thing to do—after all, all of us were supposed to be practicing yogis, and here was one of the most sacred sites in all of India. But it meant an extra hour or two before we'd get to Delhi, and everybody was tired and hungry and getting cranky. The discussion went back and forth, and finally everybody agreed that I, as the elder in the group, should make the decision.

I wrestled with it: Should we turn off? Should we go straight on to Delhi? Finally, when we were almost at the cutoff to Allahabad, I *decided*. I told the driver, "Turn right."

We drove to Allahabad and pulled into the almost-empty Mela grounds—just a handful of people walking here and there. The fellow who had been to the Mela directed the bus driver over to a little Hanuman temple he remembered visiting. As we parked next to the temple, somebody who was looking out one of the bus windows yelled, "Hey, there's Maharajji!" And there he was, walking along through the Mela grounds, holding on to the arm of Dada, his Indian devotee. We all poured out of the bus, crying and pranaming and touching Maharajji's feet. Maharajji looked unconcerned with our whole thing; he just said, "Come. Come. Follow us." Then he and Dada climbed into a bicycle rickshaw that had been waiting for them, and they started off through the narrow little streets of Allahabad, with our big bus lumbering along behind.

When we arrived at Dada's house, his wife came rushing out to the bus to greet us. "Come in, come in," she said, "dinner is almost ready. We've been cooking for you all day. Maharajji woke us up at six o'clock this morning and told us, 'Hurry up and start cooking. There will be thirty-five people here for dinner tonight.' "

Now who do you suppose it was who thought he was sitting on the bus, deciding whether to visit the Mela grounds? Long before I *made my decision,* it was already decided—Maharajji knew all about it that morning! I played my part. I "decided" to go to the Mela grounds. But my decision was inevitable.

So if it's already writ in stone, can a guru change your karma? That's an interesting one, because in many Hindu traditions there is the idea that the guru can free the student by taking on his or her karma in some way or other. One day when I went to see Maharajji, I brought him a big bag of oranges, and put it down on the tucket in front of him. Usually, he would take the fruit that was given to him and start tossing it to people, but this time he started grabbing the oranges and gobbling them ravenously—he ate eight oranges before my very eyes! I didn't know what to make of it, but afterward one of the Indian devotees told me that a guru often does something like that to take on the karma of another being.

I struggled with that one for a long time, with that question of karma and the guru. Are *we* all bound by law, but the guru isn't? What's the relationship between karma and grace? That is, if Maharajji ate the oranges to take on my karma, was he doing it because, in the grand law and design of things, it was my *karma* that I would come to a guy who would eat eight oranges and take on my karma? Or was it my karma just to schlock along eating my own oranges until this being, out of his incredible compassion, said, "Look at this poor jerk—he's never going to do anything right. I'll eat his eight oranges for him." Is it karma or is it grace—that's the basic issue, right?

I finally concluded that it was a question of perspective. That is, when you're working with the path of bhakti yoga, working within a devotional system, then the guru is your all-in-all. And in that case, he ate the oranges out of his infinite compassion. But when you're standing back in another space, you see that since the guru is one with God and so one with the Law, there would be no possible reason or motive for him to act outside the Law—and so it was just your karma to meet him and have your oranges eaten.

But surely *God* must be outside the laws of karma, right? Well, in a way, God *is* the laws of karma, and then the question becomes, why would anyone break their own laws? Sure, if you were God and you wanted to, you could act outside the laws—but you wouldn't want to. When you're in the place where you can move the mountain, you know why you put it there in the first place.

So then all of us and all the universe around us are a kind of sleight-of-hand manifestation of these life waves, of these karmic laws flowing on and on, through lifetime after lifetime. Our desires drive our thoughts, which motivate our actions, which create more karma, which determines the circumstances of our next incarnation. And on it goes. In our lives right now, we are reaping the karma, both good and bad, of incredible numbers of past lifetimes, and at the same moment we're creating our karma for the next round.

When I look back at my own life, I wonder how I could ever have imagined such a plot. It's all been too bizarre! I mean, I found myself living in an Indian village, doing sadhana, doing meditation, doing yoga—me, a nice, middle-class Jewish boy from Boston! Back when

I was on the Harvard faculty, I didn't even *know* the word "yoga." If anybody had said to me, "One day, you will be a yogi," I would have laughed at them—it was absurd. "Yogi" had no place in my professional career planning! But when I got to that place, it felt as if I were coming home. It was my spiritual connection, and so it reverberated in me with something much deeper than any of my conditioned ideas of who I was and where I was going. And so it felt absolutely right on, every step of the way.

Now—why me? What about all the rest of the people I grew up with in Newton Center, Massachusetts, who are now in the clothing business, and in the shoe business, and so forth? Why me? Hari Das (one of my teachers) once said to me, "You did a lot of yogic work in your last lifetime, but you fell." So here I am again. It was my karma that I would reincarnate into this lifetime, and if Hari Das was right in what he said, maybe it was because I fell off the path the last time and so I had to come back around again. That was one side of my karma. But in the grace I've been given with experiences like taking mushrooms and meeting Maharajji, I'm also reaping the *good* karma of my last lifetime—maybe of the "yogic work" that Hari Das said I did. This present moment is the sum of *all* that past karma. All those life waves, flowing and flowing, just to bring me to *this* place, to *this* moment.

If you're standing outside of time, it is possible to see the whole course of those life waves—past, present, and future. There are stages of development (which I have not yet achieved) where you can watch their entire pattern through time. Maharajji was in such a place. We've all seen those time-lapse movies that show flowers unfolding, and blooming very quickly. Sometimes when I was sitting with my guru, I would catch him looking at me in a certain way, and I could sense that he was watching this flower of my being unfolding, just like those movies. Since I could only see the stage that I was in at the moment, I was always caught up in reaching for this or grabbing for that or pushing away the other thing. But Maharajji could see the whole pattern evolving. When you're at that stage, you see in advance the direction the karmic waves are taking, and you know exactly why it's all happening the way it is.

For me, it's still a surprise, although I can see the connections after the fact. Here's a little example. Maybe I'm invited to give a lecture in some small town somewhere. I won't really know what leads me to accept that particular invitation, but I do. I go there, I speak to the audience, and they don't seem particularly interested in what I have to say. I think to myself, "What am I doing here? Maharajji, what on earth did you have in mind?" I finish my talk, and I take a taxi to the airport; I've got half an hour before my flight leaves, so I go in to have a cup of coffee. I sit down, and somebody comes over and says, "May I share this table?" "Certainly. Sit down." Then we look into each other's eyes, and—there it is! There's the connection that holds the whole meaning of the trip. In that moment, I know: "Oh—far out! So *that's* what I'm doing in this town!"

Or here's another one, even stranger: Some years ago, I was giving a lecture in Seattle. As I entered the hall and looked around at the audience, my glance happened to fall on someone who, for whatever reasons, aroused my prurient interests. It was momentary, just a passing thought, but my eyes lingered for a second on the object of my desires. Then I went on, gave my lecture, and thought no more about it. Sometime later, I received a letter in the mail. The letter said, "I was in the audience at your lecture in Seattle last year. I'd been depressed for months, and I couldn't bear it anymore. I planned to go home after the lecture and commit suicide—I had the pills in my pocket, I was all ready. But then as you were coming into the hall, you stopped and looked at me for a moment, and I knew that you knew what I was planning to do. And because you noticed me, and because of the way you looked at me, I couldn't do it anymore. And now it's a year later, and I'm just fine." So who thought that one up?

Then there's a story about Meher Baba. He was crossing the United States by train, and when the train stopped in Santa Fe, he suddenly got up from his seat, climbed down off the train, and walked toward the center of town. At a certain corner, there was an old Indian man standing, leaning up against the side of a building. Meher Baba walked up to him, and they looked into each other's eyes for a few seconds. Then Meher Baba turned around, walked back to the station, got onto the train, and left. He said, "Well, that takes care of my work for this trip."

Now all that may just be incredible showbiz—I mean, if he's playing at that level, he could certainly have done it all on another plane and skipped the walk to town. But it's a great story—and it's possible that that was, in fact, what Meher Baba's trip had been all about. How would we know?

Gradually, as our perspective deepens, we begin to experience our own lives in the context of a wider purpose. We begin to look at all our melodramas and our desires and our sufferings, and instead of seeing them as events happening within a lifetime bounded by birth and death, we begin experiencing them as part of a much vaster design. We begin to appreciate that there is a wider frame around our lives, within which our particular incarnation is happening.

One of the first things that kind of perspective does for us is to calm us down a great deal. The whole game isn't riding on this one lifetime! Whew! There's a great feeling of release inherent in that; it removes the anxiety and the sense of urgency. We don't have to do it all right now—and in fact we see we're not "doing it" anyway! It's the lawful continuity of karma and reincarnation flowing through us lifetime after lifetime, kalpa after kalpa. What a relief!

Once we've developed this deeper understanding of reincarnation and karma, we can see the way these ideas are framing Krishna's response to Arjuna. They are central to the argument. That's why we really had to come to grips with them. But how is Arjuna's karma playing itself out here? One part of the answer would be that it is Arjuna's *good* karma to be graced enough to find himself there in the very predicament he's facing. That is, it's *grace* for him that he's beginning to awaken to the struggle. What a blessing! Just imagine the grace that allows him a birth in which he gets to hang out with God— what a great incarnation!

But the other side of Arjuna's karma is that although he's begun to awaken, his desires—or rather, his *attachments* to his desires—are still very much hanging around.

That's not just Arjuna's predicament; that's the predicament in which most of us find ourselves, isn't it? We're caught in divided territories inside ourselves: There's that part of us which sees through the game—and then there is that part of us that is still deeply caught in all our stuff. We have a foot in two different worlds.

So although Arjuna is graced to be in an incarnation through which he awakens, he still has a way to go, and Krishna is in the process of training him to take the next step. Krishna is helping Arjuna evolve to a point where the acts he performs will no longer come out of attachment—*any* attachment. And not coming out of attachment, they will no longer create new karma. At that point, Arjuna will be done with generating new stuff for himself. He'll be done with creating new births and deaths for himself. All that will be left then will be for the old stuff to run its course, for the old, stored-up karma to run off until it's gone.

Now notice what that last sentence implies: that even though you may be fully enlightened, even though you may be fully aware of the whole game, the dance will go on until the dance is done. As long as there are stored up karmic energies, as long as there are life waves present, the five skandas, the strands of creation, will keep manifesting. The Buddha got enlightened, but then he hung around for another forty years, running off his old karma.

However, if we *want* to get done with it all, it's clear that the first step in the process is to stop creating new waves. We're never going to be finished if we keep making new waves for ourselves every day! And as Krishna explains to Arjuna, the way to go about doing that is to stop basing our actions on attachment. Once we're acting purely out of dharma and not out of any desire, we're no longer making waves.

That's the reason for all this—that's why Krishna is giving Arjuna this whole new basis for determining his actions. He's training Arjuna to stop acting out of his old, karma-creating patterns. Krishna in effect is saying to Arjuna, What matters here aren't your *feelings* toward those people on the other side. There's something bigger at stake here. You have to act out of what your *karma* demands. It's your karmic predicament to have been born a *kshatria* at this particular moment and in this particular place, where it is your responsibility to uphold the dharma by fighting this war. And so that's your way through at this moment.

Arjuna might not feel that he asked for that role, but there it is; now it's his dharma to fulfill it. In picking up this book, you may not have thought you were asking to confront these tough questions about your own life and about what it all means, but by God, here you are. By *God,* here you are. This is it—this is the battlefield. This is Kuruk-shetra within yourself. And though you may think you didn't ask for it, yet at another level, just like Arjuna, you are getting your just deserts. You are getting the benefit of all the work you've ever done up until now, which has put you in the place where you're reading this bizarre book about a peculiar topic that most of the population couldn't care less about. Doesn't that seem strange to you? What are you doing reading this book? Why you?

Whatever karma it is that brought you to this point, it's now your *dharma* to work with it. It's now your task to work with being in the situation of reading this book, and confronting these questions. You ask, "What exactly does that mean? What do I have to *do* about all this?" Well, that's something you're going to have to work out for yourself. We each have our own path. I don't know what yours is—I can hardly figure out my own. What I can predict, though, is that for you, as for Arjuna, it will probably include giving up some cherished notions about yourself, some ideas about who you are and where you're going.

Gradually, it begins to dawn on us that we are merely part of a process. Think about that: You and I are nothing more than *process.* I am a process of continuing mind-moments, each one separate from the others. There is no permanent "me," being incarnated and rein-carnated—there's merely the law of cause-and-effect, cause-and-effect, cause-and-effect, running on and on and on. It's all just the passing parade of the laws of prakriti, of the laws of nature, of the laws of an unfolding illusion of manifestation.

The more you open to that kind of perspective, the more dispassionate you become in watching your own incarnation unfold. You see that every melodrama, even the wonderful melodrama of "I'm trying to get enlightened," just creates more karma—and you can't afford that anymore. Finally, there is *no* stance you can hold on to and still go through the door—so you let go of everything.

That's the reason Krishna says to Arjuna, Let go of your models, and do your dharma. Why should you be upset about the idea of fighting your family, Krishna asks. It's their karma and yours for this battle to take place. You can't wage war against your destiny, so let the laws of karma unfold as they're supposed to. Play out the role that's been assigned to you, because when you do that, when you've totally surrendered to your dharma, when you're no longer trying for anything, that's your way through.

Krishna's argument undercuts all of Arjuna's objections by turning the very context of the discussion on its head. The rules have changed, Krishna says to Arjuna; your actions are going to have to start coming out of a new place now. All those social rules? They had their time and place. But Arjuna's feelings about family and social roles can no longer be the central values in shaping his actions, because his central value now is going to Brahman by fulfilling his dharma. He has a new purpose behind his acts.

Again and again, the Gita turns our perspective upside down, just as it does here for Arjuna. It shifts our sense of what our lives are about. So as we begin to adopt the Gita's perspective as our own, we'll notice that our focus starts to change. Instead of always preoccupying ourselves with trying to get what we think we want or need, we'll start to quiet, we'll start to listen. We'll wait for that inner prompting. We'll try to *hear*, rather than decide, what it is we should do next. And as we listen, we'll hear our dharma more and more clearly, and so we'll begin tuning more and more of our acts to that place of deeper wisdom. As that happens, all our fascination with our roles and our plans and our desires and our melodramas will begin to fall away. More and more, we will open ourselves to just being the instruments of the dharma. And then we'll discover that we've lost our lives—and found them.

3

Karma Yoga

I have been born many times, Arjuna, and many times hast thou been born. But I remember my past lives, and thou hast forgotten thine." We've seen that Krishna's whole first presentation to Arjuna, the first seed of what is called "the higher wisdom," hinges on the reincarnational perspective he spells out in that quote.

Krishna has begun to lay out for Arjuna these various alternative justifications for why he should get on with it, why he should enter into the battle of Kurukshetra, which is the struggle of dharma versus adharma, of the spirit versus the worldly, and his first argument is one you would offer to a materialist, to somebody who is very worldly: Just do your dharma, and don't worry about it. Everybody has to die sooner or later. Krishna says, "For all things born, in truth, must die, and out of death, in truth, comes life. Face to face with what must be, cease thou from sorrow." He's saying, Look: you're going to die eventually, and so are all those people on the other side. Death follows birth——that's the way the game is designed. If you don't kill them, something else will. Their karma is merely acting itself out through you——what are you getting so upset about? It's all inevitable, it's all in the cards. You're just the vehicle for its happening.

Well, that argument doesn't do much for Arjuna; he still isn't persuaded. So then Krishna introduces a second argument. He says, Look, you're going to have to do *something*. Do you think you can escape from acting? No way! Remember that Arjuna had told Krishna that he would fight, and had thrown down his bow. Krishna's reply is, in effect, You're not going to get out of it that easily. You simply *can't not act*. You have to do something or other, and whatever you do will have some kind of karma connected with it.

In saying that, Krishna was directly countering an idea that was popular in spiritual circles at the time, one which had emerged from the Sankhya philosophy. The Sankhya philosophy centered around a polarity, a pair of opposites called purusha and prakriti—purusha being the inactive principle, and prakriti the active one. The two forces had very little to do with one another; the inactive one was *always* inactive, and the active one was *always* active. The game, according to Sankhya philosophy, was to escape from the active into the inactive state, and so the highest goal was to do nothing—just *not* to act.

Krishna contradicts that philosophy; he says, "Not by refraining from action does man attain freedom from action. For not even for a moment can a man be without action. Helplessly all are driven to action by the forces born of nature. He who withdraws himself from actions but ponders on their pleasures in his heart, he is under a delusion."

That last line really gets to the core of it: "He who withdraws himself from actions *but ponders on their pleasures in his heart* [emphasis added], he is under a delusion." That's the one where you're busy *not* doing something. It's like when you meet somebody who has "Given Up Smoking!"—and that's totally who they are. "Who are you?" "I'm somebody who hasn't smoked for two weeks, four hours, and thirty-two minutes." In their thought-forms, they're smoking at least a pack an hour!

So Krishna is saying to Arjuna, You can't avoid acting, and trying to *not* act when your desires are still strong just puts you "under a delusion," it makes you phony holy. In other words, you're not going to get out of your predicament by just sitting around.

We can see the way Krishna is building his arguments for Arjuna. He's said, Look—your family, your friends—they're all going to die anyway. That's argument number one. And, he's said, you can't not act—you're going to have to do something or other. That's argument number two. And now Krishna brings in the punch line in a way that speaks very forcefully to Arjuna, because it comes from a level that Arjuna is especially tuned to hear. Krishna says to him, "Do your duty."

Arjuna is a *kshatria,* a warrior, a doer, so Krishna casts his clinching argument in the form Arjuna will best appreciate: "Think thou also of thy duty," Krishna tells him, "and do not waver. There is no greater good for a warrior than to fight in a righteous war. There is a war that opens the door to heaven, Arjuna. Happy the warrior whose fate is to fight such a war."

(Keep in mind that this is *our* war, this is the inner war that each of us faces, and hear Krishna's comment as directed to us. *"Happy* [emphasis added] the warrior"—it's our *grace* to fight this battle, because this is the war that "opens the door to heaven.")

If you don't do your duty, Krishna warns Arjuna, you watch what happens: everything will turn sour for you: "The great warriors will say that thou hast run from the battle through fear, and those who thought great things of thee will speak of thee in scorn." (The threats, you'll notice, are aimed at Arjuna's *kshatria* pride, at his ego. Krishna is using ego as a prod to get Arjuna to do his dharma, which will move him beyond ego.) Krishna goes on, "To forego this fight for righteousness is to forego thy duty and honor."

Krishna is raising the concept of dharma here, how you do your dharma and what happens if you don't. "Dharma" is a very complex word; it has many different meanings. But for now let's stick to its most traditional use in Hinduism, as meaning your duty to the higher law. Fighting this war is your dharma, Krishna says, so *not* to fight it is to fall into transgression, no matter *what* your social roles and models might seem to tell you. If you were able to grasp the whole scope of this drama, Krishna is saying, you'd understand that it's your dharma to play out your role in this struggle. It's what you're here to do. He says, "Arise, therefore, Arjuna, with thy soul ready to fight."

"Duty" is one of the highest obligations for a *kshatria;* it goes very deep. So when Krishna frames dharma in those terms and calls Arjuna to do his duty, it's a powerful argument from Arjuna's *kshatria* perspective. But although that's the power of the argument for Arjuna, it's not really where Krishna is coming from in making the argument. He's not calling Arjuna to do his duty out of a set of social demands, but out of his responsibility to a higher law.

There are subtle relationships at play between social duty and dharma, and the ways they interact. If you're trying to act dharmically, you don't determine your actions out of social duty—and yet you do use the social forms in which you find yourself as your way of expressing your dharmic path. Your karma will situate you in a particular place at a particular time so you can play out a particular role. That's why you were born a *kshatria,* Krishna tells Arjuna—so he can play out this part and, in doing that, fulfill his dharma.

In Hindu tradition, the castes (of which the *kshatria* caste was one) were divisions in society based on birth and role; therefore, your caste defined your life through one set of coordinates. Then there were the ashramas, or stages of life. There are four of those. There is the period from birth to twenty, when you're a student, when you're learning. Then there's the time from twenty to forty, when you're a householder; you make the money that supports the whole system. Next there's the stage from forty to sixty, when you do your religious study. And then from sixty on, you become a renunciate, a *sunnyas*—you let go of everything worldly, and turn your attention completely toward God.

That whole Hindu system of defining you according to those two sets of coordinates is called Chaturvarnashrama-dharma, the dharma of caste and ashrama. And between caste on the one hand and ashrama on the other, your life was laid out pretty clearly, like a plot on a grid. If you were a *kshatria* of a certain age, there would be a well-defined Vedic prescription for just what you ought to be doing today. It was called your swadharma, and it was an absolutely clear-cut structure, defining appropriate action. Krishna is standing squarely within that system when he says to Arjuna, Do your duty. Do what is appropriate.

We have more of a problem in our culture, trying to decide what's appropriate. We don't have castes and ashramas to tell us what we're supposed to be doing at any given moment—in fact, we're at the opposite end of the spectrum. There are very few clear, cultural prescriptions that are deeply ingrained in our society to tell us what to do. So we're faced with having to figure out for ourselves what our dharma might be, without that kind of comfortable matrix to guide us. We have to rely on ourselves; we have to listen, and hear how our individual differences will determine our appropriate duty moment by moment. All of our circumstances feed into that: If you have a certain kind of intellect, or if you have certain economic circumstances, it defines certain paths. If you have a husband or a wife, that defines certain possibilities, and it also defines certain limiting conditions.

Some people might say, "I can only do a job that is absolutely dharmic, and I would rather starve to death than earn money impurely." Others say, "Look—I'll do the best I can, given my circumstances." There's no judgment in either case; each of us has to hear what each of us has to do. If you are a sadhu, if you are single and a renunciate, then maybe you can afford to be more of a purist; no one is dependent on you. On the other hand, if you are a householder and you have a family, then you have certain responsibilities, and you've got to do the best you can. If you are a householder, but you are being such a purist that you don't get enough money to feed your baby, in the long run you will have done more adharma than dharma. If you're in that situation and you find you have to take a job that doesn't feel entirely dharmic to you, do the best you can to bring as much consciousness as possible into the scene. That's all you can do. You work with what you're given.

Let's say you're rich—then that defines, in part, your dharma. You can't make believe you're *not* rich. Even throwing your money away doesn't get rid of it, karmically—that's a karmically loaded act, too. Instead, you have to begin to be *responsible* about your money, to figure out your duty with regard to it; money becomes your dharma at that point.

You do that with respect to each aspect of your life. Whatever your part is, you just play it, but you play it as consciously as you can. That's the most basic form of the concept of doing your dharma: to find your little square on the grid, and then to live it out perfectly. *Why* you're doing your dharma remains to be seen. At this point, Krishna is simply saying, It's your duty—just do it.

But Arjuna, like most of us, has some trouble surrendering. He's still holding on to a lot of preconceptions about how he thinks things "ought" to be, and inevitably that gets in the way of doing his dharma. The same thing happens to us. For instance, I came to "the spiritual trip" out of an intellectual tradition, and because I was an intellectual of sorts, I got very attached to meditation practices, because they seemed so "essence-y." They were so clean, so neat, so pristine. My mind was just thrilled by a system like the *Abhidhamma,* filled with beautiful categories and intellectually so exquisite. I was *certain* that meditation was my spiritual path!

But then I met Maharajji—and my game just wasn't the same anymore. It turned out that my path wasn't what I'd thought it was going to be.

I didn't give up easily, though. For a long time, I kept trying to make it work the way I thought a "real" spiritual trip ought to work. Like I'd say to Maharajji, "Maharajji, how do I raise my kundalini, my spiritual energy?" I figured he'd give me some secret, inner teaching, like "Meditate on this ancient mantra."

He said, "Feed everybody."

I said, "Feed everybody?"

"Feed everybody. Serve everybody."

"Maharajji—to raise my kundalini??!"

He said, "The kundalini can be raised by the touch of a guru. The guru can just *think* about it and your kundalini will rise. Don't worry about that—just feed people and serve people." He was saying to me, "Do your dharma." And my dharma wasn't meditation.

Over time, it became clear to me that my yoga is devotion and service, and that it's devotion and service whether I like it or not. That's my dharma. It's what I'm given to work with. But it took a while before I would accept that, or surrender to it.

Arjuna is in the same predicament here. He doesn't like the dharma that's facing him out on the battlefield. He has his own ideas about what he'd like his path to be. But gradually, we come to realize that following our own path isn't going to get us where we want to go; we begin to acknowledge that our dharma *is* our route through, and so we start to surrender into it. And that's what Krishna is advising Arjuna to do: "Thus is the wheel of law set in motion, and that man lives indeed in vain who, in a sinful life of pleasure, helps not its revolution. But the man who has found the joy of the spirit, and in the spirit has satisfaction, that man is beyond the law of action."

That's an interesting point: That once you're acting purely out of dharma, you're "beyond the law of action." When you've totally surrendered yourself to your dharma, you're no longer acting out of striving, but out of spirit. When that happens, you are no longer creating any more karma for yourself. You only act to fulfill the dharma, not out of any personal motive, so no karma accrues.

Ram Dass (peering through fence) and Teaching Assistants: The group is pictured at the rear of the Main Hall, a recycled manufacturing and warehouse building where Ram Dass taught. (The "Service Center" designation seemed appropriate for a course focused on karma yoga.) Many of the teaching assistants went on to become leading spiritual teachers in their own right; they are, from left: *back row*—Joseph Goldstein, Dwarkanath Bonner, Krishna Das, Deena Bandhu, Vishwanath Miller, Krishna Bush; *second row*—Ramdev Borglum, Ganga Dhar Gerhard, Mirabai Bush; *squatting*—Maruti Projanski, unidentified person.

Not only that, not only do you stop building up your karma account, but your whole relationship to your life changes. It all becomes a pageant, a play. Plotinus says, "Murders, death in all its shapes, the capture and sacking of towns—all must be considered as so much stage-show, so many shiftings of scenes, the horror and out-cry of a play. For here, too, in all the changing doom of life, it is not the true man, the inner soul, that grieves or laments, but merely the phantasm of the man, the outer man, playing his part on the boards of the world."[1]

In Hermann Hesse's *Journey to the East,* Leo says, "Naturally one can do all kinds of other things with life—make a duty of it, or a battle-ground, or a prison—but that doesn't make it any prettier. Just what life is, when it is beautiful and happy—it's a game."

A game? Doesn't that change the complexion of things? It's all so much less fraught. When you're acting out of dharma, a quality of equanimity comes into everything you do. Meister Eckehart wrote, "We ought to take everything God puts on us evenly, not comparing and wondering which is more important or higher or best. We ought simply to follow where God leads."[2] As we come to appreciate more and more the exquisiteness of the total design, a wisdom begins to develop, which recognizes that no part is any better and no part is any worse than any other part—each part is just *different* from every other part. The play goes well when each person plays her or his part perfectly. Not greedily, wishing they could move into somebody else's role; just content in doing their own dharma.

In the little villages I visited in India, where living the dharma is still a real force, you don't see so much of the kind of ambition and envy that we're used to here. You find the sweeper totally fulfilled in being the perfect sweeper. That's his part. He's not even saying, "Look what a good sweeper I am!" He's just sweeping as perfectly as he knows how. And he's expecting the shopkeeper to be the perfect shopkeeper, and the prime minister to be the perfect prime minister. He isn't busy wishing he were the shopkeeper or the prime minis-ter—he knows that's not his dharma; he's living out his own dharma, and expecting everybody else to live out theirs.

Now to some degree, that's just an ideal, and it only works perfectly when everybody is living in the Spirit. But the interesting thing is that when I've been around people who are harmoniously playing their parts that way, I've often felt in them a kind of contentment that isn't very available to us here in the West, a kind of a quietness inside. Some of the desperate striving is relieved.

We can see that there are ways of inhabiting our roles without making quite so much of them. It's really not necessary to take our lives quite so personally. "The man who knows the relation between the forces of nature and actions," Krishna says, "sees how some forces of nature work upon other forces of nature, and he becomes not their slave." Your body, your mind, your personality—that's all just part of nature, it's all just lawful stuff happening. Why are you getting uptight about it? Let it be harmonious with its lawful manifestation, and don't struggle against it so hard. Live your life more lightly, more impersonally; don't get so caught, so trapped in your melodrama.

We all do love our own melodramas. We each have one. Everybody thinks they're somebody doing something, or somebody thinking something, or somebody wanting something: "I've gotta have sex tonight or I'll die." "I'm so lonely!" "I can't meditate." "I'm so high!" We all get so *involved* in our melodramas, so busy thinking we're the actors, so busy thinking we're doing it all—and it's really all just this lawful stuff running off. How funny!

But in order to see that, in order to begin to appreciate the lawfulness of the unfolding, we need to develop a little perspective. It can be a nice meditation to take a seed, and put it in a bit of earth. Put it on a kitchen windowsill, and watch it grow into a plant, into a flower. Just observe it every day. Use that as your daily meditation exercise; see the way the whole process unfolds.

Then turn the lens around. Study yourself in the same way you studied the seed growing. Observe your own life, your own actions, with that same sense of detachment and curiosity, until you can see the laws of nature working in *you*. You'll see what leads to anger, what leads to love, what leads to desire. Just watch it all—don't argue with it, don't judge it, just watch it. And as you begin to develop that perspective, you'll find that your acts gradually come less and less out of attachment and more and more out of the simple, lawful flow of things.

◎

Krishna's argument about doing your dharma and playing your part is the framework for one of the major themes of the Gita: the practice of what is called karma yoga. Up to now, Krishna has been persuading Arjuna, telling him *why* he should fight this battle. Now he's going to begin explaining to him the *way* he should go about doing it—that is, the context from which he should approach the battle. In fact, he's going to define the technique through which we *transform* our actions, and bring them into harmony with our dharma.

Here are a couple of slokas to bring the theme to mind for us.

"But great is the man who, *free from attachments* [emphasis added], and with a mind ruling its powers in harmony, works on the path of karma yoga."

"In liberty from the bonds of attachment [emphasis added], do thou therefore the work to be done, for the man whose work is pure attains indeed the Supreme."

"Do your work, but do it without attachment." That represents the first part of the formula. We're not being told yet how to *stop* being attached, but we are being told that that's the goal—to work without attachment, which means acting without worrying about the outcome. "Don't be attached to the fruit of the action" is one of the principal instructions in karma yoga. "Set thy heart upon thy work, but never on its reward. Work not for reward, but never cease to do thy work."

Mahatma Gandhi told us what that looks like in practice; he said, "In regard to every action, one must know the result that is expected to follow, the means thereto, and the capacity for it. He who being thus equipped is without desire for the result, and is yet wholly engrossed in the due fulfillment of the task before him, such a man is said to have renounced the fruits of his action."[3]

Once we've really done that, renounced the fruits of the action, we're finally free to act in whatever way we're drawn by our dharma to act. We're no longer being pulled and pushed in other directions by our attachments—we're not going to get anything out of it. We're acting solely to fulfill our dharma.

How would we know what "fruits" to ask for, anyway? How do we know what's supposed to happen? Until we're at the place where we can see the whole scope of the karmic pattern, we have no idea what outcome would be best for ourselves and for everybody else.

I'll go and give a lecture, and maybe it turns out to be a disaster—everybody gets up and walks out. That's hard on a lecturer, if you're concerned about the fruits of your action! I will go away feeling humiliated, shaken, my ego crushed. That experience will burn into me, and slowly that humiliation and hurt will keep working on me and working on me until, after a while, I come to see it as one of Maharajji's greatest teachings. Far out! The people in that audience were showing me how I was clinging to my own model of what a "good" outcome would be. If I'm really lousy, maybe that's the best thing I can do for you—maybe I'm throwing you back on yourself to get the teachings. How do I know? Because of my own ego needs, I can't stand back far enough to see what would create the optimum outcome of my own acts.

So what do I do? I do my best, but I give up the fruit of the action. If I don't know what's supposed to happen, it's probably better if I don't get too attached to one particular outcome. I listen to hear what my next step should be. I do my acts in the best way I can. And how it comes out . . . well, that's just how it comes out. Interesting, nothing more. It's a matter of letting go of expectations.

In the mid-1970s, a group of friends and I decided to put together an evening at the Winterland Ballroom in San Francisco. Winterland was a huge rock-and-roll emporium. It seated six thousand people—the circus used to be held there. So Bhagawan Das and Amazing Grace and I decided we were going to "do Winterland." We were going to have music, and a light show, and it was going to run from two in the afternoon until eight the next morning. It cost us $4,500 (that was a *lot* of money back then!) to put together the whole operation—renting the hall, getting a sound system, advertising. But we had great expectations, and great plans for all the profits we were going to make.

The day came, and we did our thing. But unfortunately for all our expectations, there was a bus strike called for the day of the show. Public transportation was shut down, and people couldn't get to Winterland. The following morning, when we counted up the receipts, it turned out that only about two thousand people had showed up, and not only had we not made any money, but we had lost about $1,100. All our fascinating fantasies of red Volvos and trips to Mexico, all the things we would do with the money we were going to make from this incredible gig—all down the tubes, just like that.

We sat there for a while in a state of shock. Then I said to the others, "Do you feel bad about it?" We thought about it, and not one of us could find in ourselves anything that felt bad about the experience. It was bizarre! In spite of the fact that all our expectations had been disconfirmed—Right! OK! How it is is how it is. We don't have what we expected; instead, we have an $1,100 debt—that's who we are now. (Of course, that was after we had all finished blaming one another.) We'd had a good time, the two thousand people all had a good time, and the outcome . . . well, it was what it was.

Such experiences are priceless. They're rich opportunities for learning how not to cling. You set up a game, and then you play it: purely, lovingly, compassionately, with total involvement but without attachment. As pure karma yoga. Then how it comes out is how it comes out—and that becomes the next condition for the next dance in the next mind-moment.

We start to see the outlines of the way a path of karma yoga might work, and how we might bring it into our own lives. We see the possibility that we can turn whatever it is we do every day into a path to God. Krishna has given Arjuna—given us—two instructions so far for how to go about doing that. First, he said, we listen to hear what our dharma is, and we try to become harmonious with that in our actions. Next, we perform each act as purely as we can, without thinking about any rewards.

But there is one more key instruction in this practice of karma yoga, and it's the one that flips the game out to another level. Not only do you do your dharma and act without regard to its fruits—in addition to all that, you act *without thinking of yourself as being the actor.* The action is happening through you, but you aren't doing it. You have stepped out of the way.

That puts you in a whole new perspective in relation to your actions. Krishna tells Arjuna, "All actions take place in time, by the interweaving of the forces of nature [the gunas], but the man lost in selfish delusion thinks that he himself is the actor." Krishna is saying, Look—you're not doing anything; it's a delusion to imagine you are. You're not the actor. What's happening is just the sum total of millions of laws playing themselves out through you. Once you see that, really see that, you're home free, because your sense of an "I" acting in the world is stripped away.

So the karma yogi is the person who uses his or her life to come to God by listening for the dharmic act, acting without attachment to the outcome, all the while knowing she or he's not the actor, anyway. That's the whole formula for turning our lives around and making them our spiritual practice.

The warrior in the Carlos Castaneda books gives us another model of the perfect karma yogi; all the things Don Juan says about the warrior refer to the karma yogi as well: "A warrior is a hunter. He calculates everything. That's control. But once his calculations are over, he acts, he lets go, and he survives in the best of all possible fashions. The mood of a warrior calls for control over himself, and at the same time it calls for abandoning himself."[4]

We can hear in that a description of some of the qualities that come into our actions when we're not attached to the outcome, and not busy being the actors. There's a sense of equanimity, for example. Castaneda talks about it as a sense of "control, yet self-surrender." There's great spontaneity, and at the same time a quality of loving attention, because each act is our offering, our flower at God's feet. If we're acting from that place, it shows up in each thing we do, even simple things, like making a cup of tea. Gurdjieff used to say, "If you can serve a cup of tea properly, you can do anything." That is, if you are able to perform *any* act in a true karma-yogic fashion, it's because you're acting from a place where you're free of attachments and not busy being the actor—and being in that place will shape *every* act you do.

The Book of Tao says, "By letting it go, it all gets done. The world is won by those who let it go. But when you try and try, the world is then beyond the winning."[5] If you're going to make a cup of tea right, you can't be busy *trying* to make the cup of tea right, because while you're busy trying, you're not present with making the tea. You can't be doing both.

The right way to make a cup of tea is to start by bringing together everything you need to make the tea, including the knowledge of how to do it. And then you make the tea. While you're making the tea, you're just making the tea—nothing else. You're not worrying about how the tea will turn out, and you're not wondering whether you're good enough to make the tea correctly, and you're not thinking about whether you should serve it with honey. You're just right there, making the tea. Now you're rinsing the kettle . . . now you're filling it . . . now you're putting it on the stove—being present with every step, and acting out of the total harmony of each moment.

The more purely we flow into our karmic circumstances, the more our acts are just happening. There's no struggle. There's no anxiety, because we don't care how the act turns out. There's no self-consciousness, because there's no actor involved. "He who sees the inaction that is in action, and the action that is in inaction, is wise indeed. Even when he is engaged in action, he remains poised in the tranquility of the atman."

But we can't fake it—that's just more attachment. We can't pretend we're right there making the tea when really we're not, when really we're lost in a thought of how well we're making the tea. We have to start from where we're at, right in this moment. So here we are: We're still stuck with all our desires. Most of the things we're doing, we're doing because we want something out of it, and we can't make believe we're other than what we are. What do we do? How do we work with our actions as yoga when we know how caught we still are? And most important of all, how do we know for sure *what* it is we're supposed to do?

The answer is, we don't. The truth of it is, until you are no longer attached to your ego in any way, every act you do will have your ego present in it. There's not a *chance* it won't! Right up to the end, there are going to be mixed motives, subtle ways in which you'll do it to yourself, again and again. That's what's so funny about this battle!

I've said before that the span of progress on the spiritual path is about one body length. We take a step, and we fall flat on our faces, because it was another impure trip. So we pull ourselves up, and we take the next step—and we fall on our faces again. That seems to be about the rate at which we go.

So when you're listening to hear your dharma, there is very little likelihood that you're going to hear the "pure message." You're just going to hear *another* message. But you keep tuning and tuning— through study, through meditation, through falling on your face. And slowly, slowly, as your methods start to work, your attachment to the whole business starts to get less and less. After all, the ego can only trap you as long as you think you *are* it; when it's just out there doing its thing—when it's just "ego-ing," like eyes seeing or ears hearing—it becomes merely a functional entity. Nothing more interesting than that.

In the meantime, you do the best you can. You look at the next step you're about to take, and you ask yourself, "What seems to be the right next thing to do?" Then you become quiet, and you listen inside for an answer. You get as quiet as you can, and you listen as clearly as you can, but you recognize that in spite of that, it's probably not going to be a pure message from beyond the beyond. Very likely, it'll still have plenty of your desire systems mixed in with it.

Once you've decided as best you can, you act, keeping in mind that you are not the actor. While you're acting, you don't second-guess yourself; you don't waste your time wondering whether you made the right decision. You're done deciding—now you're acting: Be present with your actions. After you've finished, if you want to, you can sit back and reflect and say, "Was that the right choice?" That's different. But while you're doing it, do it fully. When you're making tea, make tea. When you're brushing your teeth, brush your teeth. When you're making love, make love. Big acts, small acts, whatever it is, be fully there with it. Stop ruining things for yourself with that self-conscious, judgmental holding back.

What we're letting go of in that process is the old, self-critical inner voice, the old superego that's so afraid of blowing it, afraid of making a mistake, afraid of looking like a fool. That is not the same, you'll notice, as the impersonal inner witness, the practice of noting what we're experiencing. That's the thing we're trying to cultivate. Witnessing has a totally different quality to it—it's *observing,* not judging. The judging superego is incompatible with acting in the moment; the impersonal witness is the essence of acting in the moment.

So karma yoga turns out to be a technique for extracting ourselves from the turmoil of life not by inaction, but by shifting perspectives on our actions. No longer are our actions a means to fulfill our desires; now they are opportunities for spiritual practice: for practice in being unattached to the outcome, and for practice in getting rid of the idea that we're doing anything. We do what we do, all the time recognizing that it's just the wheel of karma, the dance of God's play, the laws lawfully unfolding through us. We see that it was only our incredible egocentricity that made us think *we* were doing it!

And as we begin to see ourselves that way—not as the actors, but as the vehicles through which the laws of nature are unfolding—we are approaching something which is much more interesting, and much more profound, than whatever it was we might have *thought* the game was about. Krishna points to it when he says, "I have no work to do in all the worlds, Arjuna, for these are mine. I have nothing to obtain, because I have it all. And yet I work."

"And yet I work"? Isn't that interesting? He's saying, Look: I don't have any karma—there's nothing I *have* to do. But I act anyway. Coming from that space of no ego and no attachment, there clearly has to be a whole different motive for acting.

You see, we've really been talking about starting with our desires, starting with our attachments, and using them as a way of coming to union. It's out of our *desire* to come to the One, out of our *desire* to be liberated, out of our *desire* to surrender, that we listen to hear our dharma, and that we do it. We do our dharma *to fulfill a desire,* within the desire system. There's an *attachment* in there—the attachment to getting liberated—and that's what motivates us to work. But if all that is true, then once we get liberated and have no attachments, why would we work?

Krishna is letting us in on a whole new basis for action here. Imagine a person who has absolutely no personal desire to do *anything*—not even to get enlightened. She's got it! She *is* it! She's not trying to develop herself—she's already there. She has no more moral motives—she's beyond good and evil. So what is she doing, *doing* anything?

Anandamayi Ma was a beautiful saint in India, someone who was living in that place, someone whose actions were totally free. Yet she set up hospitals, dispensaries, schools—what was she doing with all those ashrams and all that service? Was she doing karma yoga? Outwardly, her actions might have seemed like that, but the spirit of it, the motive from which *she* was acting, was completely different. The motive was different in that there *was* no motive. There was no intention behind her actions. She was just *being* the expression of dharma, *being* compassion.

With beings like that, beings like Anandamayi Ma or my guru, it's that spirit behind their actions which *is* the transmission. The true guru is someone whose very life is a statement of how it all is when you're done with it all, and any forms or acts that the guru uses are merely the vehicles for that transmission. Such a being is beyond the gunas, beyond the forces of nature—no longer attached at all to body, mind, reason, senses, but using them still. In that place, you're no longer doing karma yoga—you're the expression of it.

Meher Baba said, "To penetrate into the essence of all being and significance, and to release the fragrance of that inner attainment for the guidance and benefit of others by expressing in the world forms of truth, love, purity and beauty: this is the sole game which has any intrinsic and absolute worth. All other happenings, incidents and attainments can, in themselves, have no lasting importance."[6]

Yoga has been called a practice for concentrating all our faculties on a single point in order to transcend the limitations of ego. But karma yoga? Who would have suspected that the road to God would lead us by way of the household and the marketplace. The world becomes the means for extricating ourselves from the strands of worldly attachment—what an ingenious flip! Instead of entangling us, suddenly our acts set us free. The Gita says, "Who in all his works sees God, in truth he goes to God."

When we first set out to do our work as spiritual practice, we're still operating from inside the world of attachments and desires, because the desire to get free is still a desire. But as the upaya, the method, begins to work, it leads us to a deeper understanding of the reason and wisdom that underlie the whole system. We see who we are, and what it is that's going on, in a different light. And along with that understanding comes an increasing impersonality toward our own lives. Impersonality. Not less involvement, but less romanticizing of it all, less melodrama, less doer. We go on living our lives, and we live them as perfectly as we can, but we live them in an increasingly detached way. Less and less are we acting out of our motives or our desires—not even out of the high-minded ones like enlightenment. We're just acting because it's our dharma to act. That's essence karma yoga.

4

Jnana Yoga

I will tell thee a supreme mystery," says Krishna, "because thy soul has faith. It is vision and wisdom, and when known, thou shalt be free from sin." Remember what's happening here—that Krishna is now in the "how-to" part of his discourse. He's instructing Arjuna in the various techniques he can use as yogas for getting to God, and this statement of Krishna's begins a fascinating part of that dialogue. The "vision and wisdom" that Krishna is talking about belongs to the path of jnana yoga, of understanding, which comes via the thinking mind.

No matter what practice we do, in order to understand it completely we have to apply the "vision and wisdom" that Krishna is talking about. Whenever we *think* about our practices or *talk* about our practices, the thinking and the talking are forms of jnana yoga. When I *describe* to you the practice of karma yoga or the practice of bhakti yoga, the description is a jnana yoga technique. To *understand* devotional yoga, to *understand* why we meditate, to *understand* why we do mantra, we have to develop the kind of discriminating wisdom that can differentiate the real from the unreal, and the path of developing that discrimination is jnana yoga. Our meditation *practices* are meditation practices; our devotional *practices* are devotional practices; but when we *talk* about them, we've become jnana yogis.

We can see that from the way the various forms of spiritual practice rely on one another; they don't stand alone, they support and work hand in hand with one another. That's true in Hinduism, and it's true in other practices as well. In Theravadan Buddhism, for instance, panna, or "right understanding," is one of three aspects making up a spiritual practice. Sila and samadhi are the other two—sila being purification, and samadhi, concentration. The three aspects work in relation to one another in a kind of spiral fashion; you keep going around and around among them, but the practices complement one another and augment one another, and you wind up a little higher each time around. They're synergistic.

Unless you had already developed a certain level of wisdom, for example—wisdom meaning that you recognize there is something going on outside the game—you wouldn't have picked up a book like this. Maybe because of reading this book, you'll decide to start meditating. Through meditating, you'll quiet down and so you'll develop more wisdom. That added wisdom may point out to you some of your impurities, which will lead you to doing purifications. When you've purified more, that will intensify your meditation. As your meditation gets stronger, you will go deeper, and you will develop more wisdom. On and on.

In one way and another, all of the practices of jnana yoga work with our intellectual faculties and with different levels of the mind to get to something that is finally beyond the mind's grasp. It's called higher wisdom, and higher wisdom is a different thing altogether from knowledge. It's not like it's the same thing but more of it—it's a different creature altogether. Knowledge is a function of the intellect; higher wisdom goes *beyond* mind and intellect. So higher wisdom is what we're aiming for, and it's outside our minds; but we have to find ways to get there (or we think we do), and the route of knowledge and the intellect is one more of those ways.

Now every method has its traps, so let me say right off that it seems to me there is a dilemma connected with the use of the intellect as a vehicle. The intellect is like a siddhi, a yogic power, and like all such powers, it's very seductive. It's easy for us to get seduced by all the fascinating things that we can know *about*. But our knowing isn't wisdom—it's knowledge; and all of that fascination with knowing things can end up drawing us outward rather than inward. We get trapped in the world of knowing. We busy ourselves collecting more and more worldly knowledge, and focus on the matrix of the rational mind instead of opening into our deeper wisdom. And then the very tool we're trying to use to escape becomes our trap, because with knowing there's always still a "knower" and a "that which is known." You can get right up to the door and knock, but you can't get through as long as you need to know you know. "Sorry!" says Saint Peter. Only when the knower and the known become one does that One get through the door. Nobody who knows anything gets through the door—which means that the ultimate sacrifice for the *gyani,* the intellectual, is giving up knowing anything.

In saying this, I don't want in any way to belittle the intellect. I think we just have to change what we thought thinking was all about. The intellect is an exquisite tool. It's our strong suit as humans, really, and in a way, it's the most powerful tool we have at our service for getting on with our journey—once we understand what the journey is, and understand that the intellect is supposed to be the servant, not the master. Then we can use our intellects skillfully, without getting trapped by our fascination with all the wonderful things we find out, or by the subtle ego trip of "knowing how it all is." We can stop being the captives of our own minds.

Knowledge, if it is used purely enough and with fierce enough one pointedness, can certainly take you through. Einstein once said, "I didn't arrive at my understanding of the basic laws of the universe through my rational mind." He had obviously developed his rational mind to an exquisite degree of clarity; it took him right to the edge—and then . . . ahhhhh! That's where the wisdom comes—it's in the "ahhhhh."

To give you an example of the way that edge tantalizes a scientist: J. Robert Oppenheimer writes, "If we ask, for instance, whether the position of the electron remains the same, we must say no. If we ask whether the electron's position changes with time, we must say no. If we ask whether the electron is at rest, we must say no. If we ask whether it is in motion, we must say no." That sounds to me a lot like

Ramana Maharshi's practice: "*Neti, neti*—it's not this, and it's not that either. Oppenheimer's statement is so far out, and it shows how, if you push the intellect far enough, if you take your knowledge of the outside world right to the very edge of understanding, it flips you beyond intellect into wisdom. But to use your intellect in that way takes a very disciplined mind, a mind that's tuned like a laser beam, with complete one pointedness in problem solving.

Now, let's say that you'd honed that kind of intellect, and you'd decided that you wanted to turn it inward instead of outward. What would you do? The most likely thing is that you'd start by using your mind to make models of what you were experiencing, because models are something our minds can play with. What we find when we turn inward is the same for everybody, but the *description* of what we find there depends on who's doing the describing, and so there are many, many different models of consciousness which have originated in different traditions.

Here, for instance, is a model that uses one of our own cultural artifacts—a slide projector. Probably all of us know roughly how a slide projector works: There is a source of light; you put in a slide, and the light passes through the slide, which determines what patterns and colors of light come through on the other side and fall onto the screen.

Now let's say for a moment that you've been watching a slide show for a while, and that you've decided you've had enough of watching pictures and you want to know what the screen itself looks like. The problem is, all you can see of the screen is what the slides *allow* you to see. If a slide were totally filled with picture, you wouldn't see anything of the screen at all; on the other hand, if a slide had nothing on it, if it were absolutely transparent, you would see the screen perfectly.

Well, now, you could apply that to yourself, as a model. Imagine that inside you is the light, which we will call the atman—or, since you are a jiva, an individual, we'll call it the jivatman, because it's *your* atman; it's the little drop of light, out of all the light in the universe, which happens to be at *your* center. Forget for now where the neurophysiological point of that center is located; just allow that there *is* that source of light in you, and that it is sending out everything: white light, the entire universe. But what is getting through and being reflected on your screen is determined by a number of translucent veils that the light has to go through on its way out. And those veils are the veils of your mind, your thinking mind. The veils are your thoughts, the veils are your sense desires, the veils are your feelings—they're all the different parts of your personality. They're what's called your ahamkara, your ego structure. What that means is that what you end up seeing out there in the world is merely the projection of your own slide show.

That's nothing new, of course—I think we're all basically familiar with that idea; it's certainly a common one in modern psychology. Any psychologist can cite dozens of experiments that prove that motivation affects perception. If you're hungry and you walk down the street, you only see what's edible—you only notice the doughnut shops and the pizza parlors. On the other hand, if you're horny and you walk down the street, you only notice what's makeable. Now it may be that when you're horny and you walk down the street, you pass a really good doughnut shop. You'd never notice it. Later on, somebody might say, "Is there a good doughnut shop in that town?" You'd answer, "Gee, I don't really know"—but you could tell them how many sexual competitors, potential makeables, and irrelevants there were!

In other words, your desires determine what seems to be out there. *Seems* to be out there. You don't know what's *really* out there—you only know what you *think* is out there. The manas, the lower mind, is connected with sense desires and with thoughts; it's collecting now this sense desire, now that thought, now some emotion, and building a whole mosaic out of it, that we experience as our ego universes. What you think is out there, and what I think is out there, is just *us* out there. We don't know if *anything's* out there. Maybe if neither of us were here, there wouldn't be anything out there at all . . . or then again, maybe there *would* be. We just don't know. We can sit around inside our opacities and *think* about all that, but all of our thoughts will be affected by our opaqueness—by our desire that there *be* something out there, or by our desire that there *not* be something out there, whichever. Finally, the only way to get a truer picture of it all is to become less opaque. And doing that is the game of our sadhana.

We could visualize it as a series of concentric circles, with sense objects "out there," in an outer circle. (As you think about these circles, by the way—the ahamkara [or ego], the manas [or intellect], the buddhi, or even the atman—don't get caught in thinking of them as if they were fixed, solid things; they're more like Oppenheimer's electrons, patterns of energy that are always in flux. They happen to have an intensity that makes them *seem* solid for a moment, but they aren't static.)

So first there are the objects of our senses. Then come the senses themselves (the indrias), and then the thoughts, which are the manas or lower mind. Next comes the ahamkara, or ego-structure, which is the vector or the locus of all those various thought patterns, and which represents our model of the world around us.

The next circle in is this thing called the buddhi, which is the higher intellect; it's the only part of our nature package that is capable of grasping the higher realms within us. It's sometimes thought of as being related to third-eye wisdom, but actually the buddhi has a kind of "swinging door" quality connected with it, so it can go either way—it can get sucked into the lower mind and go out into the world, or it can turn back inward and aim toward the light, toward the atman, toward the source of it all. It's like a pivotal process. The dawning of wisdom comes with a recognition of the inner light, when the buddhi first turns inward rather than outward. At that point, the buddhi begins to use the intellect to search more deeply within, to move inward.

The buddhi is still part of our "package," however; it still reflects a separate "me." In the West, we would call it the soul. In the mystic Christian literature, we find the statement, "When thine eye be single, thy being will be full of light." That's the buddhi. It's still part of who we are, but it's right there on the brink. It lies between spirit and matter, and it can aim in either direction.

Then, in the innermost circle, is the atman. The Bhagavatam says: "The atman, or divine self, is separate from the body. This atman is one without a second, pure, self-luminous, without attributes, free, all-pervading. It is the eternal Witness." Think about that: It's what's inside you—right now. It isn't something external to you; it isn't something you have to acquire. It's already there! There's a Zen teaching that says, "The brilliant gem is in your hand." It's not "out there" someplace; you've already got it. You already *are* it—you only *think* you're not! Isn't that bizarre?

In the New Testament, Luke writes: "And being asked by the Pharisees when the kingdom of God cometh, he answered them and said, 'The kingdom of God cometh not with observation [not through your senses], neither shall they say, Lo, here! or, lo, there! For behold, the kingdom of God is within you.' " *Within* you! But are you living in the kingdom? Between that inner you and the you you seem to think yourself to be are all the veils of thought, all the opacities of color and form, that make up the slide projections, which create the world you experience.

Now that entire process we just went through, constructing and explaining that slide-projector model and its ramifications, was a form of jnana yoga practice. We used our intellects to construct a model, which pointed us toward that which is beyond the intellect. That's exactly what the process of jnana yoga is all about. So you begin with the lower intellect, the manas, and you start to study: You study the scriptures, you study with teachers, you read books, you attend retreats; you collect knowledge. None of that is wisdom, you understand—it's merely the *vehicle* that's going to help you get there. You use your intellect to acquire that knowledge, to get you ready to do the next thing. But then it turns out that one key part of "the next thing" is to get rid of all that knowledge. You have to let go of it. You can't be attached to *knowing;* it's just another attachment. The knowledge is disposable; it's served its purpose—let it go. Later on you'll discover that it's all still there, but it will be there in a whole new way.

And before you can get to that new way of being with it, you have to really let go of all that beautiful knowledge you've so busily collected.

Knowledge is like Joseph's coat of many colors: it's groovy, and it's fun to flash it. I mean, when I was a Harvard professor, we'd all sit around flashing our knowledge at one another. It was exquisite! "Well I know this." "But can you quote that?" "I've read the latest research paper." It was *astounding* how much we knew! Yet when I looked inside myself, I found a considerable discrepancy between my *knowing* and my *being*. You can *know* knowledge, but you have to *be* wise. I saw that I could be horribly, hypocritically, depressingly empty of wisdom, at the same time I was snowing everybody around me with my knowledge. Knowledge all by itself, without deep wisdom, ends up becoming despair.

Actually, at any given level of development, it's only possible for us to use a certain amount of knowledge anyway; beyond that, we've just overfilled the cup. We can't absorb it, because our *being* hasn't developed enough. You can get a three-year-old to recite complex mathematical formulas, but that doesn't mean the child understands them. There has to be a balance between the development of a person's inner being and the development of their knowledge in order for their knowledge to be useful. Montaigne wrote that filling the mind with too much material is like overwatering a plant, and that being "clogged with a great variety of things, the mind must lose the power of freeing itself, and the weight of them must keep it bent and doubled up."

Gurdjieff said: "Knowledge which is not in accordance with being cannot be large enough, or sufficiently suited to your real needs. It will be always a knowledge of one thing, together with ignorance of another, a knowledge of a detail, without an understanding of the whole; a view of the form without a capturing of the essence."[1] He also said, "Knowledge may be the function of one center, the thinking center. Understanding, however, is the function of *many* centers. The thinking apparatus may *know* something, but *understanding* appears only when a man feels or senses what is connected with it." What he's saying is that as we move toward wisdom, we move on a path from intellect to intuition, from knowing we know *about* something, to an intuitive sense of our interconnectedness *with* everything. Intuitive wisdom is a nonconceptual appreciation of something through becoming one with it. That's a deeper way of understanding things, and it's a doorway to becoming wisdom.

Our desire to know, which is our desire for a sense of certainty, becomes one of the hindrances that gets in the way of our developing intuition. Ramana Maharshi had a beautiful statement about knowledge as an obstacle; he said: "For men of little understanding, wife, children and others comprise the family. For the learned, there is a family made up of countless books in their minds, which are also obstacles to yoga."[2] Ramakrishna said, "Only two kinds of people can attain to self-knowledge: those whose minds are not encumbered at all with learning—that is to say, not overcrowded with thoughts borrowed from others—and those who, after studying all the scriptures and sciences, have come to realize that they know nothing." That last part is when the jnana yoga path is really working, because the "know nothing" is the next step in this trip. You learn and you learn and you learn until you realize that with all you've learned, you don't know anything—and *that's* the route through. You use your intellectual models to get you going—they're really helpful for that—but you don't cling to the models; you keep letting go of them, letting go of the intellectual structures. Otherwise they get in your way.

In *Miracle of Love,* I told about having lunch one day with Richard Feynman, the Nobel Prize—winning physicist. He asked me about Maharajji, and I proceeded to tell him a number of stories. He was fascinated, and he could allow for the truth of what I was telling him, until I got to a story about how Maharajji had appeared in two places at the same time. To that, the physicist said, "That's impossible. The very basis of physics says that something cannot be in two places at once." I said to him, "That may be true. But you see, Maharajji did it anyway."

Somebody sent me this poem:

> *The freer I get, the higher I go.*
> *The higher I go, the more I see.*
> *The more I see, the less I know.*
> *The less I know, the more I'm free.*

That's really that whole sequence! You collect knowledge, and you get just enough so it allows you to see over the next hill—and when you do, you realize that your knowledge isn't worth a thing. So you throw it away, and then you're freer than you were before you started.

As we turn in these new directions, a lot of the stuff we've filled our minds with starts to get in our way. When you sit down to meditate, you will begin to rue how much you have fed into your mind, as it all starts to pour back out again. I used to sit in the temple, trying to do my breathing meditation: "rising . . . falling . . . rising . . . falling . . ." and I would be remembering *"amo, amas, amat,"* or "area equals πr^2," or something like that. You find you have to clean house a lot. Nowadays, I try not to get caught in filling my mind up quite so much, so I won't have as much to clean out later on.

There are Eastern traditions that have developed techniques for getting rid of that mental clutter. There's the *Abhidhamma*, for instance, which is a Buddhist system of psychology; it uses a very analytical technique for studying the experiences of existence, and then uses that same analytical process to extricate you from the process itself. It's beautiful. Basically, the *Abhidhamma* is an exquisite category system. It's like having one of those old-fashioned pigeonhole desks, the kind with all the little places to put paper clips and rubber bands and messages. If you have the kind of obsessive-compulsive nature that likes that kind of desk, you will absolutely delight in the *Abhidhamma*—because there's not one single thing you can think about for which the *Abhidhamma* doesn't have a compartment. There are little places underneath and around the back, and there are secret doors . . . it's an incredible desk.

Meditation in the Main Hall: Meditation classes were held twice
a day: in the early morning, and before the afternoon talks.
The photograph gives a good sense of the gritty industrial space
that was hastily converted into an auditorium for the first year
of classes at Naropa.

What's useful about the system is that it gives you a way to get rid
of everything—so your desktop, which is your mind, is always perfectly clean. When you get good at the category system, you know
where every pigeonhole is located; something appears on your desk,
and automatically your hand reaches out and puts it in the right place,
and your desktop is clear again. You have a thought or you have a feeling, and you remember, "Oh, that's category four-six-three-sub-two."
Zip—into the pigeonhole! Gone. Besides clearing them away, that
view of your thoughts and feelings also tends to depersonalize things
very quickly, to take the romance out of the experience, and to get
rid of the feeling, "I'm really somebody going through something."

The *Abhidhamma* is only one of the practices developed in
the East for working with the mind. There are many, many exquisite

techniques that use the intellect to get beyond the veils. One of them was the method of Vicharasangraham that was taught by Ramana Maharshi, a beautiful saint who lived in southern India during the first half of the 1900s. He had an interesting history: Ramana Maharshi was someone who, at seventeen years of age, had seemed a pretty ordinary young man. He had done no sadhana whatsoever, he hadn't studied any spiritual traditions particularly, he was just busy being a high school student. One day, as he was sitting on the floor of his uncle's study, he suddenly felt very powerfully that he was about to die. Instead of struggling against his death, as most of us might do, he surrendered into it—he experienced himself as having died. He watched his body being carried away to the burning ghat and cremated there. His body was gone, his personality had fallen away . . . and then he experienced an intense sense of Presence, of the "I" that isn't part of being born or of dying. That experience transformed him.

Some of us, through whatever means, may have had experiences like that. The difference between Ramana Maharshi and the rest of us is that *he* didn't come back. Well, that's not exactly true: He stayed around for another fifty years, but *who* it was that stayed around was totally different from who he'd been before all that happened. That is, he didn't come back into his habitual thought forms about who he was.

Ramana Maharshi's practice was to continually ask himself, "Who am I?" It's a form of self-inquiry. He wrote, "If the mind uninterruptedly investigates its own true nature, it discovers that there is no such thing as mind. Such constant practice is the shortest path for attaining true wisdom." A practice like that is a beautiful method—if you can stand it! It's a practice of self-knowledge, or self-investigation that takes incredible intellectual discipline. Here's how you might work with it: You sit down in your meditative posture, and you ask yourself the question, "Who am I?" And then to whatever it is that arises, you say, *"Neti, neti"*—meaning, "I am not that, I am not that." That is, you're using your thoughts to cut through your thoughts about who you are. So you begin. You ask yourself, "Who am I?" and you say, "I am not my senses." Then one by one, you make the processes of each of your senses the object of your attention. Maybe you start with your ears—you notice your ears hearing.

Have you ever really done that, by the way—noticed your ears hearing? It's a good meditation. You draw your attention inside until you can, so to speak, watch the whole process. You observe the way waves of sound come into your auditory canal and vibrate against the cochlea and the vestibular membrane and all those little mechanisms . . . and then the way the energy of that goes on to stimulate the auditory nerves that send the signals up into your brain . . . and then the way your brain starts interpreting the signals, assigning them meaning. All that is going on, every time you hear a sound; all of it is happening, mechanically running on, even though we hardly ever notice it. So we start to notice it; we turn hearing into a meditation. We sit back and let our attention get more and more subtle, and watch that whole fantastic trip unfold.

But that's another practice altogether. In a practice of self-inquiry, instead of *attending* to the process, you notice your ears hearing, and then you detach yourself from that—you say, "I am not my ears hearing. That's not me." Then you do the same thing with your other senses, with your eyes seeing and your nose smelling and your tongue tasting and your skin feeling. As you look at each experience, you see it as object and you say, "I am not that."

After you've detached yourself from each of your senses, you move on to the next category; you say, "I am not my organs of motion"— that's your arms, your legs, your tongue, your anal sphincter, and your genitals. They're called the organs of motion or the organs of action in certain systems in India. You experience each of those parts of yourself, but in each case objectifying it, so it's no longer you. You stop thinking of it as "my anal sphincter"—it's just "look at that anal sphincter."

Then next you go on to your internal organs, and you do the same thing with them—you say, "I am not my heart beating. . . . I am not my lungs breathing. . . . I am not my stomach and intestines digesting." *Neti, neti, neti.*

Finally, after you've gone through all the physical stuff that you may think of as you, you're left with just one more thing, which is your thinking mind itself. All the parts of your physical body are gone; they've been dismissed, and your thoughts are all that's left of you. It's like you've climbed a tree, and gotten further and further out on the branches, until you're out on the final, smallest twig. All that's left is your identification with the thought "I." And then the final statement is "I am not this thought." You lop off that last little branch, and you fall free.

If you can stay homed in on that discipline, extricating yourself little by little from the body, from the senses, from the emotions, from everything, right back to the last little thought—you're through the door! You've used the intellect to beat the intellect, and you've become one with the atman. But to do that takes a level of discipline which is *incredibly* fierce! You'll get rid of your eyes, your ears, your nose, you'll be all the way to your respiratory system—and suddenly you'll hear something. At that moment, you're your ears hearing again. You've got to go back and do that one all over again, in order to cut yourself loose from it. It's the fiercest gyan method I know, and you have to be very quiet inside in order to be able to work with it. But it's a powerful technique for cutting through.

Just to round this out, let me mention another method, which at first blush seems to contradict the one we've just been talking about. Instead of a practice of saying, "I'm not this, I'm not that," and cutting off your identification with thing after thing, you can work instead with a practice of embracing everything into yourself. That is, instead of saying, *"Neti, neti,"* to each thing you experience, you say, *"Tat twam asi"*—"I am that." You expand and expand and expand who you see yourself to be, until it's all included within you.

A beautiful saint named Ram Tirth described what it feels like to be in that place. He said: "I am without form, without limit . . . beyond space, beyond time. I am in everything, and everything is in me. I am the bliss of the universe. Everywhere, I am. I am sat [absolute existence], chit [absolute knowledge], ananda [absolute bliss]. Tat twam asi—I am that." He's talking from inside, now. He went inside deeply enough to experience those places in himself, and now he's telling us who we all are—*all* of us: We're beyond space, beyond time, beyond form, and beyond limit. That's who *you* are. *Sat, chit, ananda.*

Those two methods—*"Neti, neti"* and *"Tat twam asi"*—come from opposite poles, but they end up at the same place. In the one practice, you detach from everything, and in the other practice you embrace it all, but they turn out to bring you to the same place. Empty? Full? All the same.

Practices like those of Ramana Maharshi and Ram Tirth come out of the Hindu tradition, but there's a practice that comes out of Buddhism—Zen Buddhism—that is a variation on the jnana yoga theme of using the mind to beat the mind. It's a technique most of us have heard of—the Zen koan, the insoluble riddle. A koan poses a question that the intellect just can't process, so the thought processes go "Tilt!" and that flips you outside your thinking mind.

My own introduction to the Zen koan came, improbably enough, at a Benedictine monastery in Elmira, New York. There was a gathering of holy beings happening there, and we were all taking turns doing our trips for each other. So at four o'clock one morning, I found myself seated between Swami Satchitananda and Swami Venketeshananda, as we were being taken through a Zen sitting by Joshu Sasaki Roshi—a very fierce Japanese teacher from one of the schools of Zen that uses the koan (not all of them do). First, Sasaki Roshi taught us how to sit; it's an incredibly fierce meditation posture, with the back rigid, the hands held just so, the elbows out, the chin down—very tight, a state of great tension. Then he gave us our koan: "How do you know your Buddha nature through the sound of a cricket?"

Now, what you're supposed to do is to think about that question as you're sitting in that miserably uncomfortable position at four o'clock in the morning. You're supposed to keep saying to yourself, "How *do* I know my Buddha nature through the sound of a cricket?" You sit and you sit and you sit, and you think and you think and you think. Then, later on, you get called in for *dokusan,* which is a personal meeting with the Roshi. There's a strict form to the meeting: You come in, and you bow, and you touch your forehead to the floor so many times. Then you sit down on the student cushion. He's sitting across from you, with a bell and a stick.

"Ah, doctor," he says, "how you know your Buddha nature through sound of cricket?" Well, I'd been working for several hours getting ready for this moment, right? And I had arrived at a plan: What I had decided I would do was that when he asked me the question, I would cup my hand behind my ear, like Milarepa does, when he's sitting in front of his cave listening to the universe. I figured, "Since I'm a Jewish Hindu and he's a Japanese Buddhist, I'll throw him a Tibetan answer. It'll confuse him, if nothing else." I hoped at least I'd snow him a little bit. So he asked the koan, and I cupped my hand behind my ear. He picked up his bell, looked over at me, and said, "Sixty percent." Then he rang the bell to end the interview.

Now that, of course, sucked me in completely. The Jewish achiever in me just *had* to get that other 40 percent!

Some months later, I was basking in a sauna bath in Santa Fe, New Mexico, with Allen Ginsberg and Bhagawan Das and a Tibetan nun—we were quite a colorful group of people, sitting around naked in the sauna. A telegram arrived for me. It was from Mount Baldy—Sasaki Roshi's Zen Center in southern California—and it said, "There will be a rohatsu dai sesshin, starting . . . ," and it gave the date, which was two days later. The telegram went on, "This is the most difficult sesshin of the year. It will go on for nine days. We have reserved a place for you." I thought, "Oh, my God! Nine days of *that?*" *One* day of it in New York had been enough for me! There I was, sitting in the sauna in total Sensual-ville; I'd come planning to spend two weeks just lying around, enjoying myself. But there was something in the telegram that drew me. And there was still that other 40 percent. . . .

So I called them immediately, and I said, "Well, thank you so much for thinking of me, and I certainly would like to sit with you sometime—but I'm only a beginner, and this sesshin is for advanced students." I was hoping to get myself off the hook, but they said, "Oh, you can do it." Which got me in my *next* vulnerable place.

The following day, I found myself on a plane headed to Los Angeles, and after the flight and a car ride up into the mountains, I arrived at the Zen center. I was met by a fellow in a black robe with a bald, shaved head. He asked, "Name?"

I said, "Ram Dass."

"Upper bunk, cabin four." He handed me a towel and a black robe and a pillow. I was taken to cabin four and told, "You will be in the zendo in five minutes, please, in your robe." Nobody said, "Gee, Ram Dass, great that you came." There was not one tiny bit of ego feeding in the whole scene.

I put on my robe, and walked into the zendo. There was a space with my name on it, and I sat down, and they taught us the sitting practice. And then began something that . . . well, I'll tell you, it was hard to believe that something like this was going on in America, not thirty miles from Los Angeles! We started every morning at 2 A.M., and we went until ten o'clock at night, so we had only four hours of sleep. When we got up at two, we had exactly five minutes to wake up, wash, and be in the zendo.

Once you sat down on your cushion and the bell rang, you were not allowed to move. You had to sit still—and I mean *perfectly* still. There was a man walking back and forth in the hall—a tough-looking guy with a big stick—and if you moved so much as a muscle, he'd notice. He'd come striding over to where you were sitting. He'd stop in front of your cushion, and first he'd hit the floor with the stick; now everybody knew that you'd been caught. Then he would bow to you, and you would bow to him, and then you'd lean forward in one direction, and he'd beat you three times on that shoulder with his stick, and then you'd lean forward the other way, and he'd beat you three times on that shoulder. And I mean he'd *beat* you—it really stung for about fifteen minutes afterward! Then you thanked him, and he thanked you, and you went back into your sitting position.

It didn't even have to be something *blatant* that you did that got you the stick. Imagine that you just woke up; your sinuses are full, and you're sitting there, and the mucus starts to drip out of your nose and over your mustache and down your beard . . . so you go "Snifffff."

That would do it! The first day you might get just a "Shhhh"—but the second day, you'd get the stick!

If you needed to go to the bathroom, you had to get up and go over to one of the monks and whisper, "I have to go to the bathroom." He'd say, "OK, but be quick!" And you'd say, "Yes," and run out to the bathroom. Then you'd find you couldn't go, because you were so nervous about making it back in time. Every minute was programmed and controlled—it was a *fierce* discipline.

We were given koans to solve by Sasaki Roshi. We'd see him for *dokusan*—five times a day. Five times a day, I'd have to go and see him, and he'd ask me my koan, and I'd give him whatever answer I'd been busy thinking up. The first time I went in for *dokusan* and gave him my answer he just said, "No," and rang the bell. Later he got into subtleties like "Oh, *Doctor,* I'm *so* disappointed. I expected more of you than that!" That was a nice one.

Besides all that, it was very, very cold on the top of the mountain— there was even snow on the ground at times—and by the third day, I was really sick. I had a terrible cold, I was running a fever, and my back had gone out on me. I was thinking, "I don't need a Roshi—what I need is an osteopath!" I had become totally, wildly paranoid. I mean, I was *sure* they were really out to get me. I thought, "The guy on the cushion next to me, they never beat him at all. And me, a professional holy man, they're whipping left and right!"

By the fifth day, I was so sick and so uptight and so furious that I realized I really didn't give a damn—about the koan, or the cricket, or any of it. I'd had it. I went in for *dokusan,* and Sasaki Roshi said, "How you know your [whatever it was that he was asking me that day]." I couldn't care *less* how I'd know—I just didn't give a damn, and I said to him, "Good *morning,* Roshi."

His face brightened, and he broke into a smile. "Ahhhh!" he said. "Now you are becoming beginning student of Zen."

Well, I went out of there, and I was walking two feet off the ground. I mean, I'd just solved a koan! I was so stoned by the whole scene, by the total experience, that it pushed me out into another plane. It was like an acid trip: all the bushes had flames leaping out of them, and everything I looked at was washed with a kind of luminous radiance, and no matter which koans I was given, the answers kept popping right out, koan after koan.

Now, all that turned out to be just another passing moment. I'd had what's called a minor satori, a temporary experience of increased awareness. When you still have attachments that are strongly invested, when thought-forms and habits of thought are deeply ingrained and you're still very attached to them, then even though you may override those attachments for a moment by intense sadhana practices—whether Zen koans or kundalini yoga or psychedelics or whatever—you will most likely reenter back into the old thought-forms after a while. You'll come back slightly different, to be sure, but you'll probably come back. The transformation isn't complete. You went to the wedding, but you weren't wearing the wedding garment, so you got kicked out.

Nonetheless, the seed has been planted, the awakening has begun.

☺

In each of these jnana yoga practices, we've seen tools that are able to take us outside of the rational mind *by way* of the rational mind. That's the interesting trick. The practices are carefully designed systems that use the intellect as the lever for freeing ourselves from the intellect's control. Isn't that exquisite?

When we follow any of these techniques, any of these jnana practices, and start turning the mind inward, what our intellect and our knowledge bring us to is the sense that there is within us a light . . . a consciousness . . . an awareness . . . a knowledge of how it all is. That's something already within us—already there—so we see that it's not a question of acquiring something new, that we just have to let go of all the stuff we don't need anymore, all the stuff that's getting in our way. Once we recognize that, our whole life becomes a process of shedding the veils that come between us and that Awareness.

Our yearning to do that, to be rid of whatever stuff it is that's keeping us separate, leads us to begin paying more attention to the inner voice of our intuition, because that's the clue to what we should be doing. We start to listen for the tiny, intuitive whisper that the Quakers call "the still small voice within."

In shifting our focus that way, in turning from knowledge to intuition, we actually make a shift in our whole relationship with the universe. Knowledge is objective; we know *about* something. An intuitive relationship with the universe isn't objective—anything but! It's a *subjective* relationship: We're all in it together. And that's getting very close to the concept of "Oneness," the description of the atman.

My first experience of that inner feeling of at-Oneness—or at least the first experience of which I have any conscious memory—came the first time I took psilocybin. In the course of that experience, I was ripped out of being a "knower of objective knowledge," torn out of seeing the entire world—even myself!—as an object external to me. With the mushrooms, it all became subjective, an internal matter. And that experience of inner truth was so powerful that there is a part of me that never returned from that moment.

Of course, a lot of me *did* return, just as it did after the *sesshin*. A few days later, it was all just another memory of something that had happened, one more moldering butterfly in my collection. But even though the memory faded, the experience itself had carried such a powerful sense of validity that there wasn't a chance it would be completely lost. After a breakthrough like that, we are literally never the same again. From then on, our lives are lived as a way of "getting on with it," as a way of getting rid of whatever it is that's keeping us trapped in our thinking minds. We start looking for the tools we can use to do that, using our actions in the world as karma yoga, parlaying our strengths, like the siddhi of our rational thinking minds, into techniques for parting the veils.

As all these methods start to work, they take us outside of the rational mind that created the systems. *That* is the "vision and wisdom" that Krishna was talking about: to be extricated from that flood of thoughts and sense data that is always rushing through us, carrying us along, so that we can turn back inward, turn back toward the atman. And when we can do that, when we can see beyond all the slide projections of who I am and who you are, when we can look past all the overlay of our habitual thought, we find to our surprise that there is only one of us. We find that it's all an internal matter, that it's always just God dancing with God.

5

Brahman

*W*e have been talking about karma yoga and jnana yoga, two of the practices Krishna presents to Arjuna. We have been considering them as means for getting somewhere we seem to want to go. But what is the "there" we're trying to get to?

In this chapter, we're supposed to talk about the "there"—about what, in order to have a name for it, we are calling Brahman, which is the Light Inside, which is the One of the Universe. But there's an interesting predicament with all that: We're trying to speak of something which by its very nature can't be spoken of. It can't be said, and it can't be whistled, either. Even in giving it a name, in calling it Brahman, we're trying to give form to the formless—yet the minute it *has* any form, it isn't the formless any longer. Ram Tirth said, "A God defined is a God confined." Interesting predicament.

Here we are, trying to extricate ourselves from our attachment to our thought-forms, and our description of what we're aiming toward is but another thought-form. Any label for Brahman is wrong. Any attribution of *any* form is wrong; that means even the most subtle ones, notions like Voidness or Emptiness. It is, in the Tibetan chant, *"Gate, gate . . . paragate . . . parasamgate"*: Gone, gone . . . gone beyond . . . gone beyond even the *concept* of beyond. That's Brahman.

Ramakrishna said that the one thing that can't be soiled by man's tongue (by words, that is) is Brahman, because what Brahman *really* is can't be spoken of. We can talk about it, but we're talking from one plane about something in another plane which in its very nature is completely different from anything that is "speakable about." A name or a word can be a reference point, but it can never be a definition of the thing.

(We should notice, by the way, that the word "Brahman" is used in two different ways in the Gita, referring to two different aspects of God—one of them the formless aspect, and the other that aspect which creates form. The same word is used interchangeably for both, so we have to distinguish which way we're using it; in this chapter, we are talking only about the *formless* aspect of Brahman.)

Although we can't define this thing we're calling Brahman, maybe we can approach an experience of it by immersing ourselves in a kind of collective description of it. There are mystics in every tradition who have visited that plane and then tried to convey what it's like, and even though we can't conceptualize Brahman, our minds can play around the edges by imagining it through those descriptions.

The *Tao Te Ching* is an example of that kind of mystical writing, a very pure and beautiful expression of the experience. It comes from a different lineage, so it doesn't use the word "Brahman," but you can see that it's referring to exactly the same thing.

There's a story, by the way, about how the *Tao Te Ching* came to be written. It's probably apocryphal—I doubt it's the way it really happened; but it's a good story, anyway. It's said that the keeper of the library at Peking was going home to die; he was a very old man. When he came to the boundary between his home province and the place he was leaving, the guards stopped him and said, "You have to pay a fee to cross this boundary!" He said, "How can I pay? I don't have anything." They asked, "Well, what did you do in life?" He replied, "I was a librarian." They said, "Well, go over and sit under that tree, and write down everything you learned. Leave that with us—that will be your payment." So he sat down, and he wrote out the eighty-one verses of the *Tao Te Ching*.

Here is Verse 14: "They call it elusive, and say that one looks, but it never appears. They say that indeed it is rare, since one listens but never a sound. Subtle, they call it, and say that one grasps it, but never gets hold. These three complaints amount to only one, which is beyond all resolution. At rising, it does not illumine. At setting, no darkness ensues. It stretches far back to that nameless state, which existed before the creation." That's written by somebody who's managed to come just about as close as you can to expressing the essence of Brahman.

Then there was Janeshwar, who wrote this next passage. He was an interesting fellow; he was something of a trickster. For instance, there was at one point some question raised as to whether he was a phony. Some of the priests were accusing him of being a fraud, and they came to check him out. As a test, they asked him to recite some obscure passages from the Vedas for them. Janeshwar said, "Huh— even a dumb animal could do that," and he walked over to a water buffalo that happened to be standing in the courtyard, and had it recite the Vedas for the Brahmin priests. That seemed pretty convincing to them.

Janeshwar's writing is very poetic in its descriptions of Brahman. He says, "Brahman, though existing in forms subject to change, does not undergo change. He appears to have mind and sense organs, but as the sweetness in a lump of sugar is not in its form, so these sense organs and qualities are not Brahman. . . . It is at the same time knowledge, the knower, and that which is to be known, and it is that by which the goal is reached."[1]

A Sufi mystic used a similar image when he said, "Pilgrim, pilgrimage, and road were all but myself towards myself, and my arrival but myself at my own door."[2] Ramana Maharshi said, "If it is said that liberation is of two kinds, with form or without form, then let me tell you that the extinction of the two forms of liberation is the only true liberation."[3]

The mystics of Western science have their own rational mind-take on the experience. In the 1970s, I attended a conference that was put together by John Lilly and Alan Watts, where a group of us had a chance to meet G. Spencer Brown. G. Spencer Brown was a very colorful fellow from England; he was a don at Oxford, a chess master, and a sportswriter. He also had an engineering firm, and was hired by a British railway company to set up a computer program to determine whether the number of railway car wheels that went into a tunnel was the same as the number that came out of the tunnel; they wanted to make sure of that, I guess for obvious reasons. Brown did set up the program, and it worked; but in solving the problem, he found himself using imaginary numbers, and when his counterparts at the British railway system heard about that they got a bit uneasy, because their boxcars seemed terribly real to them. So to convince them, Brown started to construct a logical sequence with which the railway company would be satisfied, tracing back from the railway car wheels going in and out of the tunnel, all the way back to whatever turned out to be the beginning of the sequence.

Well, he got carried away with going back and back and back, and he went all the way back to the beginning of the universe, and out of that he wrote a book called *Laws of Form*. But in the book, instead of starting the way he had with the railway company, he started the other way around. So on the first page he said, in the beginning there is nothing, and the first thing you must do is to make a *distinction*. He drew a line down the middle of the page to mark the distinction between the differentiated state and the nondifferentiated state. That's the first act. Once he'd made that bifurcation, he then (with a very few more assumptions) built the entire universe on it.

But then in a footnote—a very interesting footnote—he said, Of course in order to make a first distinction, you must have some kind of value system on which you're going to differentiate "this" from "that"—like, darker/lighter, better/worse, right/left, whatever. Then he said, "And since, of course, before the first distinction was made there *was* no value system on which to make the first distinction, in fact the first distinction was never made. Therefore this book is written to describe a universe that would exist had the first distinction been made." Well, if you can handle that footnote, you're already through the door into Brahman. If you balk . . . ah! There you are, clinging.

And then, finally, coming back to the Gita, here is this description of Brahman from the thirteenth chapter: "Now I shall tell thee of the end of wisdom. When a man knows this, he goes beyond death. It is Brahman: beginningless, supreme. Beyond what is, and beyond what is not. . . . From him comes destruction, and from him comes creation. He is the light of all lights, which shines beyond all darkness."

In Hinduism, the expression that is used for entering that state of Brahman is *chitta vriti naroda*—the cessation of the turnings of the mind. The image is of an ocean, on which there are waves of all shapes and sizes. The waves are thought-forms: feelings, personality traits, sense data, ideas—wave after wave. And then gradually the waves quiet into ripples, and slowly the ripples get quieter and quieter, until there is just a vast, calm ocean, out of which the ripples came, and back into which they returned. That still, endless ocean is the image of Brahman.

You can see the problem with trying to conceptualize a state of being like that. Ramakrishna, the Indian saint, used to go into very high states of samadhi all the time. There are photos of him with light pouring out of his body. He always wanted to share with his disciples what he was experiencing, so he'd try to tell them what that state was like. He'd say, "Well, now, when the shakti, the kundalini, comes up, and it gets to the third chakra, you experience this." And he'd describe the experience. "When it gets to the fourth chakra, the anahata," he'd say, "you experience this. At the fifth chakra, you experience this. And when you get to the sixth . . ." And he'd go off into samadhi. His body would be standing there, luminous, but he would be somewhere else. One of his disciples wrote, "He would differ from a dead man only in that he retained his physical life heat and that his senses were still available to him—but his consciousness was somewhere else altogether." Then after a while, Ramakrishna would come down and he'd start over again, and he'd say, "It gets to the third . . . and the fourth . . . and the fifth . . ." and out he'd go again. After three or four tries, tears would be streaming down his cheeks. He said, "I really want to tell you, but the Divine Mother won't let me." He couldn't do it, because what it *is* can't be expressed.

Ramakrishna said that our attempts to go to Brahman and report back what it's like are like sending a salt doll—a doll made out of salt—to the bottom of the ocean to determine its depth. On the way, the doll will totally dissolve, and there will be nobody left to report back. That was Ramakrishna's predicament.

But although Ramakrishna couldn't describe it, he could *be* it, he could lose himself in it. He couldn't report back, but he could experience what it was like. One of the devotees tried to describe Ramakrishna's samadhi; he wrote, "In that rapturous ecstasy, the senses and mind stopped their functions. The body became motionless as a corpse. The universe rolled away from his vision, even space itself melted away. . . . What remained was existence alone. The soul lost itself in the Self, and all ideas of duality, of subject and object, were effaced. Limitations were gone, and finite space was one with infinite space. Beyond speech, beyond experience, beyond thought, Sri Ramakrishna had become the Brahman."

What Hindus call becoming the Brahman, Buddhists call nirvana or nibbana—meaning "the blowing out of the candle." In that state, everything you and I know ourselves to be falls away from our minds completely. What remains is a profound and total sense of fulfillment—what Franklin Merrill Wolfe referred to as "a state of utter satisfaction." This isn't Mick Jagger's idea of satisfaction—the kind he can't get none of. This is like the *essence* of everything in your life that's ever given you satisfaction. It's a quality of total enoughness, or completeness, or peace. It isn't the big ice cream cone in the sky, which can never be satisfying for long; it's the *essence* of the big ice cream cone in the sky, which is totally fulfilling.

Brahman isn't an *experience*. To experience something, you have to be separate from it. We use techniques, like karma yoga and jnana yoga, to arrive at the state of Brahman, to immerse ourselves in it. A meditation practice is one of the first things we often try, in order to quiet down our thinking minds. As our meditation deepens, we will find we have many kinds of experiences, and some of them will be like an experience of emptiness. It might be a very appealing experience, but it isn't Brahman. It can't be Brahman, because no *experience* is it, and the "experience of emptiness" is another experience. Brahman is outside the realm of "experiences."

I personally arrived at the kind of states we've been talking about via the yoga of using psychedelics, and while I recognize that psychedelics might be just an astral analog of the real thing, at least they gave me a glimpse of what it must all be about. They gave me some purchase on those other states of being. I can vividly recall some of the sessions we had in a meditation room in our house back in Newton, Massachusetts, where Tim and I were living and taking LSD. Some incredible trips took place in that room. For three or four hours (by the clock time we returned to later) there was no universe, there was no experience of no universe, and yet it wasn't empty. That's paradoxical, but it's *all* paradox, because Brahman contains everything, all of it.

I'll tell you a funny story about one of those sessions. The meditation room I mentioned was sort of unusual. We had put up a false wall in the living room and situated the meditation room behind it, so it appeared that the room didn't exist. There was no door into the room; you had to come into it by way of the basement, going down the stairs from the kitchen, then climbing up a ladder and entering the room through a trapdoor in the floor.

After one of our sessions, when I finally got back into my body, I climbed down the ladder, made my way through the basement, and went upstairs into the kitchen. There was a woman in the kitchen, who had arrived at the house the day before. She'd come up from the south by bus, to get a job in the north; she had come to our house, and was thinking of working there. She was sitting in the kitchen, drinking a cup of coffee, when I came up from the basement. She took one look at me, and whatever it was she saw must have blown her mind, because the coffee cup went flying, and she came running over and fell at my feet. Well, that completely freaked me—I mean, here was this woman, in her fifties, very solid, straight, conservative-looking, kneeling at my feet; it drove me running out of the room. Later, she told me that when I came up the stairs from the basement, all she saw was a radiant, golden light. (As you can see, we had some pretty good LSD in those days!)

Now here is the way I understand the phenomenon that occurred: that whatever that Brahmanic state was which I had entered into during the trip, it was using me to blow that woman's mind and therefore to prompt her next step in her journey, whatever that might be. That was the way I interpreted what happened. I didn't take it personally.

But the point is that even after a trip like that, I came down. As long as there is stuff in us that pulls us back into *this* world (be it desires, longings, attachments—even the subtlest attachment to *knowing* something), that state of Brahman is elusive. We may be able to work with energies of one kind or another and override the system, so we can experience for a moment a little taste of what it might be like, and that's useful. But then our habitual thought patterns reassert themselves, and back we come. There were still too many things that had their hooks in me for me to be able to stay in that state for very long.

        ◎

Let's try on a few more of these descriptions of Brahman, to help us cozy up to the experience by filling ourselves with these images of it. Each passage is some mystic's attempt to describe an experience of Brahman, the indescribable.

Maybe right now these descriptions seem very abstract to us, irrelevant to our own lives. Let me suggest that the way they will become our own, the way the bones will take on flesh, is through our clothing them with our own experiences. Just hearing what other people have written about Brahman will never be satisfying. We have to feel it for ourselves.

And yet the hearing about it has its purpose. It may resonate in a place within us where we sense the validity of it, where we touch the *realness* of our identity with something other than what we think we are. That sense of validity in turn gives us faith; it's right at the point where we touch that sense of *certainty* in ourselves that faith is generated. And that faith is what makes us actually step in and consent to fight our own battle of Kurukshetra.

The Upanishads say: "An ocean One the seer becomes, without duality. This is the highest path, the highest prize, the highest world, the highest bliss. It is that bliss on but a fraction of which other beings live."

A Buddhist text describing the mind of the Buddha says, "Freed from form, sense perception, feeling, habitual tendencies and consciousness, he is deep, incommensurable, unfathomable, like the great ocean."

And here is the way the Third Chinese Patriarch wrote about the experience. He said: "In this world of suchness, there is neither self nor other than self. To come directly into harmony with this reality, just say when doubts arise, 'Not two.' In this 'not two' nothing is separate. Nothing is excluded, no matter when or where. . . . Words. The way is beyond language, for in it, there is no yesterday, no tomorrow, no today."

I'm a Westerner, with roots in the scientific tradition, so I'm attracted by the reflections of Brahman that I find in physics models. They appeal to the jnana yogi in me. Those models tell us that as we go down into smaller and smaller units of matter, what seems like our bodies, or what seems like this book, or what seems like the air, or what seems like Mars—all these turn into tiny units of energy. And when you get down to those tiniest somethings of energy (which, you remember from the Oppenheimer quote, you can't say are either this or that, but just some sort of *patterning* of the energy), then everything in the universe is made up of the very same stuff, and it's all absolutely interchangeable at every moment. The electrons of you are indistinguishable from the electrons of me are indistinguishable from the electrons in a star. It's all totally the same, and it's all totally interrelated.

What's fun is that when you're no longer attached to being one separate part of it, you get to be part of *all* of it. At that point the "all" is known to you subjectively, and you are everywhere at once, because you are no longer pinned in a space-time locus by your separateness. Metaphysics tells me that, and physics tells me that. Everything I have experienced in all of my inner work points to that. So does Maharajji's continual reminder, *"Sub ek!"* (it's all one). "Can't you see, Ram Dass? It's all one. *Sub ek.*"

When we're dwelling in that place of all-Oneness, the quality associated with it is a sense of bliss, the "state of utter satisfaction," as Franklin Merrill Wolfe called it. Wolfe was an interesting American-scientist type, who used to live with his wife in a little cabin up in Lonestar, California. These experiences happened to him in 1937, when he was in his early forties; he had been doing a lot of meditation practice up in his cabin. He wrote: "The event came after retiring. I became aware of a deepening effect in consciousness that presently acquired or manifested a dominant emotional quality. It was a state of utter satisfaction. When in every conceivable or felt sense all is *attained,* desire simply has to drop out. . . . While fused with the state, all other states that could formerly have been objects of desire seemed flaccid by comparison. . . . The secular universe vanished, and in its place there remained none other than the living and all-enveloping presence of divinity itself."[4]

Suchness . . . Oneness . . . bliss . . . the descriptions do their best to paint a picture of the experience for us, to give us a little taste of it. But "painted cakes do not satisfy hunger," and finally we have to do the work that allows us to enter the state for ourselves.

In chapter 8 of the Gita, Arjuna asks, "Who is Brahman?" and Krishna proceeds to tell him, and to describe how to get there. Were the Gita to stop at that point, I think that its Buddhist tone would be dominant: leave form behind and merge with the One. But the Gita is about to point us toward a whole new level of wisdom.

See, here is the predicament: We talked about there being those two different aspects of Brahman—the formless, and the creator of form. The question is, are they mutually exclusive, like purusha and prakriti? Does the formless one rule out the creation?

We're actually a little scared of Brahman. We figure that were we to go back into the One, were we to merge totally with it, there wouldn't be anything more happening after that. It's a good question. Would there? Would there be any more manifestation? Or would nothing ever happen again?

Krishna addresses that one for Arjuna by pushing him into deeper practice. He says that until Arjuna has quieted down, until his mind is completely cooled out, until his purification exercises are all done—in other words, until he is *residing* in Brahman—he won't even begin to recognize Krishna. You have to *be* in Brahman before you begin to recognize that something lies beyond it. Krishna is suggesting that beyond both that which is form and that which is without form, behind both purusha and prakriti, behind the Brahman and the shakti, there is still some other . . . what? Something. But what is it? It seems there is still the dharma, there is still law, there is still some kind of directionality to things.

Whatever Brahman is, we know that it is the ultimate paradox, the simultaneous presence of *all* paradoxes. In Brahman, there is no space: everywhere is here. In Brahman, time has stopped: past, present, future, all are right now. So there is freedom from both space and time.

Now we can begin to talk about *true* freedom, the real freedom that is possible on this journey. It's the freedom from limited view, the freedom from limited sensation, the freedom from standing anywhere, the freedom from holding on to any models. Beings like Maharajji are operating from that perspective all the time. They are in the world, but they are not subordinate to the world. They have transcended the gunas, the forces of nature, the strands of rope that create the world. "I have passed through the market. I am not a purchaser." If absolutely nothing entices us anymore, we are equanimous, imperturbable. We can let go of the separate self and just *be* with everything.

There are those of us who have gone in and touched that place, but have come right back because we still have more karma to unfold. Our attachments bring us back—and yet we did touch the possibility, and that changed us. I suspect that many of you who are reading this book have done that.

Then there are others. In India, there are beings who go into what's called *nirvakalp samadhi*—samadhi without form—and just stay there. After some period of time (Maharajji said forty-three days, although I've also heard twenty-one) the being totally merges into that state of *nirvakalp samadhi,* and the body disintegrates. It just falls apart, because there's nobody in there keeping it together anymore. It's an interesting way to leave an incarnation.

And then there are others still, who go into that state and reside in it, and yet their manifestation continues—only now it's different. Now it is the manifestation of Brahman coming through a human form. It's like nobody came back, and yet there is something there. For such a being, there are no more rules in the game, because the compassion has become all embracing. Any of our models of "You must do this because it's good" or "You shouldn't do that because it's bad!" come out of our limited perspective. Their compassion, on the other hand, comes out of their total consciousness of the whole of it all.

Trungpa Rinpoche talked about that—it was what he termed "crazy wisdom." Crazy wisdom, he said, is "outrageous wisdom, devoid of self and of the 'common sense' of literal thinking. Crazy wisdom is wild—in fact, it is the first attempt to express the dynamics of the final spiritual stage of a Boddhisattva, to step out with nakedness of mind, unconditioned, beyond conceptualization."

Hakuin's Zen poem—the beautiful Zen poem we used to recite at four every morning in the temple in Kyoto—says, "If we turn inward and prove our True Nature, the true self is no self, our own self is no self, we go beyond ego and past clever words. Then the gate to the oneness of cause and effect is thrown open. Not two and not three, straight ahead runs the way. . . . Now our thought is no thought, so our dancing and songs are the voice of the Dharma."

So our dancing and songs are the voice of the dharma . . . so our dancing and songs are the voice of Krishna . . . so our dancing and songs are a true harmonizing with the divine law that incorporates form *and* formlessness, life *and* death, creation *and* destruction, the law that incorporates *all* conceptual polarities and possibilities.

Operating from that space of Brahman, we come to a new understanding of karma yoga, a wider understanding. Before, karma yoga meant doing something from within our karmic predicament that we hoped would bring us to the One. Our actions were our path, our practice. Now, residing in the One, we come into a relationship with the Tao, with the way of things, with the law, such that *all* our actions henceforth are simply a pure statement of the dharma. Nothing else. We have transcended the gunas; we are *nirguna,* beyond the attachment to the strands of nature that bind us. A being residing in the Brahman is qualitatively an entirely different entity from everybody else, because there is literally nobody there. There's nobody home! That's one of the awesome and exasperating qualities, when you're around a being like that.

Take my guru, for example: from November 1967, when I first met him, right up until this very moment, in all the years I have hung out with him, thought about him, studied him, reflected about him, analyzed him—I have never been able to find anybody there! I keep projecting onto him, because there *was,* of course, a flesh-and-blood body there. And it walked and it talked and it smiled and it laughed and it did all its stuff. But when I go toward that guru, when I look into those eyes or I reside in that heart, when I quiet down and meditate on what lies behind that form, it's like I'm entering into nothing other than vast emptiness and vast fullness at the same time. I am entering into the state of Brahman, and that is the state where a being like Maharajji makes his home. Brahman encompasses a panoramic view of all form: It's the physical plane, the astral plane, the causal plane—all the conceptual levels of form, all the way back to pure idea. All of it folds back in on itself, back into that which is unknowable, immeasurable, indefinable—and yet is . . . and yet *is*. We give that state a name; we call it Brahman.

6

Sacrifice and Mantra

The subject of sacrifice plays an important role in the Gita; we find it keeps cropping up there. But it's a hard practice for us in the West to relate to. "Sacrifice" is kind of an alien concept in our culture; I've certainly always had a hard time with it myself. I think that's because most of us have a pretty limited view of what sacrifice is all about; we figure it's probably uncomfortable, and may have something to do with killing goats. Yet if the Gita keeps leading us toward it, and if we're adopting the perspective of the Gita and the Gita endorses sacrifice, then maybe we ought to take a second look at our own ideas about the subject. When we do, we discover that the Gita is inviting us into a much subtler relationship with the concept, one in which sacrifice is an act designed to lead us across the boundary between the wordly and the spiritual.

Just to set the stage, here are some excerpts from the Gita about the subject of sacrifice. You'll see that the slokas deal with sacrifice from a number of different perspectives—sometimes in very ritualistic terms, sometimes from a deeper level.

Krishna says, "Thus spoke the Lord of Creation when he made both man and sacrifice: By sacrifice shalt thou multiply and obtain all thy desires. By sacrifice shalt thou honor the gods, and the gods will then love thee. And thus in harmony with them shalt thou attain the supreme good." And then he goes on: "Food is the life of all beings, and all food comes from the rain above. Sacrifice brings the rain, and

14 Food is the life of all beings, and all food comes from rain
above. Sacrifice brings the rain from heaven, and sacrifice
is sacred action.

crifice

Symbology - easiest for us. vs. rainmaker.

15 Sacred action is described in the Vedas and these come from the
Eternal, and therefore is the Eternal everpresent in a sacrifice.

ufice *Brahma & Brahma springs from imperishable*
Brahma *around*

The world is a great Sacrifice

Here Brahma is taken to be prakrti as in 14-34.
Nature springs from the Divine & all activity traceable to it

16 Thus was the Wheel of the Law set in motion, and that man lives
one life indeed in vain who in a sinful life of pleasures helps not in
its revolutions.

& seeing interrelatedness of all in One,

Collab. competition, etc.

17 But the man who has found the joy of the Spirit and in the Spirit
has satisfaction, who in the Spirit has found his peace, that man
rit in is beyond the law of action. *No sense of duty to Work done, nor for transformation*
life. *of being but because his nature issues spontaneously in action.*

work first is training to purify — later it is fulfillment of God realization
I fulfilled - no desire, If no desire no action out of desire
Love, love. hunger.

18 He is beyond what is done and beyond what is not done, and in all
ing his works he is beyond the help of mortal beings.

*he knows that the objects of the world are essentially nothing other
than the subject sparkling upon the tossing waves of agitations
in the mind.*

19 In liberty from the bonds of attachment, do thou therefore the work
attach to be done: for the man whose work is pure attains indeed the
ork Supreme. *Work sans attach is superior to work done in a Spirit of Sacrifice
is superior than work with selfish aims.*

20 King Janaka *of Mithila* and other warriors reached perfection by the path of
action: let thy aim be the good of all, and then carry on thy
Janaka task in life. *father of Sita*
Bodhisattva
dharma

Ram Dass's Gita Notes: Ram Dass typed out the entire text of the
Gita, paragraph by paragraph, with spaces between each sloka for
recording his reflections on that passage. These are some of his
notes from chapter 3 of the Gita.

sacrifice is sacred action. Sacred action is described in the Vedas, and these come from the Eternal, and therefore is the Eternal ever present in a sacrifice."

Now there are a lot of concepts raised in that passage, but the one I'd like to lead off with is this sentence: "By sacrifice shalt thou honor the gods, and the gods will then love thee." That's a beautiful relationship that's being alluded to there, being implied there. It acknowledges that on the astral planes, there are beings who represent all the different facets of our existence. They are represented, for example, in all the many deities of the Hindu pantheon. By taking each part of our life and offering it to the particular astral aspect that's related to it, we form an alliance, if you will, across planes of consciousness. That is the beginning of an understanding of the interrelatedness in the universe of the worldly and the spiritual planes.

That's a beautiful, profound point. See, our study of karma gave us a feeling for the interrelatedness of things in a *worldly* sense, a feeling for the way in which everything in the material plane is lawfully interrelated with everything else. Now we're coming back to explore the same principle of the interrelatedness of things *after* we've transcended our attachment to the gunas, *after* we've entered into the Brahman, entered into the spiritual domain that incorporates the worldly one. Now we can look and see that not only is everything in the material plane interrelated, but that there is also an interrelatedness *across* planes.

It's from that perspective that we begin to explore our relationship to the spiritual aspect of sacrifice. Our word "sacrifice" comes from the same root as sacred, and sacrifice has to do with making something holy. The worldly and the spiritual are interconnected. And what is the connection across those domains? It is the act of sacrifice. Through sacrifice we *acknowledge* the connection. Sacrifice starts to give credence to the reality of the living spirit. It starts to give recognition in our daily lives to an awareness of Brahman.

If we accept all that, and decide that sacrifice sounds like a useful idea, what do we do next? What does it mean? What do we sacrifice? "There are yogis whose sacrifice is an offering to the gods; but others offer, as a sacrifice, their own soul in the fire of God," says the Gita. "Yogis whose sacrifice is an offering to the gods"—that's the ritualistic way we've usually thought about sacrifice: that you slaughter a lamb in sacrifice, or that you throw ghee into the fire as a sacrifice. But the Gita goes on—it says, "others offer, as a sacrifice, their own soul in the fire of God." Now we're exploring a new possibility—the possibility that the sacrifice is not of some object, but of ourselves.

So what of ourselves do we sacrifice? Krishna runs through a whole catalog of yogic sacrificial practices. He says, "In the fire of an inner harmony, some surrender their senses in darkness, and in the fire of the senses some surrender their outer light." He's saying that some yogis go into dark rooms or caves; they cut out the images that the world bombards us with. Some even go so far as to put out their eyes, to blind themselves so they'll no longer be distracted by the sight of worldly things. Still others use meditative practices to extract their awareness from their eyes, so that even if there were light out there they wouldn't see it, because they have surrendered "seeing." "Others," he says, "sacrifice their breath of life . . . and still others, faithful to austere vows, offer their wealth as a sacrifice, or their penance, or their practice of yoga, or their sacred studies, or their knowledge. Others through practice of abstinence offer their life into Life. All those who know what *is,* sacrifice, and through sacrifice purify their sins."

Remember earlier on, when we asked, If we're going to give up desires, what desire do we use to give up desires? Now here comes the answer: We use the desire to offer it all in sacrifice. All of it, even the desire to make the sacrifice, becomes the sacrificial offering. That's the return to the roots, spiritualizing life through offering up all of our acts as the sacrifice for our own transformation. We sacrifice the ego's goals, the ego's individual point of view. We throw every part of ourselves into the fire. *Swaha!* Take it, God—just let me be free.

In a way, the end product of all the yogas is sacrifice. You can even take a very intellectual practice, something like gyan yoga, and turn it into sacrifice. Krishna refers to that. "Know that all sacrifice is holy work," he says. "But greater than any earthly sacrifice is the sacrifice

of sacred wisdom, for wisdom is in truth the end of all holy work."
You learn it all, and then you offer it all up. That's the tricky predicament for the gyan yogi, as we said before, but now we're shown the
way we can work with that: Turn it into the stuff of your sacrifice, turn
it into what it is you have that you can offer.

There are, in the Vedas, various descriptions of the manifestation
of the One into form, the passage from the One into the many, and
that act of creation is always seen as an act of *sacrifice*. It's a *sacrifice* for
the One to give up its Oneness and become the many. So then our
acts of sacrifice back into the One complete the wheel; they spiritualize life, and bring the whole cycle into harmony. As we start to take
part in it, we begin to experience the entire universe as linked in one
stupendous act of sacrifice, each part offering to the other. Sacrifice
awakens us to the fact that we are part of a process, part of a divine
play. It helps us get past the pomposity of thinking about our personal,
special gratification all the time, so we can see ourselves instead as
part of what Paul called "Christ's body."

Those of you who have been in human relationships where real
love was present recognize experiences in which the well-being of
your beloved was more important than your own. You'd offer your
own discomfort to ensure their well-being. If you can extrapolate
from that experience to a time (called the Satya Yuga) when everybody makes that kind of offering in relation to everybody and everything else, you'll have a taste of what it is like to live in the Spirit.

But you know, you really don't have to worry about whether everybody else is doing it or not. You just begin to get your own house in
order. Recognizing your complete interrelatedness with all of it and
with your own spiritual source changes the meaning of each act, and
therefore both the reason and the way it's done.

For people who have not *experienced* the Brahman, who have not
experienced identity with the spiritual One behind the personality
and the body, there are limited options when they approach the subject of sacrifice. They can simply pass on it, dismiss it. Or they can rit-
ualize it. They can either say, "Well, I hear all that you're saying—and
it all sounds awfully nice. But I'm not going to do anything about it,

because that Brahman stuff is all just words to me." Or else they can adopt a kind of ritualistic sacrifice, which has a certain tradition or form to it, but doesn't partake much of Spirit.

For example, in the Indian pattern we talked about, there's a certain formalism. You study in order to arrive at intellectual understanding, and then you start to lead a *satvig* existence, a pure existence, and to do certain kinds of sacrifice. You'll see many Indians living their lives that way, according to Vedic prescriptions, and doing very ritualistic forms of sacrifice. But often the sacrifice isn't rooted in the direct experience that would make the sacrifice a free act; it's still coming out of the thought, "It's my *duty* to do this."

In the Hindu tradition, there are many categories of sacrifice, or yagya, which a Brahmin is required to perform every day. There's Brahma Yagya—the learning and spreading of scriptural texts. There's Pitri Yagya—the offering of oblations of water and rice to dead ancestors. There's Bhuta Yagya—the feeding of dumb animals and birds. There's Nri Yagya—the worship of guests or the needy.

Take Nri Yagya—that's an incredible one. Maharajji said, "Whoever comes to you is your guest. Love, respect and welcome him, serve prasad. Feeding the hungry is actual worship. First bhojan [food], then bhajan [prayer]." When I walk into the home of a friend in India, I am treated as God. I am given the love and respect and feeding that God would be given if She walked through that door. It's not because it's *me*—anybody who walks into that house is treated the same way. It's part of their practice of spiritualizing life: that every guest who enters your home turns into God. It's like Elijah in the Jewish religion, the unexpected guest who's come. So the Indians welcome you, and they worship you; they put the tilak on your forehead, they bring you gifts, and they seat you in a special place—all because you happened to drop by! That's a whole other way of looking at who it is that's come for a visit. It's a spiritual practice, because it's a reminder to stay open to the game at more than one level. That's the way all these yagyas work.

To many Brahmins, these practices are done to atone for whatever unconscious karmic acts they might have committed "while with the broomstick, the waterpot, the grinding stone, the oven, or the mortar and pestle," as they say. That is, they're acknowledging that just in living their daily lives they've been creating all kinds of karmic stuff for themselves, and their practices are a way of cleaning that up. Doing the rituals every day is a way of working out karma all the time. It's very ritualistic, but it's a useful technique.

When I talk about "ritualistic" qualities of sacrifice, I don't want you to think I'm putting down ritual itself. Far from it. Rituals can be powerful tools. They can bring the sacred into our lives, and remind us that there are many levels to our games. In fact, I think it's a useful exercise to take some part of our everyday lives, and consciously turn it into a ritual. Food might be a good one to work with, as an exercise in bringing consciousness to an area in which desire most often reigns. Other than air and water, food is the thing most critical to our survival, and so desires around it get built into us very strongly. It can be hard to stay conscious around desires which are that powerful. But there are practices for dealing with food that turn it into a sadhana, and make it part of that process through which everything in our lives becomes part of the teaching, part of the awakening process.

One way to bring that kind of consciousness to the food we eat is to make the eating an offering. In the fourth chapter of the Gita, there is a sloka that concerns sacrifice, and the notes connected with it in most texts say that the sloka is used at mealtimes by many people in India. It's the mantra I use each time I take food.

I used to have this delightful little play with my father around my doing this mantra. We'd sit down at the table, and as he was lowering himself into his chair, his hand would already be reaching for his fork. Before he was in the chair, the first bite of salad would be in his mouth, and he'd be crunching the lettuce. Midway through the bite, he'd realize that I was saying a blessing, and he'd stop in mid-crunch. But every now and then, if I took too long with the mantra, I'd hear a quick "Crunch!" It's like he was pushing me just a little bit: "Get on with it, so we can eat!" It was a beautiful, funny dance we'd go through together.

Mind you, I didn't try to lay it on heavy—I didn't care if he ate his lettuce or not; but he'd say, "Oh, no, no—I won't eat while you're praying." He asked me once, "What are you saying, anyway?" I told him, and after that he'd join in on the *"shanti, shanti, shanti,"* and then he'd say, "Amen!" It's the best of all worlds!

This is the mantra.

> *Brahma pranam, Brahma havire, Brahmagni, Brahmanahota*
> *Brahmaitan Gantabiyam Brahmakarma Samadina*
> *Gurubrahma, Guruvishnu, Gurudevomaheshwara*
> *Gurusakshat Parambrahma Tus maee shree guruvenama ha*
> *Om, shanti, shanti, shanti.*

The first two lines of the mantra say, Realize, as you're taking this food, that the food itself is part of Brahman, part of the unmanifest whatever-it-is that lies behind form. Did you remember that, the last time you had a meal? All the time you thought it was food, when what it really was is dense spirit.

Oh, but we're not going to stop there, says the mantra. The food is Brahman, but the fire into which you're offering the food (which can be the fire of your hunger, the fire of your desire, as well as the sacred fire into which you throw the ghee)—that fire is part of Brahman, too. You thought the fire of your hunger was just a fire? No, that fire is Brahman. So now you're feeding Brahman into Brahman.

Ah, but we haven't finished yet. Who do you think is doing it? Do you think *you're* doing it? Do you think *you're* going to eat the food to fulfill *your* desire? No. After all, you're Brahman, too. So now it's Brahman offering Brahman into the fire of Brahman. And who are you offering it to? Who do you think all those beings are—the gods and all of that? What is that? It's Brahman. Far out.

So it turns out that you are Brahman feeding Brahman to the fire of Brahman and offering it to Brahman—which means nothing is happening at all. See? The whole thing is an illusion—it's all Brahman playing with Brahman. It's all the play of the Lord, it's all divine lila. And you thought you were just going to eat a meal!

That's the first half of the mantra. Then the second half of the mantra offers the food to the various ways in which the Spirit becomes manifest in the universe. The food is offered to the guru, meaning to God in manifest form; it is offered to the guru as the creator, to the guru as the preserver, and to the guru as the force of change—that is, as Brahman, Vishnu, and Shiva; and it is offered to that which lies behind all those aspects—to Parambrahma, to the Ultimate. And then finally the mantra says, I touch the lotus feet of the guru; that is, I surrender once again. After that there is a silent moment, in which we can add whatever blessings or metta we want to send out into the world, and then we end by saying, *"Om, shanti, shanti, shanti"*—"peace, peace, peace."

Now after that, and keeping all that in mind, go ahead and enjoy your dinner. Every time you take a bite, remember that you're not "eating"—you're Brahman pouring Brahman into Brahman. Then, since you're not identified any longer with your hunger, and not identified any longer with being the eater, the food just is what it is, and you'll eat just what you need to eat. You'll see it all as merely the play of Brahman, in which the whole process is done as a sacrifice in order that it all may merge into Brahman.

Using a mantra like that is just one technique for working with food and making it your practice. There are many strategies for dealing with food in a way that changes the meaning of the experience of eating. There are Buddhist practices, for example; one of them, part of the punya, or wisdom, path, involves a reperception of what it is that we're eating; another is a meditation on the process of eating itself. There are examples of those meditations in "The Supplemental Syllabus," so you can experiment with them. Jewish dietary laws and Christian fasting at Lent are both familiar practices, and they are designed to reorient our relationship with food, to spiritualize it.

At retreats I've run, I've sometimes had a huge meal prepared, usually on our last day together. We'd all plan that this was going to be a final feast that we'd share; everybody would get excited, building up to the dinner. The table was laid out. We'd sit down. Everybody was anticipating the food. They'd been building up their hunger, their desire.

Then I would start by giving a long blessing of the food. You could see the cooks thinking, "But the food's getting cold!" I would ask everybody to keep doing the blessing until everybody was really *doing the blessing,* really feeling it. In order to do the blessing that way, the cooks would have to give up worrying about the food getting cold, and the diners would have to give up anticipating the food they were about to eat.

When the blessing was finished, I would say, "Now before we eat, I would like to read to you the Buddhist meditation on the repulsiveness of food." I would then read the passages about the food mixing with the spittle at the end of the tongue and eventually turning into shit and all that. At that point, the cooks wouldn't really *care* whether the food got cold or not, and the diners would decide that they really weren't very hungry anymore.

Finally, I would proceed to describe the *way* we were going to eat—very slowly, very meditatively, very intentionally. And by then, the banquet would be ruined.

At that point, I would ask people to stop and notice their reactions to the whole experience. I'd say to them, "After all the years you've been eating for your pleasure, how much does it cost you to surrender a little of that pleasure into becoming mindful of the process of eating?"

Most of us, most of the time, are totally unconscious around the subject of food. If we pay attention to it at all, it's usually to obsess neurotically about it. Those of you who have a weight problem will notice that if you focus on getting thin, you'll be suffering, suffering, suffering all the time. But if you become *mindful* in your eating, you will get thin. And those of you who are into cooking and into the exquisite subtleties of food—there's nothing wrong with any of that; it can be done as a yoga, too. But we have gone so far overboard in sense gratification that our ability to even imagine using food sacredly, merely for survival and maintenance of the body, has almost vanished. And part of our sadhana involves experimenting with each aspect of our lives for its potential as part of our awakening.

That process goes on and on, and there comes a step that takes us beyond making just our food and our eating the sacrifice. The more profound path of sacrifice that Krishna outlines is the sacrifice of one's self—meaning that we begin to do *every* act we do in the light of our awareness of Brahman. As our practice gets deeper and deeper, that awareness of Brahman takes on flesh and blood; it starts to be a deeply valid sense of *relatedness,* to something much greater than the games we've been playing. We were always asking, "Am I getting enough?" Now we start asking, "How can I get rid of all my stuff, so I can become part of everything?" That flips around the meaning of every act.

In the example of eating that we've been using, you get so that you feed your body, so that you can maintain the temple, so that you can deepen your wisdom, so that you can increase your samadhi, so that you can get through your ego, so that you can come to Brahman. Far out! And that *includes* having that pizza—I mean, it's *all* of it. Everything you eat becomes your offering. The offering, the sacrifice—that becomes what eating is all about for you.

But using food that way is only the beginning. Your offerings include everything you do—the sneaky stuff, too. Like how about when you've just bad-mouthed somebody. You're sitting around gossiping, and suddenly you think, "This is my offering to God at this moment—far out! Look what I offered God today." Gossip? Greed? Lust? Great. I mean, don't worry about it, don't judge it—the Brahman can take it all in, no problem. Just *notice* your action, notice what it is you're offering to God.

How about suffering? Are you offering your suffering to God? Ouspensky, in his book on Gurdjieff, said, "Another thing that people must sacrifice is their suffering. Nothing can be attained without suffering, but at the same time one must begin by sacrificing suffering."[1] As that happens, a shift takes place inside of you. You begin to see your suffering as grace. You don't have to get as far out as the monk, standing in the lake and crying, "God, God, give me more pain." You don't have to do a masochistic trip. But you get to the point where, when you are suffering, that suffering is your fire of purification. You say,

"Yeah. Right. Isn't this hell? Am I ever suffering!" See? The suffering is your offering into the fire.

There's a lightness which has entered into the suffering at that point, and it's important. You can't sit around steeped in self-pity and do much sadhana: "Oh, it's so hard! I'm in this temple, and the food is terrible, and—oh, how I'm suffering." Not much quality of "offering" in that. Instead, you become like Swami Ram Dass. He was thrown out of a temple, and had to spend the night by the side of the river, where the mosquitoes kept biting him. He just kept saying to Ram, "Oh, thank you, Ram, for sending the mosquitoes to keep me awake so I can think of you."

And eventually there's another thing you have to offer up: How about offering up your fascination with it all? As long as you're still doing it for the experience of it, the sacrifice is coming up short. You're saying, "Yeah, I'll throw a little ghee into the fire—that'll be interesting for me." That experiencer / enjoyer? That one has to go, too. It doesn't mean you won't enjoy it, but you won't be attached to being the enjoyer. You've sacrificed that too. Of course, you'll then make a bizarre discovery: that the more you sacrifice, the more you come into the spirit, and the more you come into the spirit, the more you get it all—the more you're *having* it all, every moment. But that can't happen until you've really thrown it all away.

So that huge mouth of the sacrifice is a gateway into Brahman. It's the gateway through which you pour your life into the Brahman, just keep pouring and pouring your whole existence into the Brahman. You forget, and you think you're in it for yourself: "Oh, yes— *I'm* going to get *enlightened!*" But then you also keep remembering, remembering that you're part of it all, part of the endless circle of sacrifice.

There is a mantra I used to work with, to awaken the energy of sacrifice. I would focus on the ajna, the sixth chakra, and I would say, "I am a point of sacrificial fire, held within the fiery will of God. I am a point of sacrificial fire, held within the fiery will of God." If you do that long enough, your ajna, your third eye, becomes like a burning fire of sacrifice. It's a power mantra; it's a mantra that turns *you* into part of the sacrificial fire.

And then when you've awakened that energy, you take everything you do, and you throw it into that fire. Every experience, every thought, every feeling—you feed it all into the fire. You're converting all your desires, all your perceptions, into an offering. It's a total conversion of the worldly into the spiritual—the mantra gives you a vehicle for doing that. You sacrifice identifying yourself as the doer, the enjoyer, the knower, the delighter, the collector, the experiencer—you sacrifice all that into the realization of the big-E Enjoyer, the merging that comes *through* that sacrifice. That Enjoyer is the atman in you; that's the real bliss, and so you sacrifice enjoyment into being the Enjoyer.

In that example, we used mantra to awaken the sacrificial fire into which we fed our offerings. And that brings us right to the second subject of this chapter, which is mantra. The word "mantra" means "mind-protecting." A mantra is something that protects the mind from itself, really, by giving it some fodder other than the thinking process. There are many, many types of mantra. Most spiritual traditions have them. There are power mantras, like the one we just worked with. There are seed mantras, like "Om," that express some essential vibratory quality of the universe. There are mantras to activate each chakra in your body.

When I was studying with Hari Dass in India, I learned mantras for every single activity I engaged in every day. I learned mantras for waking up and mantras for going to sleep. I learned a mantra for taking a shower. I learned mantras for going to the toilet—for each *type* of going to the toilet. I learned mantras for everything. And the purpose of the mantras was to keep reminding me to turn it all into a sacrifice, an offering.

Swami Muktananda used to tell a story about a saint who once was giving a discourse on mantra. A man in his audience stood up and said, "What is this nonsense about mantra? Who wants to waste time repeating the same word over and over again. Do you think if you chant 'bread, bread, bread' it will fill your belly?"

The saint jumped up from his seat. He pointed his finger at the man, and shouted, "Shut up and sit down, you stupid ass!" Well, the man was *furious.* He got red in the face, and his whole body started shaking with rage. He sputtered, "You call yourself a holy man, and you use a foul term like that in talking to me?" The saint said very mildly, "But, sir, I don't understand. You heard yourself called an ass just once, and look how it's affected you. Yet you think that our repeating the Lord's name over and over again for hours won't benefit us."

Muktananda's story relates to one of the levels at which a mantra affects us—a level at which the effect has to do with the *meaning* of sacred names or phrases. In other words, it has to do with our associations to the words. But apart from any *images* the names call up for us, the *sound* of the mantra itself has its own effect on us. It's as if there are planes of reality that have their own sounds, their own vibrations, and we do mantra to tune ourselves to those planes by tuning our own vibrations to theirs through the repetition of the sound of the mantra. That sound, or *shabdh,* is basically a spiritual sound, not a physical one—in the same way that the chakras are not physical things but spiritual loci of the various forms of energy of the body. The practice of *shabdh* yoga is a path for working with that inner sound.

Many of the holy books in various traditions have related sound to the creation of all form. In Hinduism, Om is said to be the root sound of the universe, the seed or *bij* syllable that manifests as creation. Or take the Bible: "In the beginning was the *word,* and the word was with God, and the word *was* God, and the word was made flesh." We can imagine the act of creation occurring in just that way: Formlessness comes through the causal plane into idea, which is already a subtle sound, a sound of both words and images; and then it moves from there into more and more gross sound, including, ultimately, our bodies, which are in effect a form of gross vibration. (They have a sound, though we may not be able to hear it.)

As we purify our own consciousness by extricating ourselves from the grosser vibrational planes, we turn back toward the formless. The practice of mantra is a technique for tuning us to those subtler vibrational levels. As we move more and more deeply into mantra, the sound becomes the vehicle that allows us to experience both halves of the act of creation-and-return, so we're going from the many back into the One, and then from the One into the many, all on the strength of the mantra.

Mechanical vibration alone won't do it, of course. The mantra and the reciter of the mantra are not separate from one another, and the power and the effect of the mantra depend on the readiness and the openness and the faith of the one who's doing it. In fact, mantras in and of themselves don't do anything at all—it all has to do with the beings who work with them. Mantras aren't magic spells; power mantras are just sounds, unless you're the kind of person who has the one-pointedness of mind and the particular personality characteristics that make those power mantras work. That is, what a mantra does is to concentrate already-existing stuff in you. It just brings it into focus. It's like a magnifying glass with the sun: The magnifying glass doesn't have any heat in and of itself, but it takes the sunlight and focuses it; it makes it one-pointed. The mantra becomes like that magnifying glass for your consciousness.

Mantras can be used as a way of stilling thought as well as focusing it. If you imagine the mind as being like an ocean, with waves of thought surging along on it, waves going in all directions because of the crosscurrents of the tides and the winds—in that ocean, a mantra sets up a single wave pattern that gradually overrides all the other ones, until the mantra is the only thought-form left. Then there's just one continuous wave going through your mind—going and going and going.

So say I'm driving along, I'm doing "Rama, Rama, Rama, Rama, Rama." There's a billboard coming by, and that gets chomped into "Rama, Rama, Rama, Rama." I look down at the speedometer, and that becomes "Rama, Rama, Rama, Rama." I'm thinking, "Gee, maybe I'll get a milk shake at the next restaurant," and all the time I'm saying, "Rama, Rama, Rama, Rama." It's all coming and passing, coming and passing, and it's all being mantra-ized. It's all being converted. It's all being turned into God.

If you decide to try working with a mantra, which I would encourage you to do, start out by spending some time just getting familiar with the words and the sounds of it; work with that level until you feel comfortable saying the words out loud. Then, when you feel familiar with them, start to chant the mantra. As you chant, start to surrender into it; start to merge into it, start to offer up all of your other thoughts as sacrifice into it.

Let's say you're doing your mantra and this thought comes up: "I don't think this is gonna work." Take that thought, and in your imagination, place it on a golden tray, with a silk handkerchief and incense and a candle, and offer it to the mantra. Just keep doing the mantra while you offer your doubt to it. Keep offering up the mantra, and keep offering into the mantra. Offer your doubts, offer your discomforts, offer your boredom, offer your sore throat. Offer. Keep offering. And keep doing the mantra.

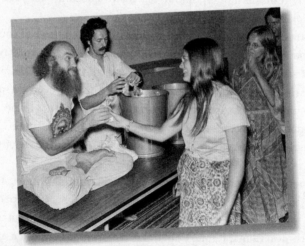

Ram Dass Distributing Malas: Assisted here by Maruti Projanski, Ram Dass gave each student a set of wooden beads and a thread from one of Maharajji's blankets. The students strung the beads to make a mala, which they then used in their mantra practice.

There's a book called *The Way of a Pilgrim,* which is about a very simple Russian peasant monk who recites mantra.[2] He's doing the Jesus prayer—"Lord Jesus Christ, Son of God, have mercy on me, a sinner"—as he's walking through the bitter cold of the Russian winter, and he says, "I don't feel that I'm walking at all. I am only aware of the fact that I'm saying the prayer. When the bitter cold pierces me, I begin to say my prayer more earnestly, and I quickly get warm all over. When hunger begins to overcome me, I call more often on the prayer, and I forget my wish for food. I have become a sort of half-conscious person. I have no cares and no interests." That's exactly the practice right there—offering each experience into the mantra, and watching the experiences get transformed.

In working with it, you'll discover that mantra is esoteric; like any profound wisdom, it doesn't disclose itself at first glance. Mantra's not a surface thing; it goes to the depths of the mind, and so as we continue the practice, different stages unfold. At first you will do the mantra with your mouth. It's on the tongue—that's in your gross body: "Here I am doing this mantra."

After some time, the mantra will start to move to your throat. When? It depends on your readiness, on how wide open you are to the mantra. Now you're doing the mantra in the subtle body, or the dream body, as it's sometimes called. When the mantra starts to enter your throat, you're likely to notice changes entering your life, coming from the mantra. You might notice that your sleep becomes more blissful. You'll feel a lightness in your body, and you'll start to experience tremendous happiness within your heart. You'll probably start to have visions of gods and goddesses and saints and siddhas. All those are qualities connected with that stage of the practice of mantra.

Then, after it's been in your throat for a while, you'll start to experience the mantra in your heart. Now it's moving toward what's called the causal body. You'll start to feel new enthusiasm, a new kind of love for everything around you. It will reflect in your physical form; there'll be a luster in your body. As the mantra starts to affect everything about you, you'll find that you're both more detached and yet more proficient in everything you do.

At a certain point, the repetition of mantra (or *japa,* as it's called) becomes *ajapa-japa,* meaning that it's going on, but you're no longer doing it. The process is on automatic. At that point, as Kabir says, "Ram practices my *japa,* while I sit relaxed." At that point you're not doing the mantra anymore—the mantra is doing you. It's a far-out moment when you notice that beginning to happen; at that point, there's no weariness in it, no effort, no individuality. That's the point where you're approaching the merging into Brahman.

I invite you to select a mantra, and to start working with it, investing it for yourself. Choose whichever one feels right to you, or create one of your own, and start to practice with it. To start, you might pick a time when you can sit at your puja, or in some other quiet space, and recite the mantra aloud for one hour. That's a good length of time to work with, for starters. By that time, you will have gone through many, many trips about the mantra. Let them all come and go. Offer them up, and stay with the mantra. Think it, do it, feel it, notice your reactions to it, sense it, experience it in your heart, think about its meaning—then forget about all that, and just keep doing the mantra. Just keep letting it move to level after level after level. And if you can empty yourself enough, when you stop doing it (if you *can* stop doing it), you will hear it being done in the universe all around you. Mantra is like a key that opens the door to a place in the universe. And since every sound that's ever been made will always exist, the voices of everybody who ever did that mantra purely are still present in that place.

I experienced that place once, with a mantra. I'd done the mantra for a couple of days, and when I stopped, it suddenly sounded like I was surrounded by the Mormon Tabernacle Choir—thousands of voices in every direction, going back over time, all doing the mantra. I freaked completely! I thought that somebody was putting me on, that they had a radio going in the next room or something. I couldn't believe that I had tuned in to that other space, where that mantra is always being chanted.

So I suggest that it could be useful for you to experiment with the practice of mantra. And I suggest that it could be useful for you to experiment with the practice of sacrifice. Both of them, mantra and sacrifice, represent ways of turning our lives into offerings. There is a deep yearning within us to complete the wheel of sacrifice, to close the circle, and through our sacrifice to merge with Brahman, to merge with the void. Sacrifice and mantra are ways we sacralize our lives, ways we make manifest our yearning to be free, and in doing that, they make us coconspirators in our own dissolution.

As I witness my own life more and more as an offering, other things in my life have less of a pull on me. Doing it for *me* isn't nearly as interesting as surrendering it outward . . . upward . . . inward. Maharajji named me "Ram Dass," and Ram Dass means "servant of God," meaning that my life is offered in service to the One. Somebody says to me, "Why do you need a weird name like that? Do you have to have an Indian name? Can't you just be Dick Alpert?" Sure. I could be. But having a name like Ram Dass is very functional, because it keeps reminding me of something all the time . . . "Ram Dass = Servant of God." Somebody says, "Ram Dass," and I hear, "Servant of God," and that immediately reminds me what my trip is all about— that it's about this process of service and sacrifice and transformation.

Sometimes when I was with Maharajji, he would say something to Ram Dass and I would be busy being Dick Alpert, and I would feel like he was talking to somebody over my shoulder. Maybe he was talking to who I will be when I cease to be who I *think* I am. And when I become that, then *all* my acts will be designed to transform my own being—and everybody else's as well.

The ultimate offering we make is the sacrifice of our own personal trips, of all the things we think we are: our bodies, our personalities, our senses, our feelings. And then, with the growing freedom that that brings, comes a deeper recognition of the Brahman, of that which lies behind, of that which is non-self, of that which is the source from which it all keeps feeding outward.

And with the full recognition of that spiritual root of the universe, sacrifice takes on yet another aspect: It becomes the sacrifice of *form itself,* the sacrifice of all worldly vibration, the sacrifice of all life and existence as we know it, into the Spirit. It's as if we are pouring it all into the mouth of Brahman, into the fire that is Brahman. We're pouring it inward, pouring it inward, and all our efforts, every act of our lives, becomes that single offering. We are, in effect, turning ourselves inside out, until finally *we* are the atman, *we* are the light within, *we* are the consciousness, *we* are the spaciousness, *we* are the presence, *we* are the . . . ahhhhhhh!

7

Renunciation and Purification

Throughout the Gita, we come upon references to the role in a spiritual life of practices that would be called renunciation. They are related in a certain way to sacrifice; they are acts of purification, designed to cut us loose from the bonds that tie us to the worldly realms. The Gita doesn't go into those practices in as much detail as we might expect, because the underlying assumption is that everybody already knows about all them. The Gita wasn't written with our present Kali Yuga mentality in mind—the mentality of the dark age in which we live, an age when we've gotten totally lost in worldly things. The Gita assumes that Arjuna would already know and practice all the acts of purification that most of us are just beginning to consider.

Practices of purification are essentially techniques for putting ourselves in a position where we are prepared to experience direct, first-hand knowledge of the Brahman. They do that by creating a structure through which we can draw back from the things that keep trapping us, the things that keep creating karma for us all the time. That is, all of the purification rituals in Hinduism (and there are rituals in Buddhism, Christianity, Judaism, Islam, and most other religions as well, by the way, and the practices all overlap), all of the renunciations, are done in order to cool us out, so we're not generating so much heavy karma for ourselves. Until that happens, we're constantly preoccupied just with the stuff we're creating every day. The minute that preoccupation lightens up a bit, we have a space where we can start to refocus, and deepen our meditation. And then, with the deepening of meditation, will come the higher wisdom. That's the principle behind the practices.

Now, in a way, purification is a hype. You take your body, just as it is, and your mind, just as it is, and your feelings, just as they are— and right here, in this very place, lies the Brahman, the enlightened state. It's right here! It's right now! It's not there or then, it's not in India or Tibet, it's not being kept secret by "him" or "her," it's not in this book or in that book. It's right here, and you *are* it—right now.

Okay, so then what's the point of purification? What, in fact, is the point of any of these practices, if we already are the Brahman? They're to get rid of whatever in us prevents us from really *knowing* who we are at this moment. See, from a practical point of view, we're faced with an interesting paradox. At one level of our intellectual understanding, we *know* that we already have all the riches—we *know* that we are the atman, that we are the Buddha, that we are free. We know all that. But if we look inside, we'll notice that although we know it, we somehow don't *believe* it. And that's what all the purification methods are about: getting us from where we seem to think we still are, to where we don't think we're anywhere anymore. Hence we have all these practices, like karma yoga and jnana yoga, like sacrifice and mantra, like renunciation and purification. All of them, by one route or another, are designed to get around that roadblock between our knowing and our believing.

Just to frame our discussion, here are a few slokas from the Gita:

"For the man who forsakes all desires, and abandons all pride of possession and of self, reaches the goal of peace supreme."

"Know that a man of true renunciation is he who craves not, nor hates; for he who is above the two contraries soon finds his freedom."

"When in recollection he withdraws all his senses from the attractions of the pleasures of sense, even as a tortoise withdraws all its limbs, then his is a serene wisdom."

The attraction of our senses is what keeps us stuck, and the purification process that the Gita seems to be recommending here is to renounce the senses—to detach the senses from their usual objects, for hither and thither the senses rove. Remember that the buddhi, which is the soul, can be pulled downward by the lower mind, the manas, which in turn can be captured by the indrias, the senses, which are fixed on the sense objects. Those are the levels of it: There is sense object, there is sense, there is mind-that-knows-sense, and there is higher mind, which can be caught in the worldly pull outward, can be drawn into the thinking mind and the senses. If it resists the pull of the senses, if it withdraws and turns inward, it becomes instead a recognizer of the atman. That process is promoted by our acts of purification.

We're gradually extricating the buddhi from being snared by sense objects, and we're using different approaches to get there. We've talked about some of them before—that we can draw the mind back from the senses, saying, "I am not my eyes. . . . I am not my ears. . . ." Or that we can work on the mind directly, as we do with meditation, quieting it down so it doesn't respond any longer to the pull of the senses. Or that we can fill our minds with the wisdom of that-which-is-beyond-all-this, because that wisdom in turn loosens the pull of the senses.

When we adopt any of these techniques—when we sit down to meditate, for example, and to withdraw our senses—we suddenly discover how agitated our minds really are, how full they are of this and that. Monkey-mind, they call it in India. The same thing happens as we enter into *any* practice—mantra, *japa,* prayer, whatever. We see how distracted we are by all the wordly desires that keep pulling on our consciousness. So we start to look for ways to quiet the agitation, and that's when practices of purification and renunciation start to attract us and to become part of our lives. Maybe we start to pay more attention to our diets, to the way we take care of our bodies. We start paying attention to who we hang out with, what we fill our minds with, what we think about when we're not meditating—because we see that all that stuff is feeding into the agitation that is keeping us from meditating.

The amount of toxin that builds up in us is amazing. Let's say you're driving down the street, and somebody cuts you off. You think, "Why you so and so!" and that—just that!—the vibration, the energy, that's fed into the system by that one thought, resonates and resonates, stirring up anger and putting all the passions to work. That's *not* the kind of mental setting that's optimal for meditation. So maybe we start renouncing that rush of righteous rage; instead, we take a situation like that and turn it into a moment of purification practice. There's a kind of fire, an inner fire, that comes with letting go of our anger at a moment like that, and that's the fire into which we make our offering. We offer our anger to our awakening. *Swaha!*

We find that we have to keep living in the marketplace until we learn how to transmute its energies—all its energies. We start to watch for the things that capture our consciousness so we can get free of them. For example, when we look at what captivates our minds, we're likely to find amid the collection our attachments to our various cherished possessions. They pull on our minds because "where your treasures are, there will your heart be also." So says Jesus. If your "treasures" are your possessions, that's where your heart will be.

Let's say, for example, that you own a very beautiful, priceless something-or-other. You sit down to meditate, but before the meditation can take you beyond yourself, here come these powerful thoughts about the need to protect that something-or-other: "Is it really safe? Did I lock it up securely enough? Can vandals get it?" Whatever. We are chained by the chains of our possessions.

Possessions don't have to be physical things, of course; possessions can be emotional possessions, or intellectual possessions. You start to meditate, and you have this really *great* idea. You think, "Gee, I mustn't forget that idea, because I'll bet I can make a million on that one." Or how about, "I have to remember that idea, because it'll help all humanity!" That's a nice one, right? Then you try to meditate. Every time your mind starts to get quiet, to get beyond thought, you grab back at the idea for fear you'll forget it. Not yet is our faith strong enough to trust that if it was a good idea, it'll come back; trusting takes deep faith.

In time, we begin to see the way the bonds of our attachments, be they physical or intellectual or emotional ones, are keeping us from something we want much more than we want the stuff we're attached to. That's when we start to see the appeal of reducing both our physical and our psychological possessions, to bring a kind of clean simplicity into our lives. I used to fill every corner of every place I lived with things. First I needed a record player and a good hi-fi system. Then there were my books—shelves and shelves of them. There were beautiful tapestries, soft things, warm things, bath salts, incense, wines, foods—I surrounded myself with a luxurious cave of stuff.

But then, as my practices deepened, I noticed it all starting to get simpler and simpler. I didn't need all that stuff around me anymore. And now, when somebody gives me an empty room with white walls, and I put my mat on the floor and sit down, I'm really just about as content as I ever was with all of that stuff. My life has gotten simpler and lighter, simpler and lighter, because I've found that the rush of experience isn't nearly as interesting as what happens when my mind gets still.

Now, just to complete the cycle about our relationship to possessions: There is a time for enjoying the romanticism of life, and for reveling in all the possessions we gather around us. There is a time when all of that is renounced and falls away. And then there is a time when we are so totally free of it all that we can *have* it all again—but without the attachment. I used to visit Swami Muktananda at his ashram in Ganeshpuri. I'd go into his suite, and there he'd be, sitting on a sterling silver chair, in front of a sterling silver table, eating off of eighteen-karat gold plates. It would take two strong men just to lift his huge, silver chair. I'd think, "What kind of a yogi is this?" Then I read the story of his sadhana and saw where his consciousness had gone, and I realized how much *nothing* all that extravagance is to him. And in that world of nothing, when people give him gold plates, he eats off of them. To him, it's the same as eating off a leaf! What does he care?

So I'm not suggesting that in order to get to God we have to give up all our possessions (although Christ did say, "Take all that you have and give it to the poor"). It depends on where we are in that whole cycle. I'm just saying that we may want to examine our relationship to all the stuff in our lives, to see if there are places where we want to let go of some of our clingings. The Ashtavakra Gita says, "The sage, who has no attachment, does not suffer, even in the world." It's fine to enjoy our possessions, our ideas, our feelings—as long as we can completely let go of them at any moment. Gold plates? That's fine. Leaf plates? That's fine, too.

Possessions are only one example. Our monkey-minds are like these agitated monsters that are wanting this and collecting that, always grabbing, grabbing, grabbing. The process of cooling out that agitation takes time, and that's hard for the agitated mind to accept. But the spiritual journey will teach us patience if it teaches us nothing else.

There are all these layers to work through—layers and layers of attachment. In the nature package that comes with our incarnation are all of the gunas, all the forces of our desires, passions, emotions, thoughts. They're all part of our package—they're all just there—and until we're completely finished with all our desires, they can recapture us at any moment. One of the Egyptian holy books says: "Let your desire be at the same level as your goal. If you aspire to superhuman joy, accept the superhuman structure in a very human body, and know that the abyss is always a near neighbor to the summit." Or as my teacher, Hari Dass, used to say to me, "Even a ninety-three-year-old saint is not safe"—meaning that there's always the possibility of the worldly stuff coming and grabbing us back again.

Right to the very end of our sadhana, as long as there is anybody at all *in* there, all the stuff that comes with that somebody-ness is lurking around, available and ready to exert its pull. Our battle, the battle of Kurukshetra that we're waging within us, is with the power of all those pulls of nature. The desires operate by using the ego, with all its deep attachments to survival and to reproduction, to capture our attention. If we're doing practices of renunciation, we have to expect to deal with the powerful pulls of those desires. That's the point of the practice, in fact—to *recognize* the power of those forces, so we can begin to cool them out.

A lot of people hear the word "renunciation" as somehow meaning that the world is bad, and that's why we must renounce it. But that's not it at all. The problem isn't that the world is evil—the problem is that we're too *caught* in the world. We're starting from a place where we are trapped, bound hand and foot, by our attachments, and through a series of maneuvers we are trying to extricate ourselves from our shackles. Renunciations and purification exercises are one set of techniques for escaping from those bonds. They're a Houdini act.

So it's not that the world is evil, it's just that we're trying to get some purchase on our desire systems so they won't be dominating our consciousness all the time, and therefore renunciation doesn't have anything to do with being a "good guy." It isn't *better* to give up sex, or *better* to fast; we don't do renunciation practices to be good—that's falling into the *satvig* trap, the trap of being attached to being somebody nice. We renounce things because we *want* to give them up. We do it because we see how they're holding us, and we've identified ourselves with something that's much more interesting than the immediate gratification, the next chocolate bar. We renounce things when our desire to get on with the journey is stronger than our desire for the next ice cream soda.

We used to do experiments in psychology about "delay of gratification." The question was, would people give up a little candy bar now for a big one later?—And how big would the later one have to be for them to give up the little one now, and how much later, and all that experimental-variables stuff. What we took for granted in those experiments was that society is essentially a training ground for the deliberate renunciation of immediate gratification—but always in order to get more of the same gratification later on.

Practices of renunciation, on the other hand, reflect a kind of "*enlightened* self-interest." We don't do a practice to get a bigger candy bar later on; we do it when we see that our attachment to our desires will in itself inevitably lead to more suffering. At the point where we see that, we decide that we want to get free of the whole bag. That kind of renunciation doesn't come out of guilt or fear, out of shoulds or shouldn'ts; it comes out of wisdom.

Ours is not a culture that has much appreciation for any path of renunciation. Ours is a culture built on the idea that more gratification, sooner, is better. Gandhi said, "The essence of civilization consists not in the multiplication of wants but in their deliberate and voluntary renunciation." That's certainly a hard sell here in the West, where everything keeps fanning the flames of our desires. Look at the way advertising is designed—it's based on the exact opposite of what we're talking about. It's built on making us feel more and more dissatisfied, making us think we want more and more things. I mean, every three or four minutes on television there is another statement designed to create in you yet another desire: "If you don't own this, you can't possibly be happy. You *must* want it! You've *gotta* have it!"

By Gandhi's yardstick, my own country, with all its affluence, is not yet very civilized. If we look at what people do with their great wealth in America, we find that they mostly use it to try and create more and more sensual gratification for themselves. And then when they're totally jaded with it all, and they begin to feel the inevitable falling away of their desires, they don't know where to turn. It's a dead-end street, because it all passes, it's all transient.

Once we see that, we're motivated to turn the process around. But as we start to do that, our minds sometimes get ahead of the rest of us, and we start giving things up in order to be "good," and not because we see that they're a hindrance and we're finished with them. We try to jump the gun on the process.

I've had my own experience of the difference between those two motivations in connection with the practice of fasting, which is a form of renunciation (we renounce satisfying our desire for food). Fasting was an interesting one for me, because I have always had an intense relationship with food. I learned from my mother to equate food with love, so by the time I was ten I was wearing pants in size double Z, with balloon seats. I was definitely *deep* into the oral trip.

Then it was 1967, and I was at the temple in India. I noticed that everybody there fasted a lot, so one day I said to my teacher, "Hari Dass, can I fast?" (Actually, I didn't *say* it—I *wrote* it on the slate I carried, because we were *maun,* silent, at that time.) Hari Dass answered, "If you'd like." I asked, "How long should I fast?" He said, "Four days would be good." So I asked him, "How long do *you* fast?" He wrote, "Nine days, on every new moon." I thought, "Well, if he can do it, I can do it." So I wrote, "I will fast for nine days." And I looked very holy.

The time came, and I started the fast. And I then proceeded to spend the entire nine days thinking about nothing but food. I thought about the Thanksgiving dinners I'd had as a child; I visualized the roast turkey, and the sweet potatoes with the little marshmallows on top, and the different kinds of stuffing, and how the gravy would smell, and what the first bite would taste like—I lived that out again and again and again. I thought about all the different restaurants I'd been to around the United States, about the cracked crab in the Northwest, and the steak at Original Joe's, in San Francisco, and the bouillabaisse in New Orleans, and the Lobster Savannah in Boston and—oh, boy! I'd been a cross between a gourmet and a gourmand for years, so I had a rich stock of memories to draw on.

I did complete the fast. I made it through all nine days. But the interesting question was, while I was so busy fasting, what was it I was feeding?

Three months later, when I did my next nine-day fast, I was getting much better. ("Better"—a new ego trip!) Now I spent the whole time thinking only about foods I could eat as a yogi. So I thought about spinach with lemon on it, and steaming bowls of rice, and fresh hot chapatis, and milk. I was doing all these fasts, thinking, "Aren't I good? I'm doing nine-day fasts, just like the book says. I'm becoming a great hatha yogi." And yet there were very few waking hours when I was not obsessing about food.

Time passed, and then a few years afterward, I was back in India again. Some friends and I were staying in a little village, and it seemed like a good opportunity to do another long fast. But this time, except for the fact that at noon, lemon and water or ginger tea was brought instead of food, I never even noticed I was fasting. I was just busy doing other things instead of eating. About halfway through, I thought, "Oh, *this* is what fasting is about. Far out!" It's not about renouncing food— it's about renouncing hunger! I hadn't even known what it was all *about* before, because I was so busy thinking that the ego-tripping I was doing was *tapasya,* that it was an austerity of some sort.

I've come to recognize that the real *tapasya* happens when we are so ripe to do it that we just *do* it. We do it joyfully, with a feeling of "Yeah—of course. That's what happens now." We do it with a feeling of "Whew! Now I can be rid of that one." It's release, not self-denial. Ramana Maharshi said, "I didn't eat, and they said I was fasting." Right there in that statement is the essence of *tapasya.* As long as we think *we're* doing the austerity—"Look at me! I'm giving this up!"—it's just another ego trip. Whatever we may think we're renouncing, we're just stuffing our egos with both hands.

In the East, there are systems of yoga built around practices of purification and renunciation. One of them is the Hindu tradition called ashtanga yoga—the "eight-limbed" yoga. It was enunciated by Patanjali sometime between 200 B.C. and A.D. 400, but it emerged from much earlier yogic practices. Ashtanga Yoga is a structured sequence of steps that help us to get the various parts of our game in order. It's a whole curriculum for going to God, and by looking at it in some depth, we can get a sense of the way practices like renunciation are meant to work within the structure of a total system of yoga.

Ashtanga yoga has an elaborate program for working with purification, and with some related practices called observances. They constitute the first two limbs of ashtanga yoga, and they're called yama and niyama, respectively.

The five yamas, which are the five purifications or self-restraints, are non-harming, non-lying, non-stealing, non-lustfulness, and non-possessiveness. The five niyamas, or observances, are purity, contentment, discipline, scriptural study, and surrender to God.

After yama and niyama comes the third limb, made up of the postures, or asanas, which is what we most often think of as hatha yoga.

Then comes pranayama, or breath control, which is also traditionally seen as part of hatha yoga. That's the first four.

The last four limbs are all concerned with meditation. First comes pratyahara, the initial stage of meditative work, which starts to withdraw the mind from the senses; it's a process of drawing back the mind, until we can watch our senses doing their trip and at the same time keep our mind on the breath. Then the last three limbs of ashtanga yoga are increasingly intense levels of deeper and deeper meditation called dharana (or concentration), dhyana (or deep meditation), and samadhi (or Oneness), which takes you right into Brahman.

The ordering of these eight steps is not random. The first things necessarily precede the last things, and you move through the sequence in order. You can't jump the line. When I was in India, Maharajji said to me one day, "Nobody does hatha yoga anymore." I was surprised; I said, "No? But it's very big in America, Maharajji." He said, "No, nobody does it anymore, because hatha yoga assumes that you've already finished with the first two practices of yama and niyama, and nobody does any of that now."

So there are eight sequential steps in the practice of ashtanga yoga, and we can see that it's the first step, yama, that has to do with the practice of renunciation. Think about it: We imagine we're so spiritually advanced because we're considering becoming renunciates, and we discover that it's the very *first* rung on the ladder. We're just beginners!

Yama, as we've said, encompasses five categories: non-killing, non-lying, non-stealing, non-lusting, and non-giving-and-receiving. The five "nons." In Hindi, they are called ahimsa, satya, asteya, brahmacharya, and aparigraha. They all sound like reasonably good ideas. The question is, what happens if we try to live by them?

Start with the first one: ahimsa, or non-killing—a subject which I've been sort of sidestepping, since the Gita is all about war. And yet there it is, an assumption in the game, the first step in the first limb of ashtanga yoga: "non-killing," it says. What are we to make of that? How does it fit into the situation at Kurukshetra, with Krishna urging

Arjuna into battle? To frame it another way, can a nonviolent person ever perform a violent act?

Mahatma Gandhi was one of the chief proponents of nonviolence, and yet he worked with the Gita and lived by the Gita throughout his entire life. One might raise a question as to the paradoxical nature of that. Gandhi said this: "When the Gita was written, although people believed in ahimsa, wars were not only not taboo, but nobody observed the contradiction between war and ahimsa."[1] I think you have to stretch pretty far to imagine how that could possibly be—how people would not see war and ahimsa as incompatible—but that was Gandhi's explanation. Then he went on to say, "But after forty years of unremitting endeavor fully to enforce the teachings of the Gita in my own life, I have in all humility felt that perfect renunciation is impossible without perfect observance of ahimsa in every shape and form."[2] In other words, Gandhi is taking exception here to the Gita; he's one of the partisans in a debate over whether you can perform a violent act without breaking your vow of ahimsa, and he says you can't, Gita or no Gita.

My understanding of the predicament here is that there is a tension between the humanitarian and the mystical perspective on the subject. The compassion of the humanitarian is that of a mortal man. The compassion of the mystic is one with the way the universe is created, survives, and is destroyed. Krishna's is a compassion that transcends the compassion that a human mind can comprehend.

There are levels of wisdom, and it is not at all inconceivable to me that just as a surgeon can perform an operation and create pain in order ultimately to alleviate suffering, so destruction can have its purpose. Krishna, in order to destroy the illusion of the separate self, might very well create a scenario which we human beings, still identified with our separate selves, would find horrifying—a scenario like war.

It's complicated. In working with ahimsa, we still have to somehow come to terms with the forces of Shiva in the world, with the aspect of God that is destruction and chaos in the universe. We as humans have to do our best to practice ahimsa, while at the same time we have to be willing to honor a dharma that might sometimes call for violence. All we can do is to listen as carefully as we can for what our next step is supposed to be.

Our whole attempt to honor ahimsa is fraught with complications and contradictions. For example, I was, for a long time, a vegetarian, which seemed like a nice, ahimsa-type thing to be. I did take milk, though. While I was on that diet, I was up visiting Ken Kesey one weekend at his farm in Oregon. Ken knew I was a vegetarian, and Ken, of course, was not. Being the prankster that he was, he said, "Come on, let me show you around." So he took me to the barn and showed me the dairy cows, and that whole scene. I was saying, "Oh, beautiful." And he took me to see the gardens: "Oh, aren't they wonderful." Then he took me out to a field, and showed me these two huge bulls. I said, "What are you doing with them?" He said, "We're fattening them up to eat them." I was trying to act cool, so I just said, "Oh, yeah. Right." But he could tell he was getting to me. He started patting one of the bulls on the head, saying, "This one'll be good—there are some really good steaks in this one," pointing right to where the steaks were. And I was looking into the eyes of the animals, trying to send love messages to them.

Then Ken looked straight at me, and said, "You know, you drink milk. If you want milk, you've got to have bulls." And suddenly I saw the reality of my predicament. I'm not a farm-boy, so none of it had been obvious to me before: That to keep a cow giving milk, she has to have calves from time to time, and every time she does, half of the calves that are born are bulls. What are you going to do with them? You could feed them until they died a natural death, but that's not a likely outcome. So there I was: a vegetarian, but still complicit in the fate of those two bulls.

I wore sandals for a long time that came from the Gandhi ashram; they had a little stamp on them that said, "These were made at the Gandhi ashram," which meant that they'd only used cows that had fallen over dead in the street. It's not like they had killed the cow to get the leather for the sandals; the cow had died a natural death, so yogis could wear those sandals in good conscience. Still, it seems a little bit . . . well, you know . . . And now we have all this new information about what plants go through when you bring a knife near them—so our diet's getting a little thin, isn't it?

All I can share, in dealing with the predicament of ahimsa, is to suggest that whatever you do, you do it as *consciously* as you can. When the Native Americans killed an animal to eat it, they offered it to their gods, and they thanked the animal for giving its life for them. They killed in order to survive in order to do their work, and that was in harmony with their understanding of how nature operates. That's bringing consciousness to the act.

But even though I don't think there are any hard-and-fast rules for a "spiritual" diet, as we go through the different stages of our yoga our practices reshape our bodies and our physical needs, and we usually find that our diet changes. When we are still very much caught in worldly thought and worldly heaviness, we will need just what the World Health Organization says we need: a certain amount of protein and a certain amount of carbohydrate, certain vitamins and certain minerals, all that kind of stuff. Later, as we get lighter and quieter, as we get more connected to a different plane in the universe, we find we're able to work with another kind of energy, and that changes our diet; the diet we'd had before seems too heavy, and so we start to eat, say, only grains and fruits and vegetables and dairy products. And then maybe the dairy products start to get too heavy, and then the grains start to get too heavy, and we're down to vegetables and fruits and nuts. And finally maybe even the vegetables are too dense and we become fruitarians. The progression is all perfect, we're healthy, and everything is fine. Now, if you had a hamburger yesterday, and you tried to become a fruitarian today, you'd probably get really sick. But were you ready for it, fruitarianism would be the right and natural thing, and anything else would feel gross.

If you keep growing spiritually, you get so you can live on light alone. Like Teresa Neumann, the Christian saint: for twelve years, she ate nothing but one Eucharist wafer a day—and she was a good, zaftig woman. They asked her, "How can this be? What are you living on?" She said, "I'm living on light."

Why not? I mean, plants do it: chlorophyll, sun, energy transformations—when you come right down to it, energy is energy. What we can *process* as energy depends on which receptors are open in us. And that's one of the things the purification trip is about—so we can start working with all the subtler energies that are available to us. If you're an energy-transmuting vehicle, you can take *any* energies and get off on them.

But all we can do is the best we can do with what we know and who we are. And most of us aren't Saint Teresa yet. I do the best I can, by trying to be as nonviolent as I can be. I try to create as few conditions as possible that would demand that things be raised and killed in order to service my existence. And yet the truth is that in spite of all that, I'm no longer a vegetarian. I stopped eating meat, fish, chicken, and eggs right after I met Maharajji, but after a while I got to wondering if maybe there was a place in me where I was caught in the *satvig* trap about my vegetarianism, caught in being the "good guy," and I felt I ought to undercut that. So I decided that what I was going to do was to break my vegetarian trip—just break it. And if I was going to do it, I figured I might as well *really* do it up right, and since I had been raised as a Jew, I decided I would break my vegetarian diet by having spareribs, which would sort of hit it from both angles.

I found a Chinese restaurant. I went in and sat down and ordered the spareribs. The waiter put them in front of me, and I blessed them; I gave a particularly *long* blessing. I offered the spareribs to Maharajji, and I said, "I know you think this is strange, but . . . it's the way it is. You know my heart, and you know why I'm doing this, and—well, I'm just going to do it!" And I then proceeded to thoroughly enjoy the spareribs. I mean, they were *every* bit as good as I had remembered them being!

While I was eating, I noticed that there was a man sitting about two booths away, in a suit and a tie and a gold wristwatch; he was drinking tea all through my whole meal, and he was watching me. Finally, just as I finished, he came over to my booth and he said, "May I sit down for a minute?" I said, "Sure." He said, "I'm a traveling salesman for an electronics outfit in Boston. I was just about to leave the restaurant when your food was served. And you know, I couldn't help watching the way you blessed the food. It was . . . well, the blessing was so powerful that I haven't been able to leave the restaurant without talking to you." It turned out that he was a fundamentalist Christian, and we got into a beautiful rap about the Bible and Christ, and we talked for around an hour and a half, and drank a lot of tea. Finally he said, "Well, I'm just so delighted to have met you, it's been wonderful. There's just one more thing I wanted to ask you. I've had a lot of questions about my diet, what I ought to be eating and not eating, so I'm just curious—what's your diet like? What do you eat?" And I looked down, and right there in front of me was this big pile of bones. I would have done anything to be able to push it away and say, "Well, of course *I'm* a vegetarian, and . . ." But there it was. I had to face the fact of who I was at that moment.

When I was in India, during my vegetarian days, I stayed at this hotel called the Palace Heights; it was the hippie hangout in Connaught Circus. It turned out that the window in my room overlooked the alley next to a fancy restaurant, and (since the Indians in Delhi were "going Western") they were serving chicken at that restaurant. Every afternoon around four, out in the alley, they'd wring the necks of the chickens they were going to serve that night for dinner. We would come back from shopping and be lying there peacefully, and suddenly: Cluck, cluck, cluck—*awwwwk!* I felt all my chicken-karma coming home to roost—it was all those Sunday chicken dinners I was paying for, you know. There was another one, and there was another one . . .

But what's interesting is that even after all that, I've sometimes visited Colonel Sanders. I see the horror of it all—I mean, not only the physical horror of the way the chickens are produced, but the absurdity of the fact that I'm asking somebody to produce a chicken, a living creature, so I can eat it. But nonetheless I *do* eat it. And I enjoy it. And I sit with that horror.

I can't be phony holy anymore. I've just got to be where I'm at. I don't really *want* to eat the chicken, and yet there I am eating the chicken. And who knows whether eating chickens or not eating chickens creates greater violence in the long run? Which is more ahimsa? Maybe in pushing away eating chicken, I would end up being so frustrated, so filled with rich, sadistic fantasies, that I'd psychologically destroy everybody around me, and create incredible suffering, just because I didn't eat that last chicken. I'm not offering that as an excuse, or as a practical suggestion. I'm just sharing with you the psychological dilemma we face in deciding when we renounce and when we don't renounce. Now we're getting to the nitty-gritty of all these practices we're talking about.

We'll move a little more quickly through the other yamas, but I think it was worth taking the time to explore a practice like ahimsa deeply enough to get the full flavor of it. We can get a little facile in the way we accept these practices in principle, without confronting the issues we actually wrestle with when we try to implement the practices in our lives.

The second yama is satya: truthfulness, non-lying. Gandhi said, "Truth is God, and God is Truth," and his life was the statement of someone who was trying to live as close to truth as possible. A woman once came to Gandhi with her young son. She said, "Mahatma-ji, please tell my little boy to stop eating sugar." Gandhi told the mother, "Come back in three days." Three days later the woman and the little boy returned, and Mahatma Gandhi said to the little boy, "Stop eating sugar!" The woman was confused, and she asked, "But why was it necessary for us to return only after three days for you to tell my little boy that?" Gandhi replied, "Three days ago, I had not stopped eating sugar." That sets the bar pretty high; that's a high level of truthfulness to demand of ourselves, and the practice of satya has to do with shaping our lives to that level of inner truth.

Now, at the point where most of us are, we don't have a deep enough connection to Truth to be straight at *every* level, but we start out by being straight wherever we can. We learn to listen for the truth, and to live by the truth, even if there's some cost to it. Mahatma Gandhi was leading a march once; many people had left their jobs and come long distances to take part in the march, but after the first day Gandhi called his lieutenants together and said, "This is wrong. This march is not a good idea after all. I'm calling it off." His lieutenants got very upset and said, "But Gandhi-ji, you can't do that! People have come from all over to take part in this march. We can't stop it now!" Gandhi replied, "I don't know absolute truth—only God knows that. I'm human; I know only relative truth, and that changes from day to day. My commitment must be to truth, and not to consistency." That is, I have to honor my commitment to the truth, even if it means reversing myself to do it.

We often find, as we go merrily on our spiritual way, that we have to reverse ourselves if we want to stay with our truth. Finding our dharma is a little like finding a floating crap game; it doesn't stay in one place, it's always changing its location. You think you know what your route is. You've just gotten all your new outfits and beads and brownie badges, all the things that go with your new schtick—and then suddenly, the whole thing turns dead and empty and horrible. What are you going to do? "My commitment must be to truth, not to consistency." Give the outfits to the nearest Salvation Army thrift store, and go on. After a while you get so you just *rent* the costumes; you don't buy them, because you see that you're going to be moving through the trips very, very quickly. You just keep staying as close as you can to your living truth.

Maharajji was always admonishing me to tell the truth. It was one of his regular dialogues with me: "Ram Dass, tell the truth."

"Yes, Maharajji."

That alternated with Maharajji's other dialogue with me. He'd call me up to the tucket and he'd say, "Ram Dass, give up anger."

"Yes, Maharajji." Sounds like a nice thing—give up anger.

He went back and forth between those two injunctions: "Ram Dass, tell the truth." "Ram Dass, give up anger."

Now there were at the temple all these Westerners who had come to India with me. It was my own fault they'd come—Maharajji had warned me not to tell anybody about him. But I had, and now there they were; they were all hanging out with me, and I was really bugged, because I wanted to be hanging out with the Indians. So I was growing to detest them all.

So I started thinking about Maharajji's instructions, and I thought, "You know, the truth is that I really don't like these people." I wanted to do what Maharajji said, and give up my anger. On the other hand, what I'd always done in the past was to be the nice guy, and pretend I wasn't angry; I'd been giving up truth in order not to appear angry, but inside I was always this bubbling cauldron. So I decided, "Why don't I do it the other way around this time? For a change I'll tell the truth, and the truth is I can't stand any of these people."

So I started to be *very* honest. Somebody would come into my room and I'd look at him and say, "Get the hell out of here. You make me sick!" The guy would say, "What did I do?" I'd say, "I don't know. You're too nice." Well, after about two weeks of my "truth telling," I wasn't talking to any of them, and they were all busy plotting to throw me in the lake.

Now, we Westerners were staying at a hotel in town, and every day all of us would go by bus to the temple. It happened that I was at that time performing a *tapasya,* which was that I wouldn't touch money. It's an interesting austerity to experiment with, because you begin to see how powerful the little game is of having some change in your pocket. Without it, suddenly everything is all out front. You can't sneak off for an ice cream cone if you don't have any money. Furthermore, you're dependent; you need a bagman to carry your money if you're going to buy your lunch or ride a bus. But by that point in my relationships I was so mad at everybody that I wouldn't even *let* them pay my bus fare, which meant I had to walk to the temple, which was about eight miles away.

So I walked to the temple. It's a beautiful walk, actually, through green hills and woods, but I was so angry at everybody that I didn't enjoy the walk at all. I was busy being furious the whole way there, because they were all at the temple, enjoying Maharajji, while I was having to spend hours walking there—and all because I was so good that I wasn't touching money. But I certainly wasn't going to let any of *those* bastards pay my fare and . . .

By the time I got to the temple, I was *seething.* I arrived there just after they had taken lunch. One of the fellows—one with whom I was *particularly* furious—brought over a plate of food, and set it down in front of me. I wasn't about to take food from *his* hands, so I picked up the leaf plate, and I threw it in his face.

Across the way, Maharajji was watching. "Ram Dass!"

I went over and sat down in front of him. He said to me, "Something troubling you?"

I said, "Yeah. I can't stand adharma. I can't stand that in all of us which takes us deeper into the illusion. I can't stand it in them— they're all so impure! I can't stand it in myself. In fact I hate everybody in the world—except you." And with that, I started to cry—not just to cry, but to really weep and wail. Maharajji tried to comfort me; he patted me on the head, he sent for milk and fed it to me. He was crying, and I was wailing and wailing. And when I got all finished with my wailing, he said to me, "I thought I told you not to get angry."

I said, "Yeah—but you also told me to tell the truth, and the truth is that I'm angry."

Then he leaned toward me, until he was nose to nose and eye to eye, and he said, "Give up anger, and tell the truth."

I started to say, "But . . ."—and then, right at that moment, I saw my predicament. See, what I was going to say to him was "But that isn't who I am." And in that instant, I saw in front of me the image of a coffin, and in the coffin was an image of who I thought myself to be. And what Maharajji was saying to me was "I'm telling you who you're going to be, after you're finished being who you *think* you are."

Then I looked over at all those people, all of whom I *detested,* and I saw that one layer down, one tiny flick of the lens, I loved them all incredibly. I suddenly saw that the only reason I was angry with them was because I had a model of how I thought it *ought* to be, which was other than the way it was. How can you get angry at somebody for being what they are? You're trying to outguess God. They're just being what God made them to be—what are you getting angry about? Somebody lies to you? They're just doing their karmic trip. Why are you upset? "Well, I didn't think they'd lie to me!" Ah, expectations—there's your problem. The next time you get angry, look closely at what you're angry about. You'll see you're angry because God didn't make the world the way you think it should have been made. But God makes the world the way She makes it!

So the practice of satya requires that in all our doings—in our dealings with other people, in steering our spiritual course, whatever—we stay as close to the truth as we possibly can. Maharajji said to me, "Truth is the most difficult *tapasya*." It's the hardest austerity, the toughest one to do. He said, "People will hate you for telling the truth." And sometimes they do. "People will laugh at you and taunt you, they may even kill you," he said, "but you've got to tell the truth."

The trouble is, we can only tell the truth when we cease to identify with the part of ourselves we think we have to protect. If we're *afraid* of being laughed at or taunted or killed, we can't tell the truth; we can't tell the truth if we're busy guarding some position. It's only when we realize that we're not as vulnerable as we fear we are that we can afford to tell the truth. Let's say I tell you the truth, and you don't like it, and you get up and walk out. That's your problem, not mine. But if I need your love, your interpersonal love, then I can't risk having you walk out on me, and so I can't tell you the truth. I can never be straight with you if I need something from you. So in order to tell the truth to you, I have to give up whatever that need is in myself. That's why satya is a practice of renunciation; what we're required to renounce are the attachments that keep us from speaking the truth.

There is a very far-out thing about Truth: That when you are rooted in Truth, *really* rooted in Truth, your word takes on power (and this in fact is exactly what "powers" are all about), such that when you say something, it is so. When you give someone a blessing, the blessing is given; it simply happens. When you say, "Be healed!" the person is healed. That's the power of the word, *if* the word comes out of the place of total Truth—because then it comes out of the place in you where you are so connected to the deepest core of Truth itself that everything that comes out of you is straight at every level. The purifications of the satya practices prepare us for that kind of Truth.

The third yama practice I want to talk about is the one called aparigraha. It literally means "non-hoarding," but it's also variously interpreted as meaning non-coveting, non-possessiveness, or non-giving-and-receiving. "Non-giving-and-receiving" doesn't mean that nothing is passed back and forth; it has to do with the spirit in which the giving and receiving are done. It recognizes that giver and receiver are the same, so there's a freedom from any greediness in the transaction. That's the core of the practice of aparigraha.

I used to go through a little dance with my father all the time around the subject of money. My father was a very loving, wonderful, wealthy guy, and I was a very loving, wonderful, *poor* guy. He'd say to me, "Rich [which was a funny name, considering], is there anything you need?" And I'd always say, "No." He'd never say, "Rich, here's a thousand dollars," to which I would have said, "Thanks." Instead, he'd ask, "Is there anything you need?" All I'd have had to say was "Yeah, I need a thousand dollars," and I'd have had it. But once I had to ask for it, that thousand dollars would come with a whole set of strings, like fine spiderwebs, attached to it—things like: "The kid still needs me," or "Damned kid, still can't earn a decent living," or "Sure, all they want me for is my money."

With all the paranoia connected with money, most of us can't afford to be in the giving-and-receiving business. Most of our giving, most of the time, happens because we want something in return. That's not generosity; that's greediness. Even if we don't want something material, we at least want somebody to *appreciate* our gift; we want them to thank us for it. Or maybe we want the return of having a good image of ourselves, as somebody who gave something. Even if

The Puja Bazaar: A bazaar sprang up outside the hall, where people brought religious photos, craft items, and ritual objects to sell and barter, everyone trying good-naturedly to bargain and at the same time to remain mindful that "everything is God." It was a creative attempt to stay conscious through the temptations of the marketplace.

we give anonymously, it's just a subtler hype: "Look at how good *I* am—I gave *anonymously.*" See? Just more ego-feeding!

In dealing with money, it's useful to try adopting the notion that you're merely the bookkeeper in the firm. It's not your money; you're just there to administer it in a responsible way. It wasn't really my father's money, he was merely the keeper of that energy at that moment, because it was his karma to play that role. It's your karma to work with your money, or with whatever other corner on the energy market might have been given to you, but the energy doesn't belong to you. We're all just moving God's energy around from hand to hand.

People often bring me little gifts of one kind or another. Sometimes someone wants to give me something, and I find I can't take it, because I feel they *want* something while they're giving the gift. Other people just have some beautiful thing that they want to share with me; then I'll take it, and I'll use it for a while, and I'll pass it on to somebody else. It's just a sharing of energy; it's not yours or mine—whose is it, anyway?

When the United States gives food as foreign aid, like sending wheat to Biafra, we stamp on it, "Gift of the United States of America." It's like we're demanding gratitude—and so everybody ends up hating us, and we can't understand why. It's not our gift to give in the first place—it's God's wheat! Why are we making such a big deal about it? Because it grew on our land—*our* land? What's that about? My mother used to go around "our" property and say, "That's my tree and that's my tree and that's my tree." Far-out concept, "*my* tree." They're all *God's* trees. Nobody owns anything—how absurd! We're just working with the energy that's passing through us.

If we have the energy, we're responsible for it. We can use it to create more heaven or more hell; we can relieve the suffering of sentient beings, or we can take them deeper into illusion. Which way we use it will depend on whether we think the energy belongs to us, and whether we think the other beings *are* us. We can't simultaneously be protecting our little stash, hoarding it away, and at the same time opening our hearts to other people. Practicing aparigraha is about renouncing first-chakra stuff like possessiveness and greed, so we can start playing in a more conscious way with whatever energies have been given to us.

Asteya—non-stealing—is obvious: If everybody's "us," who are you going to steal from? Are you going to rip yourself off? Are you going to steal out of the cookie jar at home? You're just taking it from yourself. When there's no "them" in your universe, you can't steal—it's that simple.

So in order to steal, you have to see your victim as "other." That means stealing takes us deeper into the illusion of me / you, which is the illusion of identity, which is the illusion of separation. That, from a spiritual point of view, is why non-stealing is part of the practice of ashtanga yoga; it's not because of our usual ideas about morality, it's because in order to steal we have to turn the other person into "them," which rules out our seeing them as "us." That takes us away from the One. It's just that straightforward.

When you come to a place where you're absolutely clean in your relations with other people, you start to recognize what fun it is not to be feeling paranoid all the time. There's such a sense of freedom in it! You see that you really don't want to create all the stuff that comes from getting into relationships with other people that have elements of dishonesty in them.

It's like the difference in the feeling you have coming across a border carrying dope, and then coming across the border *not* carrying dope. Because of my nefarious psychedelic past, I was on "the List" for a long time, and so when the customs agents would punch in my name at the border, lights would flash, and bells would ring, and the agents would make hurried telephone calls—because I was a really *bad* guy, see? Then they'd proceed to go through everything I was carrying; they'd look inside my sneakers and turn all the pants pockets inside out. And I'd just sit there, doing mantra and enjoying the whole scene. I was watching good public servants doing their work. After a while they'd notice that I wasn't buying into the whole paranoia that their scene usually creates, and we'd generally end up being really loving buddies. It would take about two hours, but that's OK—you just learn to move more slowly. After all, it's always just Maharajji, coming to put us on.

So to avoid separating ourselves from other people, we stop ripping them off. We practice asteya. And while I think that most of us have already renounced stealing in its most literal, obvious form, the practice of asteya, in ashtanga yoga, goes much deeper than that. It's a much subtler practice. It's not just the physical stuff, like not stealing somebody's wallet. Practicing asteya includes things like not accepting undeserved praise and not taking credit for somebody else's ideas. It means in the very broadest sense possible that you don't appropriate anything, material or otherwise, that isn't rightfully yours. That's asteya.

I've saved non-lusting for the last, because I don't think most of us really want to hear about it. The word that's used for it, "brahmacharya," literally means "behaving like a disciple of Brahma," and it entails abstaining from lust in all its forms. It means renouncing the passionate desire for an object, in thought, word, and deed, in all conditions, places, and times. Now *that's* a heavy one! Saint Augustine, as you know, prayed, "Lord, give me chastity and continence—but not yet." That may be the appropriate motto for us at this moment. Given the fact that we have been born into an incarnation as an animal that reproduces the species through mating, all those desires surrounding it are really strong in us. It's all second-chakra stuff, and there's a lot of energy localized there.

Within our own society, everything conspires to make the second chakra a temple of worship, with *Playboy* as its Bible. Gandhi said, "The only reason one would have sex is to reproduce," but I've found that very few people in a Western audience are ready to hear that. When I read that quote, people just get uptight and say, "Don't lay that moralistic trip on us. These are the days of sexual freedom."

(The first time I ever used that Gandhi quote was at a lecture I was giving in Berkeley, at the beginning of the sexual freedom movement. There were about fifty people in the audience, and one couple, up in the first row, was screwing, right there in front of me. They were making a sexual freedom statement, I guess. As I read Gandhi's quote to the audience and started talking about his philosophy and the reasons behind it, I saw the couple growing more and more uneasy, and after a few minutes the guy lost his erection, and their whole "statement" ended kind of abruptly.)

But brahmacharya isn't about doing a moralistic trip on ourselves. It's the same as with fasting—we don't do it because we're good, we do it because we're ready to be finished with the lusting game. It's interesting to consider that if somebody is falling off a cliff, or if his car is flipping over, it's probably rare that he would be feeling sexy. When it's a matter of survival, lust seems to disappear—it just sort of goes out the window. At that moment, you're completely one-pointed on staying alive.

Now imagine that you could get so preoccupied with coming to God that the same thing would happen—that your lust would simply vanish. Not that you would *make* it happen, anymore than you make yourself lose your sexual desire when the car is rolling over. It just goes. That's what real brahmacharya is—when the lust just goes, not when you're pushing it this way and that, because if you're pushing it this way and that, you shove it under here and it pops up there.

When you work with powerful drive systems, like sex or fasting or breathing, you're working with stuff that's deeply built into us. It's the primordial stuff of our incarnations, and we can't treat it lightly. Each of us has to deal with different levels of energy within those systems, and with different levels of attachment, and so what is right for one person is absolutely wrong for another.

We have to approach a purification practice like brahmacharya with all of that in mind. That's why, for some of us, the absolute necessity in this incarnation is that we marry and have children, and that is right on. And for some of the rest of us, that would be right *off*, and we would struggle all the way. If we get a model in our heads that in order to get holy we've got to do it this way or we've got to do it that way, we're stuck with our models, and we can't see the truth about what in fact we need to be doing.

All that said, there are still good reasons for the emphasis on brahmacharya in ashtanga yoga. One reason has to do with the way lust poisons our relationships with other people. Let's be clear that we're talking about *lust* here, and not about a sexuality that is rooted in love. Lust turns the other person into an object; love does just the opposite. When you lust for another person, you are focusing on them as a body, as something to satisfy your second-chakra demands. Whenever you see another person as an object to be manipulated for your own purposes, you have forgotten that what you're dealing with is another manifestation of God.

A second reason for the focus on brahmacharya rests in the fact that sexual energy is just that—*energy*. It's merely one more form of energy, and there are stages in our sadhana when the amount of energy we have available to us is very important. At those points, you will want to conserve the sexual energy to have it available for other uses. And so you adopt a practice of brahmacharya. Hinduism isn't the only tradition that teaches that, by the way. Many spiritual paths suggest that at certain stages of spiritual development, it's wise to minimize sexual activity, because it expends so much energy that could be used in a different way.

And it's true; I can vouch for it. When I was doing very intense hatha yoga and pranayam practices, where the breath would stop for long periods of time and the energy would travel up the spine, I was using all the energy I could get my hands on. But the passions are always lurking! Even though I was eating pure, light, *satvig* foods, and even though I was living in a very unsexy environment in a temple in India, still, every now and then the sexual juices would flow and there would be either a wet dream or masturbation. For a while after that, my whole pranayam practice would change; it just wouldn't work very well. The energies weren't available for it. I could see for myself the rationale for practicing brahmacharya; I had experiential evidence of the way the process worked.

Now, there is, of course, an alternative approach to the spiritual use of sexual energy, one which is at first glance very different from the brahmacharya practice of conserving the energy; it is the practice we call Tantra yoga. Whatever prurient imagery that phrase may call up for us, Tantra is in fact a highly technical form of spiritualized sexual activity. To begin with, it has nothing very much to do with orgasm. It has to do with bringing together polar opposites in order to create a prolonged liberation of energy, and then using that energy to come into clearer and clearer, and emptier and emptier, spaces. Tantra yogic techniques are methods for getting that energy generated, and then for staying with it over long periods of time by not being eager for the rush of orgasm. Sexual Tantra is not a personal gratification trip. It's not that you won't enjoy it, of course—and that's the paradox of it. But anytime you get caught *being* the enjoyer of it, you've lost. Sexual Tantra is based on the assumption that you are using the sexual dance as an upaya, as a method for coming to

God. That's what it's about. And when it's really used in that way, it's a powerful tool for awakening.

Tantra, however, lends itself to a lot of self-deception. A lot of people don't want to give up sex, but they do want to appear holy, and so they say, "I'm doing Tantra." It is certainly true that all the energy in the universe, including sexual energy, is yours, anyway. And it is true that when you finally figure out who you really are, you can make it every day and stay right with God, all the way through. But until you *get* to that place, Tantric sexual practices are a hot fire to play with. You have to be a pretty conscious being to use Tantra as a practice and not as a diversion. Just because there are Tantric masters who can do it doesn't mean it's easy. As Kalu Rinpoche liked to say about Trungpa and his students, "When you go to the top of a mountain with a bird, and the bird flies, don't think you can, too."

There is one more reason for including brahmacharya in the list of yamas. Besides objectifying the other person and depleting our energy reserves, lust is sticky; it tends to trap us in our desires. Every time we perform an act in response to a desire, we end up strengthening the likelihood of having that desire again in the future. This isn't metaphysics—this is just straight learning theory from psychology. You satisfy the desire, you reinforce the motivation. Or as the Buddha said, "Defilements are like cats—if you keep feeding them, they keep coming around."

Every time we get lost into thinking we are the desirer, we feed the desire. If I eat a pizza, and I am busy being the pizza eater and the enjoyer of the pizza, I increase the likelihood that I will desire a pizza in the future. But there is another way to eat a pizza. If all the while I'm eating the pizza I'm right here, eating the pizza, but I'm not busy being *The Pizza Eater* . . . and if, although the enjoyment of the pizza is there, I'm not busy being *The Enjoyer of the Pizza* . . . then my quiet spaciousness around the act of eating of that pizza is not ensnaring me. Instead, it is *extricating* me more and more from my attachment to being the pizza eater, and therefore it's *decreasing* the likelihood that my attention is going to be pulled by the smell coming from every pizza parlor as I walk down the street. Same act: eating a pizza. And yet totally different.

Well, it's the same with sexuality. When you practice brahmacharya, when you renounce your sexuality, it doesn't necessarily mean that you will stop the game, or push sex away. Brahmacharya is less about changing what you do with regard to your sexuality than about developing a different *perceptual* stance toward your actions, such that those actions are feeding into your awakening rather than putting you back to sleep. True brahmacharya and true Tantra are *both* acts of renunciation, and what you are renouncing in both cases are your desire systems. "Know that a man of true renunciation is he who craves not," says the Gita. *Craves* not—that's the deeper meaning of brahmacharya. It's the same principle I talked about in my experience with fasting. On a shallow level, renunciation means renouncing the object itself. But the more profound meaning is renouncing our *attachment* to the object, our craving for it. Then, whether we engage in the act or not is really irrelevant because there is no attachment, and an act done without attachment does not create more karma. It's as simple as that. The Gita says, "Satisfied with whatever comes unasked . . . even *acting,* he is not bound."

Well, that's an overview of this one system, ashtanga yoga, and the way it uses the practices of renunciation and purification. By looking at our own lives in relation to that system, we've begun to appreciate the delicacy of the practices, and the intensity of our dance with all these desire systems we have. We'll take a desire and say, "Well, I'm ready to renounce that one." So we'll stop doing it for a while. And then maybe it will be just like me with my vegetarianism: I found out I'd done it a little too soon. I'd head-tripped it; it hadn't come out of my inner being. I wasn't *ready* to give up meat, I just *wanted* to be ready to give it up. But there was still all that stuff in me . . . and I went back to eating meat.

But as we're *drawn* to them, we start practicing the purifications that we see will release us from the obvious stuff that we know is keeping us stuck. We start purifying because it feels right to do it. And the more we get into it, the lighter our lives become. And the lighter our lives become, the more our inner work can go ahead. We purify because we see that if the waters are too wild outside, we can't get on with our inner work. If we're ripping people off, if we're hating this person and lusting after that one, if we're filled with greed and passion and anger, it's really hard to meditate; it's hard under those conditions to quiet the mind and open the heart. And so we begin the work of purification.

If you want to play a little bit with a renunciation practice, pick some desire that you encounter every day. You decide which one: the desire to eat something or other, the desire for a cigarette, whatever it is you want to play with. Pick something that you usually give in to every day—like, let's say, a cup of coffee in the morning—and for one day, don't do it. Then the next day, do it much more than you usually would—have *two* cups of coffee. Start to study your reactions. Notice the difference in your feelings toward the desire on the first day and on the second day.

Maybe another time you'll want to take *two* desires to work with; one day don't satisfy one and doubly satisfy the other, and then flip them around. Try to be very attentive to what's going through your mind about it. If you're keeping a journal, write about it in your journal. Start to relate to your desires as something you can scrutinize, rather than as things that totally suck you in all the time, things that consume you. Get into a friendly relationship with your desires. Play with them, instead of being driven by them all the time. Desires get to be fun, really, once we're observing them instead of mechanically reacting to them.

The whole game of renunciation and purification is an *experiment*—an experiment in how quickly we can extricate ourselves from being attached to our desire systems. Notice that it isn't a question of getting rid of desires—that's a misunderstanding. Trust me, the desires will stay around! We're just loosening their hold on us, getting clear enough of them so we can see them in some sort of context.

Renunciation is like all the rest of our practices. We're engaged in a kind of hunt-and-peck system. We keep experimenting with various practices and asking ourselves, "Am I ready for this?" We quiet, and we listen. Then maybe we renounce—or maybe we decide to go on with things as they are for a while. We bring as much consciousness to each system as we're able to muster, without getting all uptight about it. We just keep learning to live with ourselves, as truthfully and as consciously as we can.

8

Devotion and the Guru

We come now, in our journey through all the many and varied routes to Brahman, to the path of bhakti yoga, or devotion—which means we're going to be talking, among other things, about the ins and outs of gurus. We'll talk about the method of the guru: how it works, what you do, and what the guru does or doesn't do. And we'll talk a lot about *my* guru, Maharajji—because, although you may not believe it, he is the man behind the scenes here. All this is really his trip; I'm just the windup robot.

Bhakti, by its nature, is not a practice that we can sit down and figure out intellectually. Devotion has to do with the heart, and there is something a little absurd in *thinking* about heart trips. Devotion is something experienced in a realm that is not necessarily conceptual, and so it doesn't lend itself very easily to words. Hafez, the poet, said, "O thou who are trying to learn the marvel of love from the copy book of reason, I'm very much afraid that you will never really see the point."[1] He's telling us that to the extent that we try to *think* our way through the issue of devotion, we're not going to get very far, because devotion isn't thought about, it's felt. And to feel it, we have to experience it directly: through doing *japa,* through singing kirtan, through ritual and mantra and prayer, through remembering—through all the practices of merging in love, and letting love happen to each of us. That's the only way we will come to know about bhakti practices.

So if you want to know about bhakti yoga and you aren't already doing devotional practices, you might want to take this as an opportunity to start exploring them. Do it, and see what it feels like. There are some suggestions in the syllabus for setting up a puja table and working with *japa,* for example; you can start with that, or find some practice of your own that feels right to you. Begin nurturing the quality of devotion within yourself. The devotion can be directed toward some form of God that draws you toward itself (which is what in India is called the Ishta Dev). It can be directed toward a guru. It can be directed toward Gaia, or toward the Void, or toward your pussycat. It can be directed toward whatever form of God it is that opens your heart. Set aside a little time every day and spend a few minutes doing some devotional practice in relation to that being. Sing. Pray. Offer a candle flame or some food. Begin opening your heart, cultivating feelings of love and appreciation.

The Gita is rooted in devotion. Although it mostly concerns itself with service to God and with the higher Wisdom, all of that is set within a framework of devotion. At one point, Krishna says to Arjuna, It is because of your *love* that I am allowing you to hear and see all this. The vision that Krishna bestows on Arjuna, the vision of the cosmic form of the universe, is the vision that comes when the third eye opens and we "see without looking." It is incredible grace to be given that vision, and the awesome and aweful nature of that vision was bestowed on Arjuna, Krishna tells him, only because of his love, because of his devotion and the purity of his relationship to Krishna.

Tracing the sequence laid out in the Gita, we start with what we call lower knowledge, which leads to a certain kind of faith: the lower mind's faith in the possibility that there might be something the higher mind knows, even though the lower mind doesn't. That's quite a leap of faith for the lower mind! That faith leads us to do practices, through which we start to open a bit, which allows us to have some visions or some direct immediate experiences, which in turn lead us to deeper practices, which ultimately bring us to the higher wisdom, the wisdom of Brahman. But that entire sequence, which involves jnana yoga and karma yoga and purification and all the rest of it, takes place

Evening Kirtan in the Main Hall: In the evening there were
sessions of kirtan, a devotional practice of singing the names
of God or the Goddess. Kirtan is like a meditation practice that
deepens with time, so a single chant would often continue for
half an hour or more, repeating the same names again and again:
Sri Ram, Jai Ram, Jai, Jai Ram or *Kali, Durga, Namo, Namah.* (The
musicians here are Ganga Dhar Gerhard on tabla, Dwarkanath Bonner
on harmonium, and Krishna Das on ektara and vocals.

within a context of devotion, which is the prerequisite for all the rest
of it. The practices all bear fruit because of Arjuna's love for Krishna.

In the literature about the practices that bring us to Brahman—
what we would call the mystical literature—there are descriptions of
what seem to be two very different categories of mystical experience.
In one of them, the dominant feature is escape from the phenomenal
world and all that conditions it—what in Buddhism is known as
"attaining *nibbana.*" In the other, equally frequent, type of mystical
experience, love is the central phenomenon. It's characterized by the
quality of being absorbed in an all-enveloping love. Those represent
two alternative experiences of the Brahman.

Often times it may seem that there is a tremendous struggle going
on between the jnanis and the bhaktis, between what we might call

the head-trippers and the heart-trippers, between the people who say, "Don't buy into all those emotional trips," and the people who say, "It's OK—drown in the ocean of love." In the contrast, devotion can look pretty sloppy and mushy, while the intellect looks so clean and tight. But one of the sages in India, when he was asked to compare jnana and bhakti yoga said, "Jnana yoga is like a lamp; bhakti yoga is like a gem. The gem only glows by reflected light, while the lamp is its own illumination. But a lamp constantly requires attention—more oil, a new wick—while the gem goes on glowing without any effort on its part."

The main objection jnanis usually raise about bhakti is that it is dualistic: there's the gem, and there's the light source. That's the crux of their opposition to devotion—that devotion is, by its very nature, a dualistic practice. To be a bhakti, you have to be devoted to *some-thing*, say the jnanis, and since eventually you're going to have to give up subject-object distinctions, wouldn't it be better not to get sucked more deeply into them in the first place? That's a general outline of the way the argument runs.

That criticism of bhakti hinges on thinking that the vehicle for getting to the top of the mountain has to look like the mountaintop itself. A bhakti like me, on the other hand, would frame the question a different way; I would ask, "Can I afford to use dualism to get to *nondualism?*" It's certainly true that dualism can be a trap, and that we *can* get hooked on the object of our devotion. Jnana can also be a trap, as we have seen; we can get hooked on our need to know. *All* methods are traps. We just have to choose our traps wisely, and hope they'll self-destruct after they've served their purpose. A dualistic method, if it's used with wisdom, can be a first-rate vehicle into nondualism. As the method works, you go beyond the method, and the whole thing falls away.

So we can acknowledge the problem, and still use the practices of bhakti yoga. Krishna says in the Gita, "It's very difficult to go the route of merely identifying with the unmanifest." That's known as "the high path that has no railing." It isn't easy to make the leap from our individuality directly into nondualism. In order to come to the wisdom of the direct experience of Brahman, we have to be intensely one-pointed about where we are going. The lubrication that can grease that process, and so make the whole thing much easier, is an intense feeling of love for what it is you're moving toward. Whether you call that a love of Truth, or a love of God, or a love of guru, or a love of the Mother, or a love of the Void—it doesn't matter. What matters is what happens in your heart through that kind of intense emotional commitment to whatever it is.

We gravitate toward the experience of that kind of love, and it makes the opening of the heart happen very easily, very naturally. And that heart opening then allows us to break out of our identification with the manas, the lower mind, because we're so busy focusing on thoughts of our beloved. Your thoughts turn naturally toward the one you love, don't they? If you love someone, you can hardly stop thinking about them. If you're in love with God, and your thoughts are constantly turning toward Her, they're no longer trapped in the stuff of the ego. In the Psalms, David says, "Because my heart was enkindled, my reins were also changed." He's using the chariot image, as the Gita does, in which the reins are what control the mind. So David is saying, When my heart was opened, that made it easier for my mind to turn to God. That's the way devotion bolsters jnani practices—it becomes easier to turn the mind in a certain direction, by using the reins of the heart.

My relationship to Maharajji is a relationship of the heart, a relationship of love. My love for him started out in a very dualistic place; I wanted to rub his feet and look at his form and be around him. Then, as time went on, it was not that the love grew less, but that the love grew different. It kept growing deeper and deeper, until I didn't really care any more whether I was with his form or not. And then, as the love went deeper still, I was no longer relating at all anymore to "that man in India"; I was relating to the essence of "guru-ness," and I began to experience it *within* myself, in relation to him. The whole quality of the relationship kept changing and changing, as I grew in wisdom, as my heart opened, and as my surrender went deeper. I've kidded about it by saying that I worshipped his form until I finally realized that it was just the doorpost to the real thing. I was rubbing the doorpost, worshipping the doorpost; and then I saw that it was just the doorpost, and beyond it . . . ahhhhhh!

That's the way devotional practice works. We make use of the guru and of the love the guru awakens in us to bring us to the doorway. Then we look through—and what we see there draws us in, and in, and in. Devotion, as a method, takes us right back into the innermost part of ourselves, right back into the unformed—but it greases the skids for us. Practices like sacrifice or renunciation, which can seem really difficult if you're coming at them in a rajasic, *"I* can do it!" way, become incredibly easy in the presence of love. Sure you'll do it. Again, it's like something we see in a powerful love relationship, when you care more about your beloved than you do about yourself. Your favorite food is brought to the table, and your main concern is that the other person gets enough of it, even if it means that you don't; you are fulfilled by her eating it. It's what you experience when you're a parent; somebody says, "You do so much for your child—aren't you the self-sacrificing one!" But to you, it doesn't feel like sacrifice—it's joy.

Well, it's the same way with practices. Austerities, done with a dry heart, are heavy. But when done with love, you say, "Oh, yeah—I'll gladly do this for my beloved. I'll give that up, because that will get me closer." When you're eager to get close to your beloved, you can't give things up fast enough: "That's getting in the way—I don't want to have anything more to do with *that.*" That's the way bhakti yoga works. It's the yoga of the heart, a yoga of loving openness to God, and it uses all our emotions to keep us working on the stuff that will eventually bring us to the Brahman.

It should be clear, I hope, that the love we're talking about here is not romantic love. It isn't at the level of "I love so-and-so because he has a great personality." It's a different species of love. It's the *place* of love where you meet every other being in your heart of hearts. It's what's called conscious love, or Christ love, or agape. It's the kind of love that, like the sun, shines on everything, whether it's "lovable" or not. It doesn't sit around judging whether it can afford to love this being or that being—it just loves everything, regardless. C. S. Lewis, in *Perelandra,* conveyed the spirit of that love; he said, "Love me, my brothers, for I am infinitely superfluous. And your love shall be like His [meaning God's], born neither of your need, nor of my deserving, but just bounty, plain bounty."

When a being *becomes* love, everything that person touches *is* love; it all rests within the aura of love. Meher Baba described one of the qualities of that kind of love when he said: "Love has to spring spontaneously from within. It is in no way amenable to any form of inner or outer force; love and coercion can never go together. But though love cannot be forced on anyone, it can be awakened in him through love itself. Love is essentially self-communicative. Those who do not have it catch it from those who have it. True love is unconquerable and irresistible, and it goes on gathering power and spreading itself until eventually it transforms everyone whom it touches."

Meher Baba's comment that love is not amenable to any kind of coercion is true down to the subtlest levels, the little psychological coercions. Even when it comes out of the best of intentions, coercion still doesn't work. Say I'm sitting with somebody, and I sense that that person's heart is closed. What I want to say is "Open your heart—you need to love more," but I know that won't be heard. So I turn on the manipulation; I say, "Tell me about this or that in your life. How does that make you feel?" By coaxing out the emotions, I'm really trying to subtly coerce that person into opening his or her heart. And of course it doesn't work. So after a while, I give up; I stop trying so hard. Instead, I just hang out with the person, and love her or him. I'm just there with the person in love. He may say, "Well, I still don't feel anything!" but then he gets up to leave and he asks, "Can I hug you?" "Why do you want to hug me if you don't feel anything?" "I don't know. I just do."

When people say to me, "I don't feel any love. I don't feel any of this stuff you're talking about," I think about that Thomas Merton quote from *Seeds of Contemplation;* he said, "Prayer and love are learned in the hour when prayer becomes impossible and the heart has turned to stone." It's only when our despair reaches rock bottom that the opportunity occurs for the heart to open. So if someone says to me, "I feel nothing; I feel dead inside,"—that, to me, is a critical moment. It's a moment when there is the possibility of the heart opening.

But that only works when the despair is deep enough. Sometimes I'll see that it isn't, that the person is still trying to *think* her or his way out. Then I'll usually say, "Go away and suffer some more, and come back in about a year. You haven't suffered enough yet."

Often people don't seem to think that that's compassionate advice. That's because it's so hard for us to hear the truth of the matter: that suffering *is* grace. The suffering born of the feeling that our hearts are closed will ultimately open our hearts. Reason will never allow us to understand that one!

When we've got our troubles, our sorrows, our difficulties (which every one of us has), it's hard for us to hear that all of that is a measure of *grace* that's being given to us. It sounds so Pollyannaish, or so masochistic, or something. It's only in the space of complete love and faith and trust that it starts to make sense to us. Maharajji said, "I love suffering. It brings me so close to God. You get jnana—wisdom—from suffering. You are alone with God when you are sick, you call on God when you suffer."

Devotion is what brings us to the place where we can embrace suffering in that way, because our love is so strong. "Thou shalt love the Lord thy God with all thy heart, and with all thy soul, and with all thy might," says the Bible. Now consider: Could that line possibly actually *mean* something? Could it possibly be talking about something real, something that is actually there for me to open to—loving God with all my heart and soul and might?

The history of devotional yoga is rich with examples of the most intense love, examples of beings for whom the love gets overwhelmingly powerful. In Isaiah, the Bible talks about those who are "drunken, but not with wine. They stagger, but not with strong drink." There are beings like that in India, beings who are completely lost in love, totally drunk with it. They're called masts, or God-intoxicants. In this country, people like that would probably be considered psychotic and sent to mental hospitals. However, there is a difference between psychosis and God-intoxication: The masts are not in the world, but all screwed up about it because of their anxieties, the way psychotics are; in a way, masts are no longer *in* the world at all. Their fifth chakra is wide open, and they are flooded with the experience of God. They have turned inward toward God, and they couldn't care less about their bodies or their role in the social scene. All of that has just fallen away, and so they can't keep their scene together anymore.

In India, it's understood that people like the masts are undergoing a spiritual transformation. Meher Baba used to go around and bathe the masts; he'd build places for them to stay, and take care of them in ashrams. Nobody else wanted to be around them, because they were so crazy and flipped out and wild. When people are going through stages like that, it's often inconvenient to have them around. We say, "That person is too neurotic; I wish he would go away." But with our own quieting, a different sort of recognition comes, and we honor the fact that the person may be going through some sort of very profound spiritual awakening, and that he must be treated with a lot of love and compassion.

Ramakrishna had that kind of intense, devotional love. He said, "Cry unto the Lord with a longing and yearning heart, and then you shall see Him. People would shed a jug full of tears for the sake of their wife and children, they would drown themselves in a flood of tears for the sake of money, but who cries for the Lord?" Think about what you have cried for in your lifetime. Was it when somebody put you down? When you lost something? When you made a fool of yourself? Whatever it was, it probably wasn't because you weren't close enough to God. When you cry out for God with that same kind of desperate yearning, "then you shall see Him."

There was a beautiful devotee of God, a sixteenth-century saint, born in Rajasthan. Her name was Mirabai, and she sang of her devotion, and created incredible bhakti love songs. Here's an example of one of her poems: "Oh black vultures, eat away everything of this flesh—but discriminately. Leave these two eyes, for they still hope to see the Lord. Oh black vultures, pull out these eyes as well, and take them to His presence—only make an offering of them to the Lord before you devour them."[2] That's certainly an *intense* kind of love. In fact, if you look at it from a hardheaded place, it seems absolutely grotesque. But if you can imagine loving something so much that nothing else matters—*nothing* else—then you can experience what Mirabai is singing about. The body means nothing at all—just the love. Just the love.

Tulsidas was a Hindu poet who lived in Banaras (Varanasi) in the late sixteenth century. He was a great devotee of Rama; and he wrote a kind of folk version of the Ramayana, called *Ramacharitamanasa;* it is total, liquid, bhakti love. Just to give you the flavor of how drunk with love Tulsidas is, here he is talking about his beloved, about Rama: "I adore the Lord of the universe bearing the name of Rama, the chief of Raghu's line and the crest jewel of kings, the mine of compassion, the dispeller of all sins, appearing in human form through his maya, his deluding potency. The greatest of all Gods, the bestower of supreme peace in the form of final Beatitude, placid, eternal, beyond the ordinary means of cognition, sinless, and all pervading. There is no other craving in my heart, O Lord of the Raghus: Grant me intense devotion to your feet, O Crest Jewel, and free my mind from faults." You can feel his way of relating to God—just love and devotion and yum-yum-yum. The overwhelming outpouring of love.

The point of all the bhakti practices is to kindle that kind of love, and then to direct it toward God or toward the guru. One can connect it with some concept of a Supreme Being—the Lord God Jehovah, or Purushatma, or Krishna, or Rama. Or one can find some form on the physical plane to love, someone to use as a doorway and eventually, through the love, to pass beyond. Whatever the form, we open our hearts to it. We use singing, we use praying, we use chanting, we use remembering, we use any and all of the practices of bhakti devotion to fan the intensity of our love for that Being who has awakened our heart.

Guru Kripa, or the method of the guru, is one form of bhakti practice. It is the specific form of bhakti that focuses on the guru, and

Puja Table:
Each student was
encouraged to create
a sacred space where
she or he could do
personal spiritual
practices, including
meditation, mantra,
and puja. This puja
table was one of the
shrines created at
Naropa. The
background is a
prayer shawl with
the name of Ram
inscribed on it. The
large picture shows
Ram, his wife, Sita,
his brother
Lakshman, and the
monkey-god Hanuman.
On the altar are
pictures of
Maharajji and
Hanuman, flowers, a
bell, and a bottle
of water from the
Ganges River in
India.

on the guru's grace or the guru's blessing. It happens to be the method I personally follow, although it's kind of a strange one here in the West. We in the West generally don't take well to the idea of gurus. A few years ago, I was asked to review a book by a couple of American social scientists who were writing about "primitive phenomena," in which context they were discussing the guru. Here was the sentence where they lost me: "The Guru is a real or fantasy authoritarian figure whose basic function seems to be to represent a cultural sanction for the wanted or desired activity, and by his presence to help bring it about." I guess that's about as much as the intellect can ever understand about the guru, because that's what the guru looks like from the outside in. And that is precisely the *limitation* of an objective view of the guru, because the relationship with the guru is totally an *internal* matter, and has nothing at all to do with that kind of intellectualized process.

The essence of a relationship with a guru is love: The guru is a being who awakens incredible love in us, and then uses our love to awaken us out of the illusion of duality. The relationship between the guru and the chela was beautifully described by Ramana Maharshi (see if you can catch this image): "It's like an elephant waking up upon seeing a lion in a dream." The elephant is asleep, and *in its dream* a lion appears, which jolts the elephant awake. Ramana Maharshi goes on: "Just as the appearance of the dream-lion is enough to wake the elephant, so also is the glance of Grace from the Master enough to waken the devotee from the sleep of ignorance to the knowledge of the Real."[3] Notice the implications of that: that the guru, as a separate entity, exists only *within the illusion of separateness,* within the dream. The minute the method of the guru has worked, it's awakened you, and it ceases to be anything at all. It has an automatic, built-in self-destruct mechanism. You use it until it opens you in a certain way, and then you see through it and let go of it. The guru becomes irrelevant.

I've mentioned the way my relationship with my own guru became less and less rooted in dualism as time went on. Sometime after I'd first met Maharajji, I was sitting across the courtyard from him, and I thought to myself, "What am I doing here? That body sitting over there isn't what it's all about." At that moment, Maharajji called an old man over, and said something to him, and the man came running over to me and touched my feet. I asked him, "Why did you do that?" He said, "Maharajji told me, 'Go touch Ram Dass's feet. He and I understand each other perfectly.'" Just at the moment when I thought, "That guy in the blanket isn't it," Maharajji responded by saying, "Good! You got it. Go, go, go!"

Now none of that detracts one bit from the incredible love I feel for Maharajji. Once the awakening begins, you can't help but feel profound love for all the beings who have helped you along the way. But my neurotic *need* for love has diminished, and what has replaced it is a kind of conscious, present love, in which every time I love you, I am loving Maharajji, because he is everyone and everywhere.

When I talk about Maharajji, someone will usually ask me, "How will I know if someone is my guru? How do I know when I've met her or him?" Somebody asked Maharajji that question and he said, "Do you feel he can fulfill you in every way spiritually? Do you feel he can free you from all desires and attachments? Do you feel he can lead you to final liberation? When you feel all these things, then perhaps you have found your guru."

I think my own short answer to that question is "If you're not sure, it isn't." When it is, there won't be any doubt. You can never intellectually decide, "Well, this person fits all my rules of guru-hood, therefore she will be my guru." The real guru will always undercut all of your expectations. You may decide, "That shoddy slob! I wouldn't have anything to do with *him!*" Invariably, that turns out to be your guru.

The other question people usually ask is "Does that mean that I have to have a guru in order to get to God?" Well, it's certainly useful to have an external teacher to help you cut through your stuff, but The Guru, that which beckons from beyond, is God/Guru/Self as one. You may find your path through relating directly to God, you may find it through a guru, or you may find it by going deep enough into your Self. Maharajji said, "The guru is not external. It is not necessary for you to meet your guru on the physical plane." If a guru presents her- or himself to you, wonderful. If not, then that isn't your path, and you'll need to work with some other practice.

While it may be given to only a few of you to pursue the path of Guru Kripa, that doesn't mean you won't have gurus along the way. Hindus make a distinction between what are called upagurus and what are called satgurus. A satguru is what we've been talking about here as the guru; it's the one who *is* the doorway. The satguru may take many forms, but there is ultimately only One of it.

Along the way, however, there are the upagurus. They are teachings for us; they are there like marker stones along the road that say, "Go this way, Go that way." I think, in fact, that it is much more productive to look at those beings that way—as teach*ings* rather than as teach*ers*. That way, we can take a teaching here and a teaching there and then go on, instead of getting hung up in deciding, "Is this *really* my teacher?" The whole teacher-trip leads us into making The Big Commitment, and then we sit around judging and comparing and worrying whether we've made the right choice. None of that intellectual analysis is conducive to getting the bhakti juices flowing.

The more our inner wisdom develops, the more we see that we are not being left alone to deal with our situation. We look around and see that we are being guided, protected. Even while we thought we were doing it all ourselves, there were these beings nudging us along. Besides the satgurus and upagurus on the physical plane, there are astral guides, beings on all those other planes as well. We're sitting in the midst of all the many levels of relative reality, with physical beings and astral beings all helping us along in their various ways. We are surrounded by a web of well-wishers, all wanting to help us get free.

Mount Analogue, by René Daumal, is a lovely metaphor about climbing the mountain of consciousness. First, the travelers have to deduce the existence of the mountain, and then they have to figure out how to get there. Finally, they start to climb the mountain, and the narrator says: "By our calculations, thinking of nothing else, by our desires, abandoning every other hope, by our efforts, renouncing all bodily comfort, we gained entry into this new world. Or so it seemed to us. But we learned later that if we were able to approach Mount Analogue, it was because the invisible doors of that invisible country had been opened to us by those who guard them. . . . Those who see us even though we cannot see them opened the door for us, answering our puerile calculations, our unsteady desires, and our awkward efforts, with a generous welcome."

So although an external guru is not necessary, assuming that one happens to have one, what does one do with him or her? That is, what is the practice of Guru Kripa all about? To begin with, I would suggest that the very essence of the relationship between a guru and a devotee is a sense of complete, utter trust. You trust that whatever the guru does will be for your good. I know that may raise some hackles, and bring up images in our minds of Jim Jones and the Kool-Aid, but the truth of the matter is, it's only that quality of absolute, trusting openness that allows us to receive the transmission from another being. It was my *love* for Maharajji, and through that love my total opening to him, that allowed the blessings to come through. It's like the Grace is flowing in a continuous stream, and as each person opens in love . . . ahhhhh, then it comes through. The moment you open to it, it just pours into you.

But once you've opened that way, there's absolutely nowhere to hide. Your life is completely transparent. I remember one time when I went to stay at an ashram, at a "rent-a-cave." You could rent a cave for eighteen rupees a week; you'd pay your eighteen rupees, and the attendants would show you to a cave. They'd close you in and pass food in to you through a little opening. It's a way to do some really intense inner work. It was summer in India, and it was very, very hot in the cave, so I stayed naked the whole time. Usually, you're supposed to wear at least a loincloth when you're meditating, but I was too hot to care; I was all alone, I was very hot, so I was naked. Afterward, when I went back to Maharajji, one of the first things he said to me was "It's good not to wear any clothes." "Oh yeah, Maharajji? Thank you."

I went to Bombay for a while. I was visiting the home of the president of the board of trustees of an ashram, and I was a yogi. The first evening I was there, the man said to me, "The doctor has said that for my heart, I have to take a little Scotch every night." I said, "I understand." Then he said to me, "Perhaps you'd join me?" Now, in India it's not considered good form to drink alcohol—certainly not for yogis and ashram board members.

But this was medicinal, after all, so, being accommodating, I said, "Sure," and we adjourned to his room. I expected him to bring out a little medicine glass of Scotch, but what appeared instead was an ice bucket, a soda dispenser, a bottle of Scotch, and two large tumblers. And I suddenly remembered the days when I used to really *love* Scotch and soda. So he poured a hefty shot for himself, and another for me. He asked, "Would you like some soda water?" He filled the glasses with ice and soda, and he handed me one. Well, I drank my Scotch and soda, and I got completely crocked. I stumbled my way through dinner—I couldn't even find the table without help; his wife was feeding both of us. And that was on just *one* drink. The next evening, we started a little earlier . . . and so it went.

After about three days, I went back north to Vrindaban, to Maharajji's ashram. The evening I got back, he called me up to his tucket. He started talking to me about this yogi who had gone to America, and who was being taken care of there by some very devoted women. Maharajji said, "He's with *women*." I said, "Yes, I know, Maharajji." He said, "What does he call them?" I said, "He calls them his mothers." "Oh? How old are they?" I said, "Well, one is twenty years old." "Mothers!!?" he said. Then he asked, "Do you know what his mothers give him?" I said, "No, what do they give him?" He said, "They give him milk." I said, "That's wonderful, Maharajji. 'Mother's milk'—that's perfect." He said, "Every night they give him milk." I said, "Isn't that nice." Then he leaned up really close, and said in this conspiratorial way, "Do you know what they *put* in the milk?" I said, "No, Maharajji, what do they put in the milk?" He looked me right in the eye and said, "Liquor!" Then he laughed and laughed.

So where am I going to hide? You think now, because he's not in a body, that it makes any difference? Not if he is who I know him to be! When you can't hide, it's all out in the open; and if it's all out in the open, well . . . here we are. I've got to be whatever I am; I can't make believe I'm something else—who am I going to fool?

The way I see it, the minute you know that there's somebody who knows it all, you're free. You're done hiding—what a relief! All your secrets become absurd, because somebody already knows *everything* about you, and that somebody is saying, "Yeah, right. Just look at all that horrible stuff. And here we are." Maharajji knows about all my dirty laundry, and he still loves me.

❊

Those qualities of being known and loved, of trusting and opening, are what the relationship with the guru looks like to me, the devotee. But what does it look like to the guru? If the guru is the "finished product," what might it look like from inside the guru when he or she is sitting with a devotee? I've heard it said, "Though the master and the disciple appear as two people, the master alone enjoys himself under the guise of the two." It's like a flower turned into a nose to smell its own fragrance. That is to say, from the guru's point of view, nothing at all is happening. I used to sit in front of Maharajji, and the best way I can describe it is that I felt like I was Charlie McCarthy. I felt like he had created me out of his mind in order to play with me. You say, "But why would he do that?" Well, you'll have to ask him. I have no idea.

Although to the guru nothing at all is happening, the laws or processes that are manifesting through the guru call forth certain actions from him. Sometimes those actions include the use of what are called siddhis, or powers. Maharajji used a certain kind of siddhi with me when he told me, the first time I met him, how my mother had died a few months earlier—something he had no "rational" way of knowing.

We have to understand that when those powers are used, it's not like the guru is sitting there thinking, "I'll use this power and blow his mind." It's that a being like Maharajji is so totally a statement of the laws of dharma, the laws of the universe, that at an appropriate moment, with a particular person, he will say or do something that causes a certain flip to happen, which leads that person to the next new stage. The guru is just there, doing whatever the dharma of the moment demands.

Most of the time, gurus use siddhis to break a person loose at the point where he or she is ripe for a certain change to happen. Ramakrishna said: "Dislodging a green nut from its shell is almost impossible. But let it dry, and the slightest tap will do it."

If you hang around these beings, you'll notice the way they're tuned in to some kind of readiness in people. Hundreds of people would come to Maharajji, and touch his feet; he would ignore them, and go on talking. They would be given food, and they would leave the temple. Then somebody else would come. That person, by my standards, would be someone who should just be given food and sent away; he didn't fill the bill at all. But Maharajji would stop what he was doing, and turn to the person; he'd carry on a long conversation with him, give him a special blessing and everything. I had to realize how unfathomable it was for my rational mind to comprehend what the guru was doing to whom or why. Somehow, he had sensed in that person a moment of ripeness, a readiness for that little tap.

Sai Baba from Shirdi, who was born in India around the middle of the nineteenth century, was a "siddhi baba"; that is, he was known for having incredible powers. He was the one who would go down to the stream and pull out his stomach and intestines and wash them in the water, then hang them over the trees to dry.

An old couple once came to see him. They were crying because all their money had been stolen and so they wouldn't get to see the holy Ganges River before they died. Sai Baba said to them, "Don't worry about it." He raised his foot, and the Ganges started to pour out of his toes.

Sai Baba would wander around from town to town. He came to one little village, and because he seemed kind of weird, the people shunned him at first and wouldn't have anything to do with him. He ran out of oil for his arti lamp one day, so he couldn't do his rituals. He went from door to door in the village, begging for oil, but no one would give him any. So he gave up on them. He took some water, and blessed it, and poured that into his arti lamp. And it burned. Well, that convinced the villagers that *something* was going on, and they started to honor him and to come to him for his teachings. At that point, they were ready to hear what he had to tell them. You get people shaken up a bit, and they are open to new possibilities. That, roughly, is the way siddhis are generally used.

There's another story about Shirdi Sai Baba that gives us an interesting insight into the question of *when* powers are used. A woman's
young son was bitten by a cobra, and she begged Sai Baba for some
sacred ash to save him; but he wouldn't give it to her, and the child
died. The woman was grief-stricken; she was weeping and wailing,
and one of Sai Baba's devotees begged him, "Please, Baba, for my sake,
revive her son." Sai Baba replied, "Don't get involved in this. What has
happened is for the best. Her son's soul has already entered another
body, in which he can do especially good work—work that he could
not do in this one. If I draw him back into this body, the new one he
has entered will have to die in order for this one to live. I might do it
for your sake, but have you considered the consequences? Have you
any idea of the responsibility, and are you prepared to assume it?"

See, that's an example of the guru's true compassion in the exercise of powers. The devotee was seeing only the death and the
mother's grief. Sai Baba's was the compassion that comes from seeing
a bigger picture than the one defined by our human emotions.

Siddhi stories feed our faith by reminding us that there's more
going on than meets the eye. Swami Nityananda, Swami Muktananda's guru, was a really beautiful yogi, and also quite a colorful
character, like Sai Baba. Thousands of people would come to see him
every day; Nityananda would just sit there, humming to himself, paying no attention to any of them. People somehow learned to interpret
his movements, though, so they would come up to him and say, "Shall
I buy this stock, Baba-ji?" "Hummmmmmmm." They'd say, "Baba says
I should buy it." They'd buy it, and they'd make a killing.

Nityananda used to put up the money to have the roads paved in
the areas around his ashram. The workmen would come, and they'd
dig and grade and spread gravel, and at the end of the day Nityananda
would say to them, "Go home now, and on your way home, pick up
any rock you like, and your pay will be there." Two rupees a day. So
the men would start for home, and they'd pick up any rock along the
way, near or far, whichever one struck their fancy, and there would
be their two rupees, always in crisp, new rupee notes. There wouldn't

be rupees under any *other* rock; you couldn't pick up a second rock and find two more rupees—you'd already been paid.

Well, after a while, the situation came to the attention of the authorities, and they were, to say the least, curious. It's a little delicate to go to a guru and ask him where his money comes from, but finally they felt they had no choice but to look into the matter, and the police—an inspector and his sergeant—went to the ashram to see Nityananda. They said, "Uh, Baba-ji, we've come because we're a little concerned about where all those brand-new rupee notes are coming from." Nityananda said, "Oh, no—I certainly don't want you to be concerned. Come along. I'll show you where they come from." Nityananda took off into the jungle, with the two policemen trailing along behind him. He led them deeper and deeper into the jungle, and finally brought them to a lake, which was infested with crocodiles. Nityananda went wading into the water. The policemen were standing on the bank, looking anxious, saying, "Please be careful, Guru-ji!" Nityananda ignored them. He motioned to one of the crocodiles, and it came paddling over to him. He pried open its jaws, reached in, and started pulling out handfuls of crisp, new rupees. The police went running out of the jungle and never bothered him again. They'd met their match.

Gurus must enjoy playing with our fixations on money, because there's a money story that's told about Maharajji, too. A sadhu came to the ashram and began berating Maharajji, saying that he was too attached to possessions. Maharajji just kept nodding and heard him out. Then he said to the sadhu, "Give me the money you have tied inside your dhoti." The sadhu said, "What do you mean? I don't have any money." Maharajji said, "Give me that money inside your dhoti!" The sadhu reluctantly pulled out some rupee notes, crumpled inside a corner of his dhoti. Maharajji took them, and threw them into the fire. Then the sadhu started to berate Maharajji all over again, this time for destroying the possessions of a sadhu. Maharajji said, "Oh, I'm sorry, I'm sorry! I didn't know you were so attached to the money," and he reached into the fire with a pair of tongs and started drawing out fresh ten-rupee notes. He looked at the sadhu and said, "All the money in the world is mine."

◎

These siddhi stories are so much fun, and they give us the kind of tangible evidence that our minds love that the guru really is who we think he is. But as much fun as they may be, the stories are finally just words, not experiences, and it's in the *practices* of bhakti that the feelings of devotion are cultivated. For the devotee, the essence of yoga is doing whatever bhakti practices it takes to keep the heart and the thoughts focused on the guru. And to do that, we use all our different devotional strategies.

Swami Muktananda's method of relating to his guru, his practice of Guru Kripa, was a form of meditation. He meditated on his guru. In his autobiography, Muktananda described how he would do it: "Meditating on the Guru, install him in all parts of your body, from the toes up to the head. Thus installing the Guru throughout the body, finally begin to meditate, feeling you are yourself the Guru. The Guru is in you, and you are in the Guru. Meditate daily in this manner, without the slightest doubt."[4] As he kept doing that meditation, Muktananda got to the point where he started to fully identify himself with Nityananda, his guru. Muktananda would get so flipped out that most of the time during his sadhana he wasn't even sure which one he was.

A meditation practice like that is a technique for bringing ourselves into identification with the guru. It's a way of turning our consciousness around, of arriving at the place where we are no longer separate from the guru. It's a meditation, but it's a meditation rooted in devotion, and it's the love that drives the entire process.

So you take a being like Nityananda, a being like Maharajji, a being that's formless, a being you can't pin down anywhere, and you start to incorporate him into yourself. It's a lot like the way a child identifies with a parent. You incorporate this other being more and more fully, until there is no difference between you. You can do that with Christ, you can do that with Buddha, you can do that with Muhammad, you can do that with Maharajji, you can do that with whoever opens your heart. Just imagine that being sitting right there in front of you, and then slowly begin to draw him into yourself; draw him bit by bit into each part of your being, until, in a certain way, he has replaced you.

That kind of meditation is a very powerful practice. And yet for me, the practice of Guru Kripa is really nothing at all like that. For me, it's simply a process of hanging out with my guru, moment to moment, and seeing my life reflected through his consciousness. I can't tell you how many times a day I encounter him. I have pictures of him everywhere: in my puja room, on the dashboard of my car, by the refrigerator, above the toilet. I really dig hanging out with this being!

Ram Dass Offering the Arti Light: The ceremony of arti is performed daily in Hindu temples. A puja hymn is sung, and there are offerings of flowers and incense to the deities and holy beings represented on the puja table. The light of a butter-lamp is offered, after which the lamp is passed among the worshippers so they can "take light"—i.e., draw the sanctified light into themselves. Afterward there is generally a distribution of prasad—a sweet or a piece of fruit that has been consecrated during the ceremony.

My love for Maharajji is my way of opening myself. Maharajji is constantly there, constantly reminding me. When I'm talking to someone, she turns into my guru. When I get mad at someone, he turns into my guru. Moment by moment, I'm just hanging out with this incredible being: this being of consciousness, of love, of light, of presence.

My love for Maharajji is a process of surrendering. I'm willing to let go into whatever he thinks is best for me. I surrender to his version of my story line in place of my own. Saint John said, "He that sent me is with me, he hath not left me alone. I do always the things that please him." And gradually that practice of surrender is changing me. It's turning me into him.

I think that what I found in Maharajji was something that satisfied both my intellect and my heart. There was an intense degree of love, an oceanic love feeling that pervaded the space around Maharajji. There was an aura; there was a presence so powerful that you felt bathed and purified just by being anywhere near it. Even now, as I bring him into my heart, it does the same thing. I feel bathed in his presence.

That's the essence of my relationship with Maharajji: to love him, to open myself to his presence, to surrender to him. That's my bhakti practice, a practice of Guru Kripa. But those qualities of love and openness and surrender are the essence of every bhakti practice. We find some being that draws our heart: it could be Maharajji or Anandamayi Ma, Christ or Krishna, Allah or G-d. You pick the name. Then we invite that being in. We install that being in our hearts, and we offer ourselves to it: We sing to it, we chant to it, we pray to it, we bring it flowers. We love and we love, and we open and we open. And then we watch, as slowly, slowly, but surely, surely, we love our way into *becoming* it.

9

Social Aspects of Sadhana

*W*hen we look back at where we've come from, we see that we have been constructing a whole new outlook on our lives, a perspective that transforms our acts into karma yoga, and that leads us to develop practices like meditation and purification and devotion. But as I reflect on all that, I find that it feels as if there's a place where we've left some work undone, an area to which we've given short shrift thus far. It has to do with all the personality stuff, with all the emotional / interpersonal / cultural stuff in our lives. It's what I'm calling, for want of a better word, the "social" aspects of our sadhana. I think it's time now to go back and take a closer look at those parts of our lives, because they, too, will have to be transformed in the course of this journey. Nothing can be left out of this particular stew.

When we talk about "personality" in the way we usually think of it, we're looking at a peculiarly Western invention. Personality has much less pizzazz in a society like India, where everyone relates to every-one else much more in terms of their roles and their souls than in terms of their personal identities. But we in the West are completely in love with personality.

To focus on personality means to focus on individual differences: I'm me because I'm like this and not like that. The sum total of all those differences is what defines us in our own minds: "I'm depressed." "I'm self-confident." "I'm *such* a good mother." "I'm laid back." The process of cultivating those "personalities" for ourselves meant that we grew up preoccupied with individual differences—our own, and everybody else's. Now, if our attention to our individual differences were simply neutral, if we were just noticing them and appreciating all the myriad ways God can manifest, everything would be fine. But instead of that quality of appreciation, our discrimination more often than not has an edge of judging connected with it, and that leads both to a lot of tsk-tsking about other people and a lot of neurotic self-concern about ourselves.

It seems as though many of us—maybe most of us—have come through childhood with some deep sense of inferiority, or impotence, or incompetence, that's built deep into the core of who we see ourselves as being. It's so deep that it has an almost theological quality of original sin associated with it. It's at an emotional, nonconceptual level—just some gut feeling of not being good enough, which came out of our early childhood training. We don't have to get into the dynamics of how it developed, but it certainly seems to be a pretty common thing.

Now, instead of searching for a source of that feeling within ourselves, instead of tracing the roots of it in our personality development, we accept the feeling as a given, and then look around and attach it to some particular characteristic in ourselves. We take one of our individual differences, and blame it for our feeling of inadequacy or wrongness; we find some quality or trait in ourselves that we can blame for the way we're feeling. The trouble is, that leaves us working against what a psychologist would call a negative core-ego concept.

When I was a psychotherapist, I was always amazed by the fact that each person had his or her own "Thing." Each person said that if it weren't for that Thing, their lives would be OK. If I didn't have a nose that was shaped this way. If my breasts were bigger. If my breasts were smaller. If I were having better orgasms. If I had come from a richer family. If my parents hadn't broken up when I was young. If I hadn't fallen and gotten this terrible scar when I was little. If my hair were a different color. If I'd lived in a neighborhood where I'd had more kids to play with. If I'd had a more compassionate father. Everybody's got their Thing. I may not have hit yours, exactly, in that list, but I'll bet I hit at least a good 40 percent of us there—and the other 60 percent of us get the idea.

We get so emotionally preoccupied with the thing that is "wrong" with us that it starts to color all the ways we see the world around us. If you are preoccupied with your nose, then you notice noses. You notice all the successful people and what particularly *nice* noses they have, and so on. Each one of those negative self-descriptions is a way of expressing the feeling that who we are isn't enough; and if we feel that who we are isn't enough, it makes us very vulnerable to any unflattering perceptions of ourselves that come to us from the people around us.

Let me tell you an interesting sequence; this happened back around 1964. Tim Leary and I had been colleagues for several years, but we had come to a point where we were disagreeing about a lot of strategies of one sort and another. We had, in fact, separated for a while, but we still had a lot of involvements in common; I was the treasurer and director of our nonprofit, and we were jointly running Millbrook, our commune in New York. And because Tim had been away traveling a lot, I was at that time the legal guardian of his children.

I came back to Millbrook in 1964, after spending some time in Europe. Timothy was running Millbrook at that point, while I was away; I had run it during the previous year, while he was traveling in India. Although Timothy and I were at great odds with one another, I was very close to his kids. He came in one evening while I was sitting there with them and he said, "Kids, there's something I have to tell you. Uncle Richard [which is who I was to them] is evil." His son said to him, "Oh, come on, Dad! He may be a schnook, but he's not evil." Tim said, "No, no—Uncle Richard is *evil*." Well, I lost my cool at that point (which I was prone to do back in those days), and I said to him, "Well, Timothy, if I'm evil, you are psychotic." Which got to him, just as I knew it would. So then we were *both* totally freaked.

I left Millbrook at that point, and went out to California. But Timothy's statement started to work away inside my head. Those deep feelings of inadequacy inside of me had been awakened full blast. I thought, "Gee, maybe it's true. I've certainly done my share of rotten things in my life. Do you suppose that I *am* evil? Do you suppose there is something just basically corrupt and depraved in me?" I kept turning it over and over in my mind.

That fall, I took an LSD trip with a woman I was living with at the time, and in the middle of the session, I told her the story about Timothy. I said, "So Timothy thinks I'm evil." She looked at me, and in the state we were in at that moment I can't imagine what she saw, but she said to me, "Well, you know, maybe you are."

That was pretty much the end of that relationship; I became impotent with her, and she ran off with another man. But her statement had reinforced what Timothy had awakened in me, and now it really kept gnawing away at me: Do you suppose I really am evil? Two people have said so—I guess maybe I must be.

Then, in the late winter of the following year, I took a very deep acid trip, all by myself. I went in and in and in, going for the place in myself where I felt truly evil. I stood in front of a mirror and I became as evil as I could; I went through every one of my evil thoughts. I was really scaring the hell out of myself—literally!

But I didn't stop there. I kept going in, deeper. I went beyond the place where I saw myself as evil. I went back and back and back . . . and I came to the place in me where I just am. I just *am*. I do a lot of crummy things, and I do a lot of beautiful things, and I'm neither good nor evil, I just am. There is good, and there is evil, and here I am.

I had touched that place before. But I had never before been in a situation where my friends had said that I was evil, so I had never before had the opportunity to work with my "evilness" as intensely as I did then, and so I had never before experienced that place *beyond* good and evil quite so clearly. From then on I was pretty much liberated from the whole issue of the good and evil in myself, so the whole episode turned out to be a very great gift for me.

It was about a year and a half later. Timothy had been busted in Laredo, and I was working with a group of people who had set up a defense fund for him. Tim and I were still very cold toward one another, but we were working together. I was living in New York City then, and Tim was up at Millbrook. At about two o'clock one morning, I got a phone call from someone at Millbrook who said, "Tim has taken a trip and he's been calling for you all night. He wants you to come to Millbrook, so he can talk to you." At that point, I hadn't seen Tim for probably six months or so.

So the next morning, I rented a car and drove up to Millbrook, and I went in to see Timothy. I walked into the room; Timothy was lying on the floor. He got up, and came over and embraced me. Then he said to me, "Richard, I just want you to know one thing." I said, "What's that, Timothy?" He said, "You're not evil." I said, "Well, thank you, I already found that out. But I appreciate what you did for me. Because if you hadn't laid that trip on me, I would never have done all the work that brought me to that understanding."

◎

This may be something of an aside, but since I've opened up the whole psychedelic can of worms, we might as well take the occasion to talk about psychedelics, and about the way they fit into a spiritual journey. Their use goes back further than most of us may think. In the Bhagavad Gita, Krishna says, "I am the Soma." The "Soma" that Krishna is referring to was a plant extract used by the ancient Hindu yogis to achieve mystical experiences. We don't actually know anymore exactly what Soma was; that knowledge was lost centuries and centuries ago. Whatever its chemistry, it was the elixir, the ambrosia of the gods, the drink that transmutes, the drink that "Spirit-izes." In the Rig-Veda, there is a poem honoring Soma, calling it "a drop of crystal with a thousand eyes." The poem goes on to describe what a Soma trip was like; it says.

> *We have drunk Soma*
> *And become immortal;*
> *We have attained the Light,*
> *The Gods discovered.*

Those of us who were involved in research with mushrooms and LSD in the sixties experienced similar effects through those psychedelics. They opened us up spiritually; they were a sacrament, really. Aldous Huxley said they were "a gift of gratuitous grace."

Soma-like substances are mentioned in many Hindu systems. In Patanjali's ashtanga yoga, for example, there are references to the use of chemicals for altering consciousness. Some have speculated that psychedelic mushrooms were at the very root of yogic practices. That's Gordon Wasson's theory, at any rate. Gordon Wasson is a mycologist, but before he was a mycologist he had been a vice president of Morgan Guarantee Trust Company in New York City. Then he got interested in the sacred mushrooms, known in Mexico as Teonanacatl—"the flesh of the gods"; they are the psilocybe mushrooms, which, like a few other varieties, are able to bring about altered states of consciousness. After he started working with *Teonanacatl,* Wasson retired as vice president of Morgan Guarantee Trust Company, and started traveling around the world studying mushrooms and their religious uses. He found that there were "mushroom stones"—stones carved into mushroom shapes—that were connected with very, very ancient religions. His thesis was that the original yogi mystics of India were mushroom eaters from the mountains in the north who'd come down into the Indus Valley; but the sacred mushrooms didn't grow there, and so they then developed all the yogic practices—pranayama and hatha yoga and raja yoga—to try to reproduce the same states of consciousness to which the mushrooms had originally given them access.

Nor was knowledge of such things limited to India. Carl Heinrich, an ethnobotanist in Santa Cruz, California, suggests that the "bread" Jesus offered at the Last Supper was, in fact, a psychedelic mushroom called fly agaric, which looks somewhat like pita bread and was appreciated for its taste as well as its effects. Psychedelic substances were used in the West as well. There no longer seems much doubt that rites among the ancient Greeks included ways of altering consciousness for "better living through chemistry." It seems that an ergot-based potion called kykeon was used in the Eleusinian Mysteries. Some three thou-

Kirtan Dancing:
Dancing was a common
accompaniment to the
evening kirtan sessions.
The energies of a group
chant become very
powerful, so for many
people kirtan became a
highly charged
experience. Very often
the energies expressed
themselves through
beautiful, spontaneous,
ecstatic dance.

sand people at a time would take part in the rituals at Eleusis, and Plato and Aristotle were among the initiates.

And, of course, in the New World there was peyote—the psychedelic cactus. I have taken part in the peyote ceremony, a beautiful ritual that comes out of the Native American tradition. The value of ceremonies like that is that the psychedelic experience is totally ritualized; there are social forms to it. So if you start to get uptight and have a bad trip, for example, there are ways for the group to help you work with that. We spent many hours one night, all of us together, working with one person who was stuck, because the sun couldn't come up until that person was clear. It was four in the morning; it had been a long, cold night, and everyone yearned for the sun to rise, but it couldn't happen until that person broke through. It became the task of everyone in the group to help make that happen, and the intensity of the love and attention that were directed toward that person was incredible. It's a powerful ceremony.

Not long after I first met Maharajji, he asked me one day about what he called my "yogi medicine"—LSD. So I rummaged around in my bag, and I pulled out the box of pills I was carrying, and I showed him the three LSD capsules I had with me—about nine hundred micrograms, a very respectable dose. He took the pills from me, and I saw him seem to toss them into his mouth; and then afterward, all afternoon long, he just continued talking and doing what he always did, and nothing seemed to happen.

Later on I came back to America, and I wrote about that experience, and talked about it in my lectures. But inside of me was this gnawing little doubt: Do you suppose that, through sleight of hand or hypnotic suggestion or whatever, he hadn't really taken the pills at all—that he'd actually just tossed them over his shoulder or something? (See? There it was: My thinking mind, busy at work!)

When I went back to India the next time, Maharajji called me up to his tucket one day and he said to me, "Did you give me some medicine the last time you were in India?" I said, "Yes, Maharajji." He asked, "Did I take it?" I said, "Well, I think so." He asked, "What happened?" I said, "Nothing." Then he said, "Jao, jao!"—go away.

The next morning, Maharajji called me up to his tucket again and he said, "Got any more of that medicine?" I said, "Yeah, I do." He said, "Bring it, bring it." So I brought the LSD that I was carrying in my bag. This time I had *five* pills, one of which was broken; he took the four that weren't broken, which was a *very* high dose, some twelve hundred micrograms of pure LSD. He took the tablets, and he very elaborately placed each one on his tongue, doing the whole thing almost in pantomime, so there could be no doubt at all in my mind that he had taken them.

When he had swallowed all four of them, he asked, "Pani?" (Can I take water?) I said, "Yeah, sure." He called, "Pani, pani"—bring me some water—and he drank a little. Then he asked, "Will it make me crazy?" I said to him, "Probably. Whatever you want, you can do." (You've got to remember whom you are talking to, you know.) He asked, "How long will it take?" and I said, "About an hour." So he called an old man over, and the man had this *huge* pocket watch, like an old railroad watch, on a chain. Maharajji had the man sit down next to him on the tucket; he was hanging on to the man and staring at the watch—it was a whole Marx Brothers routine! At one point, after half an hour or so, Maharajji ducked down under his blanket for a few minutes, and came up looking absolutely deranged, with his tongue lolling out and his eyes crossed. I thought, "Oh, my God! What have I done? He really *hadn't* taken the LSD the first time, and because he's a good mind reader he knew that I knew that. So he figured he'd better really *do* it this time—but he didn't know what he was letting himself in for, and now he's gone crazy. This nice old man—I'm going to have all this on my head!" At that point, Maharajji looked over at me, and he started to laugh. He laughed and laughed at the way he'd put me on. Then he went back to doing the things he always did, talking to people and tossing fruit at them.

At the end of the hour, Maharajji pointed to the man's watch and said to me, "Well, what do you think?" I said, "I guess it's not going to work." He asked, "Don't you have anything stronger?" I said, "No, Maharajji, I don't." He just shrugged. "Most yogis would be afraid to take that medicine," he said. "Those things were known about long ago, in the Kulu Valley, but all of that has been lost now. They don't know anything about this anymore."

Later on, I asked him, "Maharajji, is it all right to use these chemicals?" He said, "If you were to take it in a cool place, and your mind was feeling much peace, and if you were alone and turned toward God, it could be useful. It would allow you to come into the room and pranam to Christ." (Meaning, you could come into the presence of Spirit.) "But you can only stay two hours," he said, "and then you have to leave again. It would be better to become Christ than just to pranam to him, but your medicine won't do that for you. It's not the ultimate samadhi."

However, that doesn't mean it isn't useful. Maharajji said, "That kind of experience can be very helpful. To visit a holy man even for a few hours will strengthen your faith. But, he added, "love is a much more powerful medicine than LSD."

(I once told one of Maharajji's Indian devotees the story about giving Maharajji the acid and he said to me, "That's nothing." He told me that a couple of years before, a sadhu had come to see Maharajji. In India, some sadhus take arsenic for devotional purposes. They take tiny, tiny amounts of it, and in those doses it's not lethal, but instead it acts like a psychedelic; it gets you high. This sadhu was carrying something like a two-year supply of arsenic, which would be a lethal dose for maybe ten people. Maharajji said to the sadhu, "Where's your arsenic?" The sadhu said, "Oh, Maharajji, I don't have any arsenic." Maharajji said, "Give me your arsenic!" The sadhu fished around in his dhoti and handed over the packet. Maharajji opened it up and swallowed the whole thing. Everyone started to cry and wail . . . and nothing happened.)

The first time I took LSD again after I came back from that second trip to India was at a motel in Salinas, Kansas. It was a cool place, I was feeling much peace, I was alone, and my mind was turned toward God. The conditions felt right.

I started the session with a total Grade-B melodrama—that is, I panicked. A "bad trip," it's called. I was just about to run naked out of the motel room and into the manager's office and say, "You've got to help me—I'm dying!!" As I reached for the doorknob, I had a flash of what was about to occur. I saw myself running into the office, and I saw the manager sitting there, and I saw what I'd look like in his mind: Here's this middle-aged, balding, naked man running out of Room 125 wailing, "I'm going to die." Then I saw the police, and the psychiatrists, and the tranquilizers, and all that would follow. And I thought, "There's got to be a better way than that."

So I turned away from the door. I sat down on the bed and I thought, "Is there any way I can *avoid* dying?" And I realized that the answer was no—that there *wasn't* any way at all. Some of the ways I thought about might take forty years or so, but still I would die. I really realized, deeply experienced, that it was absolutely inevitable: that as long as I thought I was anybody—*anybody*—I was going to die.

So I gave up. I said to Maharajji, "Since it has to happen, please let it happen now. I'm ready—I want to die." I lay down in front of the television set. I'd taped a picture of Maharajji right in the middle of the screen, so it looked like all the images were coming out of his head. I lay there, and I waited to die.

In the session that followed, I had the darshan of Maharajji. He manifested in the exact way that is written about in the eleventh chapter of the Bhagavad Gita, and the room filled with the entire universe. Maharajji kept emerging into all these other beings, and absorbing everything back into himself. He was sitting there on the bed in the motel, laughing and laughing, and the universe was pouring into him and out of him.

Following that, there was a blank space—a moment of no-thought.

The first thought that occurred, after that interstice between mind-moments, was, "Wow!—you can be anything you want to be this time around!" And with that thought, I started to reincarnate again. That is, my karma made the state of no-thought only momentary, before the "I" reasserted itself. I'd had the darshan of Christ, but I hadn't become Christ.

True. *But* . . . when I came back, I was freer than I'd been before.

Psychedelics have been a dominant theme in our cultural landscape for quite a long time now. I think they warrant our considered reflection, because for so many of us, they were a pivotal element in our journey. They certainly played a major role in my own awakening process, and I want to give them their spiritual due.

◎

Well, going back to that story about Tim and me, you can see that I was beginning to take a different stance toward the way I related to my own feelings. I started out with Tim's negative projections toward me, and with all the feelings in myself that those projections aroused. Then slowly, slowly, I let all that become my teaching, and that transformed all the personality games. At that point, instead of being something that brought me down, my personality stuff became the very vehicle for my getting free.

That's the flip. That's the way we turn our emotional games around on themselves. There are techniques like that that we can use to work with *any* of the stuff that catches us—with anger, with depression, with boredom, with loneliness, with whatever emotional state arises. Instead of trying to push it away, or getting angry with God about it, we invite it in, we appreciate the teaching it brings. We turn the situation around, so it frees us.

Take another example—anger. When somebody makes me mad, I am really fierce! But as I am doing my "fierce thing," as the adrenaline is starting to pump, and I'm getting into my *roaaaarrrrr!*—suddenly, the cosmic humor of the situation starts to sneak in. I hear Maharajji saying, "Got you again!" Because we only get angry when someone disconfirms our expectations, when they upset our models of the way we *think* things ought to be. And since our strategy in this game is to ferret out exactly those places in ourselves where we are *clinging* to models of this or that, what more could we ask than for people to come along and wake us up yet again? If they can get us furious—isn't that nice of them? Isn't that a compassionate act? It's not necessarily a *consciously* compassionate act on their part, but from our point of view it's a compassionate act nonetheless. "You really got me bugged. Thank you."

Now, the question is, how long does it take me, in that sequence of little mind-moments, to go from the "Grrrrrr!" (which is at the level of individual differences) to the "Ah—there I am in an incarnation going 'Grrrrr!'" (which is at the level of the witness)? Our practices are about shortening that sequence. We're learning to wake up as quickly as we can, before we've created too much extra karma for ourselves through our reactivity.

(One little humorous aside on this subject of anger: A New York City friend of mine wrote to me and said, "Downtown on the East Side, I saw an angry woman leaning out of the window of her car, shaking her fist at a truck driver who had cut her off. She was sputtering with rage, trying to find words adequate to her fury. Finally she shouted, 'You . . . you . . . you . . . *weird* expression of God, you!'")

So we can use unworthiness as a practice, and we can use anger as
a practice. How about loneliness? There's one that's familiar to a lot
of us. If we wanted to look at it from a strictly clinical point of view,
we could say that we feel something we call *loneliness,* when we get
into certain psychodynamic psychological spaces where we don't have
contact with others. Describing it that way already strips it of a certain amount of its juice, doesn't it? Just seeing it in those totally
detached terms loosens its grip on us.

Loneliness is part of the personality's melodrama. Say you're alone
in your room; everybody's left you, and nobody cares; you feel
unloved and full of self-pity. From a spiritual point of view, what do
you do with all that? If you have some centering practice, like meditation, it will give you some purchase on the situation; and then, as
you quiet down, you'll begin to hear the little voice of cosmic humor
inside yourself that says, "Wow—just *look* at that self-pity. You can cut
it with a knife." That is, once you look for it, you see that right there,
along with the loneliness, there is a connoisseur in you, appreciating
the essence of the loneliness, savoring the intense quality of the suffering. It's right there, all the time, that other part of yourself.

If we start to work from that kind of perspective, our notion of
loneliness begins to shift. We discover, for example, that there is a difference between being alone and being lonely. On a spiritual journey,
there are points when we will enter into experiences of the most
intense aloneness—because it turns out, in fact, that we *are* all alone.
Sometimes, very early in our spiritual practices, there begins to be a
flickering recognition of that "all aloneness." If, when we have those
experiences, we perceive them through our old patterns of thinking,
they arouse old emotional patterns in us, and that often creates a kind
of reflexive pulling back—because "all alone" is very scary to who we
think we are. If we have a practice that lets us put a little space around
the fear, one that lets us relax a little and examine it, we discover that
it's a different kind of aloneness altogether, one in which "loneliness"
plays no part. We aren't lonely—not because there are others there,
but because there is no one at all, *including us.*

Ⓖ

Many of us who are reading this book are in a peculiar predicament. We have built a whole ego structure about who we are and how we function in the world that's based on the emotion-laden models about individual differences that we've been taught to think define us. But now we're experiencing realms of the universe and perceptions of ourselves and others that are totally inconsistent with those old ways of thinking. How do we bring the two together? How do we understand what's going on? How do we respond?

Let's play a little game. Let's imagine that our whole perceptual field, everything that we might be experiencing from moment to moment, is like a television set, where we can change our reality by flipping from one channel to another. If we look at another person when we're tuned to channel 1, we see them the way we've habitually seen them, which means we're seeing them first and foremost in terms of the way they fit into our own desire systems. So, as I've said before, if you're horny, you see who's makeable, who's a competitor for who's makeable, and who's irrelevant. That's your way of dividing up the universe. If you're an achiever, a power-oriented person localized in your third chakra, you see everybody in domains of power and control. You see who's beatable and who's going to beat you out; you see who's where in the power hierarchy. If you are a gymnast, you look at people in terms of their body development. If your preoccupation is with the color of your skin, that's what you're aware of. All of that is on the first channel.

Now give the channel selector one little flip. We look a little deeper into other people, and what we begin to see now are their personalities: that's a cheerful person, that person is very surly, that one seems depressed. Those of us who are preoccupied with the planes where our personalities exist are inclined to see other people that way as well: "That person was kind to me—she's a nice person, sort of motherly." Those are psychological variables, and when we're focused on them in ourselves, we're also looking for the psychological dimensions in other people.

If we flip channels once more, we come into the astral planes. That's where our perceptions of ourselves and one another have to do with our mythic story lines—with things like our astrological types, for instance. Then there are only twelve basic permutations in the world, and we see everybody as a Leo, or an Aries, or a Libra. When we look at another person, that's who we see. We say, "Well, I can tell I'm seeing a Sagittarius here." The person may say, "I'm not a Sagittarius—I'm Fred!" We say, "Well, that's what *you* think, but really you're a Sagittarius." That's reality on that plane.

As we start to experience the whole show from channel 3 and up, and to discover that behind the physical plane there are all these other planes on which we *also* have identities, it's easy to get seduced by all the new possibilities. They all have more shakti connected with them than this plane does, so when we get into one of them it seems even more real than *this* one did, and we get sucked right back in. The minute we start to acknowledge our identities on other channels, there's the immediate tendency to start casting the new identities in starring roles as part of our romantic image of ourselves. We finish with our physical-plane identity; we say, "Well, I know I'm not Joe anymore." But then we immediately follow that with "Who I *really* am is the Messiah." A lot of us, through various means, have moved into other planes, flipped TV channels, and then gotten very much enamored of our new identities. We've traded in one costume for another. The new ones may be more fun, but we're still just as much caught in individual differences as we were before. The game isn't to create exciting new roles to inhabit, but to keep letting go, letting go, letting go.

Channel 1—physical identity; channel 2—emotional identity; channel 3—astral identity.

If we give the channel selector one *more* flip, we come to what we could call the soul level. And now what we're seeing when we look at another person is another soul looking back at us. We look in another's eyes and we see another being, just like us. "Are you in there? I'm in here! Far out." We can still see the packaging—the packaging that includes the body, the personality, the astrological sign, all the individual differences. There is still somebody separate from "me" in there, but the individual differences now are more like veils, like packaging for the real product. Here we are: We are two beings; we have our individual characteristics, and we are also just alike.

So you take a relationship—say, to your parent, or to your child; someone you have a long history of treating solely as her or his role: "That's my mother." "That's my father." "That's my son." "That's my daughter." "That's little Mary Jane—hello, little Mary Jane." Now flip the channel. You look at Mary Jane, and suddenly there is another being inside Mary Jane who isn't Mary Jane at all. It's not *not* Mary Jane—it's not like it's Sarah Lou or something. It's the soul, another part of her being, saying, "I'm in here, and I'm just like you."

What we've described are four channels—four different "takes" on reality. For efficiency's sake, so we can sleepwalk through our lives, we generally confine our perceptions to channel 1, or maybe channels 1 and 2. Furthermore, we make the assumption that our individual differences, whatever they might be, are a constant, and that we can therefore treat everybody as being exactly the same today as they were yesterday. If you were Mary Jane yesterday, I'm going to assume that you'll probably be Mary Jane today, which means I'm going to deal with you on the basis of past history. If I have pigeonholed you as someone who is a slob, I might as well continue to treat you as a slob, because it's most likely that if you were a slob yesterday, you will be a slob today. That's known as "efficiency of social relationships."

But what if, when I meet another person, instead of being preoccupied with our individual differences or with who I remember her as being last time, I go beyond all that, I see the soul, I see that other being who is just like me? Then every moment is a fresh moment. And then it's a whole new ball game every time we meet. Now it gets interesting: Who are you this time?

Once we discover we can look at the world on channels 3 and 4, we start consciously trying to spend more time hanging out on those planes with other people. We don't demand that the other person be there—that's up to them. It's a perspective we begin to cultivate *within* ourselves. We see the other person as a fellow soul; we don't have to *say* anything to him, it's just who we are. But in the process of seeing ourselves and the other person from that perspective, we create a space in which the other person is free to join us, should they wish. We become the environment in which optimum growth is available to all the beings with whom we come in contact. And from that perspective comes the recognition that in every relationship, it's all possible, all the time.

Take, for example, my relationship with my father. My father was always busy thinking he was my father. He knew who he was, right? He had all his identities solidly in line. He was a Republican, he was somebody who loved his family, he was somebody who owned this and that; and when he and I were together, he was first and foremost my father. That meant I had to be the son. But from where I was seeing it, he was just another being, one who happened, in this particular round, to have taken on an incarnation that made him my father and made me his son. It was our karma that we would be in that relationship; we were each other's karmic predicaments, if you will. But behind it all was "You here? I'm here! Far out."

That's what it was from where I was sitting. Now, were I to say to him, "You here?" he'd have said, "Oh, you're talking that nut talk again." And it wasn't my job to try to foist off my views on him. Chapter 3 of the Gita says, "Let not the wise disturb the mind of the unwise in their work. Let him working with devotion show them the joy of good work, and those who are under the delusion of the forces of nature bind themselves to the work of these forces. Let not the man who sees this, disturb the one who sees it not."

So my job wasn't to say to my father, "Look, you're not really my father"; he had the birth certificate, and that was his reality. My role was to add an additional dimension to our relationship *within my own perception*. I saw him as my father, and I *also* saw him as another soul like myself—but a soul who was in an incarnation in which he was totally identified with the thoughts connected to that incarnation. He was so deeply identified with those thoughts that they were completely real from where he was sitting. That's OK. I didn't have to tell him how I was seeing it. We'd sit down together and talk father-and-son talk, and all the time I'd be doing my mantra. I'd be talking father-and-son talk, but I'd also be sitting in that place inside myself where we were just two souls, doing this dance together.

Of course, the plane that I added was merely one more plane. It was no better or no worse than the plane my father was on, but at least it did present an alternative. My mind was creating a space in which, if he chose, he was free to give up the limiting conditions of his role, which were making him think that that was all there was to him.

And what would sometimes happen between us in that space was very far out. We would talk father-and-son talk for a while, and then we'd run out of that, and we'd just sit quietly together. If you're caught in your roles, you freak when the role material runs out, when you've exhausted the script lines. But Dad and I got so we'd just sit together in silence, and pretty soon it was as if we were at some meditation retreat together. We'd left the words behind. We were just there, together.

When operating from channel 3 and up we automatically start to change the way we deal with one another. There starts to be a certain evenhandedness in the way we treat other people. Whatever our relationship is with someone, the same general rules will apply. It doesn't matter if it's our parents or our child, our enemy or our friend; we start treating them all the same way. Everybody becomes "Uncle Henry." We treat everyone with appreciation for the fact that we are all beings who are in incarnations, and that we are all God at play as the many. The Gita says, "The man whose love is the same for his enemies or his friends, whose soul is the same in honor or disgrace, who is balanced in blame and praise, whose home is not in this world, and who has love, this man is dear to me."

Kirtan in the Park: Afternoons in the Main Hall were often very warm, so Krishna Das moved the kirtan class to a nearby park and conducted the chanting circles there.

When we're seeing other people on channels 3 and 4, we aren't nearly as likely to be judging them all the time. We see the perfection of their being exactly who they are, and we stop laying so many trips on everybody. We're not always sitting around saying, "You should be this way," or "You should be that way." "If you were a good father, you would . . ." "My child is going to be a . . ." "I'm hoping my therapy patients will . . ." "A good employee would never . . ." Can you hear all the judgments, all the expectations? "I think my husband should . . ." "I expect a wife to . . ." What could be more corrosive in a relationship than that?

If we go out into the woods and we look at all the trees, we don't say, "I wish that oak tree were an elm." Somehow, we can allow trees to be what they are; we can grant that each tree is perfect just the way it is. But when it comes to people, if everybody isn't the way we think they ought to be, all hell breaks loose! We sit around judging and judging, having opinions about everybody.

See, the predicament with all our judging is this: Everybody is always doing the best they can. Maharajji kept saying to me, "Ram Dass, don't you see it's all perfect?" Everyone is perfect, *exactly as they are.* There are all these gunas, these strands of the universe, weaving back and forth, interacting with one other. And in each individual manifestation, those strands have woven themselves together in a unique way so as to produce yet another perfect statement of the unstatable. So someone comes to you, and she's hung up, uptight, and angry. You see the perfection in that. You say, "Far out! There's God as an angry person. You weird manifestation of God, you." You give each incarnation the space to manifest exactly as it needs to manifest.

When we're just beginning to remember that we have identities on those other planes, it's helpful to be around other people who are engaged in the same game we are. It's fun to play with other beings who are working on themselves, who are getting conscious, like us. We call those people members of our satsang, or our sangha, or our fellowship, and they're so important in the journey that Buddhism makes them one of the three "jewels": "I take refuge in the Buddha, I take refuge in the dharma, I take refuge in the sangha."

Satsang is important because it keeps us from getting so lost on channels 1 and 2. When you're with satsang, you may go "Grrrrrrrr!" and the other person may go "Grrrrrrrr!" but at the same moment you're both thinking, "Far out! Look at *this* one!" That's why it's so juicy to hang out with satsang. There is an assumption that everybody is on the trip together, and that we are all really here to help each other wake up. We may still get caught in *incredible* melodramas, but at the same time we know that behind them there lies the cosmic joke.

It turns out that we can have, that we are beginning to have, a satsang, a community of the spirit, that isn't based in space and time. We are so habituated to thinking of our relationships with other people in terms of time-and-space dimensions that we keep running through our old dramas, even though we've used them up. Say somebody leaves; that person is going away, and we run through a whole melodrama: "Good-bye! I'll miss you!! It's horrible that you're leaving!!!" And we're really deeply caught up in *feeling* all of that. Yet a few minutes later, we are fully involved in whatever it is we are doing right then, with no more thought of the melodrama; and when we see the person again, it seems like only a moment has passed.

One night I phoned a fellow in Texas. I had last seen him maybe twelve years before, I'd visited then, with him and his wife. I called him, and we started to talk on the phone, and within two minutes— we were right *here*. Those twelve years were like—swoosh! They were gone. But the fellow kept saying to me, "It would certainly be wonderful to hang out with you again." I thought, *"Would* be? What do you think we're doing right now? Here we are!" Do you think if our bodies—these big, grotesque, decaying bodies—were to get together and hug, that it would somehow be more "real" than it is right now? (Or what about the telephone in that situation: Was *it* really necessary? They were here, and I was here, so . . .)

I tell people, "There is nobody I could ever miss again." That's because nobody could ever get away from me again—nor I from them. See, I don't live exclusively on the physical space-time plane anymore, and when you break out of that identification with channels 1 and 2, you realize that our comings and goings never really *were* what it was all about. When you're experiencing the world as channel 3 and up, you can never be lonely again. You couldn't possibly be lonely—where could you *go* to be alone? How can I get away from Maharajji? I've already told you what *his* trip is all about—do you think that if I go in the bathroom and lock the door, I can be lonely? How silly.

It's always just one thought away. The living spirit, the community of our consciousness, the guru within—whatever you want to call it, is always just one thought away. One *thought!* If you're busy being lonely, all you've got to do is to sit down and meditate. One thought away—no loneliness! The moment you give up the thought of yourself as *separate*—which is the one that's lonely—here we are again. And in the "here we are again" there are other beings just like me— and there is also only one of us. Because it turns out that channel 4— that "You're here? I'm here!"—isn't the ultimate channel, either. It turns out that if you want to go even further still, mystically speaking, and you give the dial another flip, you'll discover that when you are looking at a "somebody else," you are really looking at nothing but yourself. All form, all separateness, is just passing show. All emotion, all relationship, is just illusion. Bodies, personalities, astrological signs, souls—it's all just yourself dancing with yourself, by making believe that you are separate.

10

Dying

The subject of death is a topic it seems most of us would generally rather avoid. The Gita tells us, "As the dweller in the body experiences in the body childhood, youth, and old age, so passes he on to another body. . . . Certain is death for the born and certain is birth for the dead. Over the inevitable, you should not grieve." That's the basic position the Gita puts forward, but people have been reading the Gita for years, and at the same time grieving over death and remaining incredibly afraid of it. Most of us try hard to keep any thoughts about death at arm's length—especially thoughts about our own death, because if there is anything that is a panic trip for most human beings, for most entities, it is the thought of losing their entity-ness as they know it to be. Our deepest root fears and anxieties concern our survival, and while we may be willing to talk about death in a sort of abstract, academic way, we're not overly eager to bring it up close and personal. We don't want to let it in at a level where we're really feeling it.

So in order to personalize the issue, to bring it home and relate it to our real feelings, what I'd like to do in this chapter is to share with you a series of experiences—experiences that led me to a change in my own perceptions about death. They are the experiences that have taken me from what I believed back in, say, 1960, to what I believe now. I'll just share these stories with you, because it is the sum of those experiences that changed my perspective.

Back in my psychologist days, I was very much attached to seeing the personality and the body as "real." And because as far as I was concerned they were not only real but the *only* reality back then, I believed that when you died, you were dead—that was that. And since there was nothing to be done about it, you might as well ignore death and enjoy life while you had it. The game of life, as I saw it then, was to be optimally happy at every moment; death clearly didn't seem to have much to do with happiness, so the topic was best avoided or denied. (The psychologist back then wouldn't have said "denied," of course; I would have said, "realistically coped with.")

Then I started taking psychedelics. They turned out to be my first real teachers about dying. In the course of my explorations with psychedelics, I had a number of experiences in which I ceased to be as I ordinarily knew myself to be, and then, after a time, reentered my ordinary awareness. That is, in a certain psychological sense I had died and been reborn, and those experiences changed my relationship with death in a very profound way.

One of those death-rebirth experiences was the motel trip that I've already told you about. Another happened during my initial experience with psilocybin. I'd taken the mushrooms at Timothy's house, as I mentioned before. At one stage in the trip, I was sitting alone in the semidarkness of the living room, when I saw across the room from me, some eight feet away, a being who, I was surprised to realize, was in fact *myself*. That "me" was standing over there, and he was dressed up in a mortarboard and an academic gown; I thought, "Oh, wow— there's Richard-Alpert-as-Professor." And from there, one by one, the being took on each of my social roles: a professor, a pilot, a cellist, a lover, an achiever—role after role. I saw it like a series of costume changes: Richard wearing a pilot's helmet and goggles, Richard in a tuxedo playing the cello. And each role I let go of, let go of, let go of. Finally, what I saw, over across the room, was whoever Richard was way back when I was a child, when my parents first started labeling this entity: He's a good boy, or he's a bad boy, or whoever Richard was. It was now "essence Richard-ness" standing over there. I got a little anxious when I saw *that* one; I thought, "Will I have amnesia if I give this one up?" But I reassured myself; I thought, "Well, it'll be okay, because I'll still have my body."

That, however, turned out to be a premature conclusion, because as I looked down at the couch where I was sitting, I saw the entire couch—the whole thing, from one end to the other—and there was nobody sitting on it.

Now, there was nothing in my psychological training that had prepared me for that moment. I was about to freak and yell for Tim—to "bad trip it," you might say—when I suddenly thought, with my Jewish-humor-mind, "But who's minding the store?" That is, "Who is it who's about to scream?" If everything I thought I was, including my body, *wasn't,* then who was left to scream? Who was *that* being? Suddenly, all the anxiety was gone; it just drained out of me. I felt I had met a new being in myself, one that wasn't connected with who I'd always thought myself to be.

With that, the "who I'd always thought I was" started to lose its power to scare me quite so much. When Harvard kicked me out and I lost my professorship, it wasn't like I was losing my self-ness; I was just losing my professorship-ness. When I lost my hair, it wasn't like "I'm losing my hair!" It was like "Look at it go!" My identity started to be less and less connected with my body, or my personality, or my social roles.

It turns out that the process of dying is all about letting go. So I treated my psychedelic experiences like little inoculations, opportunities to practice letting go: letting go, letting go, letting go, one by one—and then the Big One. The psilocybe mushrooms and the other psychedelics I used gave me the chance to work with that letting go process—letting go of my personality, of my ego, of everything I thought I was. And through those death-rebirth experiences, my understanding of dying changed.

If you would like to see the way doctoral dissertations confirm that which we already know, a dissertation done at the University of California in Berkeley demonstrated that people who had taken psychedelics, and people who had meditated for more than three years, were significantly less anxious about dying than anybody else in the whole population. Anyone who's done either of those practices could have told them that!

One researcher, Eric Kast, did some pioneering studies at Chicago Medical School using LSD with terminal cancer patients. One of the patients, a nurse, said, "Yes, I know that I am dying of cancer, but look at the beauty of the universe!" At that moment, she had extricated herself from identification with that which was dying, and had identified instead with the universe, in which her death was just one small part.

At around the same time that I took that first mushroom trip, Tim and I began working with Aldous Huxley, who was then a visiting professor at MIT. Aldous introduced us to *The Tibetan Book of the Dead. The Tibetan Book of the Dead* is quite extraordinary. It's an ancient text which is read to Tibetan lamas at the time of their death and for forty-nine days thereafter, to guide them through the experience of dying and what follows. It's like having someone at your elbow as you're dying, whispering, "Right here, stay right here. Stay with each moment, be with your dying. Let go . . . it's OK. Let go . . . it's all right." What a support system! If the process of our death permits it, it would probably be a good idea to arrange to have such a person around.

The Tibetan Book of the Dead is concerned with the bardos, or "islands," which are the states of consciousness or planes of reality that one passes through after leaving this physical plane. It's not that those bardos just suddenly *appear* at the time of death. They are planes of reality, and they're around all the time. They exist right here, right now; all of the bardos that are mentioned in the *Book of the Dead* are right here, could we but see them. As long as we're alive, however, the ego screens us from those planes—that's one of its mechanisms for keeping us focused on everyday states of reality. But once we've died, our egos aren't around doing that anymore, so we suddenly become aware of those other planes. Were we open to them, we'd be experiencing all the bardo states right now.

What was extraordinary for me, in reading *The Tibetan Book of the Dead,* was that I kept coming across descriptions of bardo states and thinking, "My God—that's what happened to me last Thursday night, when I took that psilocybin!" It was pretty weird to have a twenty-five-hundred-year-old book describing the things that we were experiencing on psychedelics, which we were calling "indescribable" or "ineffable." Here it was, and it had all been written out and choreographed twenty-five centuries ago.

Tim and Ralph Metzner and I subsequently did a "translation" of *The Tibetan Book of the Dead* into the language of a psychedelic trip, and published it as a book called *The Psychedelic Experience.* We treated the *Book of the Dead* as a guide for dying and being reborn through the use of psychedelics; we wanted to begin to make manuals available for using psychedelics in a sacred way.

At about the same time as I was going through all those changes via my early experiences with psychedelics, my mother was dying. She had had a blood condition, which had led to an enlargement of her spleen, and when the doctors finally had to remove the spleen, she died. Going through all that with her became another rich teaching about death.

I saw in the course of my mother's dying the way we try to cover up the decay of the body, the way we try to mask it. It's part of our way of hiding from what's happening. I remember visiting my mother when she was very close to death; she had an infection in her gums, so her bridge didn't fit anymore, and the nurses had removed it. In all the years I had known my mother, I had never been allowed to see her without her teeth. Now there she was, at the point of dying, and with the little bit of energy she still had left, she was holding a fan up in front of her mouth, lest her son should see her without her teeth. Little vignettes like that show us how hard we try to push away any acknowledgment that the body is decaying.

I saw the denial that exists around death. As my mother got closer to dying, I began to spend a lot of time with her at the hospital. I would come to the hospital stoned on this or that, and she, being kept from her pain with various medicines, would also be stoned on this or that (although she would never have called it that; the doctors were "treating her"—that was the way she would have put it). Mother and I would sit quietly together, and we would share moments of incredible presence, just meditating, being silent together, holding hands. As we sat there together, other people would come into the room— nurses, doctors, my father, my aunts and uncles. They would all be involved in hysterical denial of what was happening. They would say, "Gert, you're looking *much* better." Then they would walk out into the hall and say, "She won't last a week." It was horrible—nobody could be truthful with her, because they were all so afraid of acknowledging death.

Denial permeates the whole system, and all the relationships in it. A young nurse once told about her experience with a patient who was dying of rheumatic heart disease. She talked about how guilty she would feel as she entered his room each day, knowing she was going to live, while he, a man of her own age, was about to die. She said, "I knew he wanted to talk to me, but I always turned it into something light—a little joke, or some evasive reassurance which had to fail. The patient knew, and I knew—but as he saw my desperate attempts to escape, and felt my anxiety, he took pity on me and kept to himself what he wanted to share with another human being. And so he died and didn't bother me."

Another nurse wrote in her diary about the usual responses to a patient's direct question, "Am I going to die?" This was her list.

Moralizing: "You shouldn't talk that way, Mr. Jones. No one knows when he is going to die."

Stating facts: "Your pulse is strong and steady, and your color is good. I don't think you are going to die today, Mr. Jones."

Direct denial: "I don't think you will die today, or even tomorrow."

Referring the patient to another person: "I am unable to tell you that. You should ask the doctor; he's better able to tell you."

Philosophizing: "No one really knows what the future holds."

Changing the subject: "Who is that in the picture on your nightstand?"

Kidding the patient: "Oh, come on now, Mr. Jones. You're probably going to outlive me!"

And finally, there is simply avoiding the question altogether, and turning away.

At one point, when my mother and I were alone in the room, she said to me, "Rich, I know that I'm going to die. But nobody will talk to me about it." So I said, "Yeah, I think you're right. I think you are going to be leaving your body soon." She said, "What do you think is going to happen then?" I said, "Well, I don't really know. But I've noticed that as your body has been slowly decaying through this illness, it hasn't changed anything very important. You are still who I know you to be, and I am still who you know me to be, and here we are. Yet all this decay is going on." Then I said, "And from what I have read and from what I have experienced, I have a suspicion that when you drop your body, it's all going to continue in pretty much the same way. There may be some confusion at first, but when that sorts itself out . . . there we'll be."

We had moments like that, moments when my mother and I found a place where we could be very peaceful together. But the minute she came down off the morphine or whatever it was they were giving her, she would go right back into her Jewish middle-class mode. Instead of acknowledging that she was dying, she would be "all better, getting healthier." She would get busy controlling her scene: "Move this, do that." In fact, the very last time I saw her alive, I was up in her room and we were having a beautiful visit together. But just then, the plumber arrived to fix her toilet. She completely forgot I was even there in her zeal to order the plumber around and get the toilet fixed. That's who she was busy being, at the moment when I last saw her.

I took LSD to go to my mother's funeral, which made it interesting, because, of course, she was at the funeral, too. She and I were hanging out together, and seeing it all as really quite beautiful. We enjoyed all the loving people coming together, and it was a very happy occasion for both of us. That put me in a rather peculiar position, though, because according to the customs of funeral showbiz, they had seated the mourners of the family on one side of the casket and everybody else on the opposite side, so they could look at the mourners mourning. I was in a state of great happiness, being there with my mother, but I realized that one smile, and it would all be over. "Look at that!! He's the one that takes drugs. Wouldn't you know? He laughs at his own mother's funeral. The depths of depravity!"

There was an interesting moment, though, later in the funeral service, when Mother let the rest of the family in on the game. On each of their wedding anniversaries, my mother and father had always exchanged one red rose, as a token of their continuing love for one another. At the funeral, my mother's coffin was covered with a blanket of roses; when the coffin was being wheeled down the aisle, just as it passed the row in which my father was sitting, one red rose fell off the blanket and landed at my father's feet. Now, seated in that row were my father, a very conservative Boston attorney and ex-president of a railroad; my oldest brother, a successful New York stockbroker; his wife, a Long Island wife-of-a-successful-stockbroker; my second brother, who, at the time, was under the impression that he was Christ; and me. All of us looked at the rose—we all knew the story about the anniversary roses, of course—and as we started to file out, my father bent down and picked up the rose.

We went out and climbed into the Cadillac limousine to go to the cemetery. My father was holding the rose, and nobody was saying a word. Finally my brother, Christ, said, "Well, I guess she sent you a message"—and everybody in the car agreed! Can you imagine that? Not just Christ and me, but the attorney and the stockbroker and the Long Island matron all agreed. They all said, "Yes, that's right. She sent you a message." It was a beautiful moment, in which the emotions of the situation had led everybody to transcend all their cynicism and doubt, and to allow for the possibility that something like that had actually happened: that a message had come from my mother "from the beyond," which meant that some part of her was still around.

Of course, my father's immediate question was "How can we preserve the rose?" He's a materialist, right? It isn't enough that we got the message—we have to preserve the rose. Well, that started a frenzied plan of action, which led to numerous phone calls, which ended up with our locating a company that said it could encase the rose in a plastic bubble full of some kind of liquid that would preserve the rose "forever," so that we, for all eternity, could have this red rose. We air-mailed the rose to the company, and when it came back in its plastic bubble we put it on the mantelpiece.

Well, the years passed. It turned out that the procedure for preserving the rose wasn't *quite* foolproof, so the rose got all deadish and the water got all black. And now on the mantelpiece was this globe of brackish water.

Eventually, it came time for my father to marry again (to a wonderful woman; I gave the bride away), and now there was some question about what to do with this eternal memento sitting on the mantelpiece. That whole clinging thing of "preserving it for eternity": Now that you've got it, what do you do with it? Well, the rose gradually made its way to less and less prominent places, and then eventually was relegated to a closet at the back of the garage that was set aside for all the things we were preserving eternally. (I did later rescue it from there, and for a long time kept it on my puja table, but somewhere in my many moves it vanished, and I don't know where it is now.)

My deepest teachings on the subject of death came from Maharajji, my guru—but interestingly enough, my mother cropped up several times in the course of my connecting with him. First of all, she appeared to me on the ceiling of my hotel room in Nepal, while I was lying there trying to decide whether to go on to Japan with my friend David Padwa, or to go back into India with Bhagawan Das and do temple pilgrimages. Going to Japan would be secure, and first class all the way. Going back to India, on the other hand, meant that I would be without much money, and it would all be kind of nitty-gritty and wild. As I was sitting there trying to figure out what to do, my mother appeared. She looked down at me with a look that was both peeved and pleased at the same time. The middle-class mother-role was peeved, saying, "When are you going to settle down and become a responsible member of the community?" But the other, pleased, part of her was saying, "Go, baby, go!" I'd always suspected that the other little part of her was in there, but I hadn't been able to see it because I was so used to dealing with the middle-class woman and with all the Freudian stuff about mothers (all of which was totally applicable to her and me). But there she was, in a hotel in Kathmandu, encouraging me to go on to India—where, as it turned out, Maharajji was lying in wait for me.

A few months later, when I first met Maharajji, it was through an exchange regarding my mother that he blew my mind and opened my heart to him. The day I met him, Maharajji said to me, "Your mother died last year." He closed his eyes and he said, "She got very big in the stomach before she died"—which was true, because of her enlarged spleen. I said, "Yes." Then he spoke the only word that he said in English; he looked directly at me and he said, "Spleen." That is, he named, in English, the organ that had killed my mother. That one word brought my mind screeching to a halt. How did he know? *How did he know?* My mind was like one of those pinball machines going "Tilt!"—it stopped dead in its tracks! And then my heart could open to him.

The next day, Maharajji said to me, "You know, your mother is a very high being." I said to the translator, "Didn't he say she *was* a very high being?" The translator asked again, and Maharajji said, "Nay, nay—she *is* a very high being." I suddenly experienced a whole figure-ground reversal: I saw this high being, who had taken on an incarnation as a middle-class Jewish woman from Boston, but who had, in some subtle way, been supporting my going out and out and out, while all the time keeping up a veneer of total middle-class respectability—in fact, fooling herself with the disguise most of the time. I began to reperceive her, through that comment of Maharajji's, and to appreciate the *being* behind the temporary roles we'd both been playing.

Maharajji totally reoriented my attitudes toward dying. He often spoke about death. He said things like these: "The body dies, but not the soul." "The body passes away. Everything is impermanent, except the love of God." "You can't take anything with you when you die, because the world is just a dream, an illusion." For Maharajji, death was an escape from the prison of that illusion—"escaping from Central Jail," he called it.

One day, walking along with one of the devotees, Maharajji said, "So-and-so—this old woman devotee—just died." Then he laughed and laughed. The devotee who was walking with him said, "You butcher! What are you laughing about, if she just died?" Maharajji looked surprised and said, "Do you want me to pretend to be one of the puppets?" He was saying, Should I make believe I'm sad? She just finished her work, and left the stage.

Maharajji was lying on his tucket at the temple one day. Suddenly he sat up and said, "Somebody's here." The people around him said, "No, Maharajji. Nobody's here." He said, "Yes, yes, someone has just come. Nobody thinks I know anything." A few minutes later a man came into the compound, and started toward Maharajji's tucket; he was the servant of one of Maharajji's old devotees. Maharajji yelled at him, "I won't go. I won't go. I know he's dying, but I won't go." The man said, "How did you know this, Maharajji? Not even the family knows. But yes—he is dying, and he is calling for you." Maharajji said, "No, no, I'm not going to go." Everyone begged, "Maharajji, please go! That man has been your devotee for so many years." Maharajji just kept saying, "No, no. I won't go."

Finally, Maharajji reached over and picked up a banana. He handed it to the man and said, "Here, give him this banana. He will be all right." The servant pranamed and thanked him, and ran home with the banana. He mashed up the banana and fed it to the dying man; the man ate the banana—and as he took the last bite, he died.

Now, what are we to make of that story? What's "all right"? Maharajji didn't say the man was going to live—he just said he'd be all right. Why do we think that has to mean remaining in this incarnation?

When I first went to India, in 1967, I was still in my Land Rover phase. My friend David and I were driving around India in a big Land Rover, with Vivaldi concerti on the tape recorder, eating canned tuna fish and drinking chlorinated water and keeping the windows closed so the germs wouldn't get in. When we arrived in Banaras, we stayed

Hatha Yoga Class: Near the end of one of the yoga sessions, the students practice a deep relaxation posture called *savasana*, or the corpse pose. The open, relaxed pose facilitates the release of any physical or mental clinging.

at a first-class English-type hotel. But when I went out into the streets of Banaras, there it all was.

Banaras is the city of dying in India, and death isn't hidden away there the way it is in our culture. In Banaras, when somebody dies, he is wrapped in an orange cloth and placed on a kind of wooden stretcher. Then he's carried through the streets to the burning ghats, right out in the open, all to the chanting of Ram's name. Quite different from our funerals, which have made the whole thing so antiseptic. Hindus try to go to Banaras to die, because if you die there, Shiva comes and whispers the name of Ram in your ear at the moment of your death, and that brings enlightenment. In other words, once you understand what the game is all about, it's a very auspicious place to die.

The scene in Banaras, like the Tibetan monks reading the *Book of the Dead,* reflects an understanding that it's important how we orient our minds at the time of our death. Both of those systems are reincarnational, and they both include two of the main ingredients in a spiritual view of death: first, that it matters what you are thinking about at the moment of death; and second, that the key to not being reborn is not being attached. Banaras and *The Book of the Dead* each creates a context through which you could, at the moment of death, go straight through the door and be in the arms of God. They each create a set of symbols and a set of rituals that at the time of death are right there to remind you what it's all about. Krishna says in the Gita, "At the time of death, think of me." These are techniques for making that more likely.

But none of that was I seeing, that first time I was in Banares. As I walked around the streets, what I saw then were all these human beings who were literally down to skin and bone, many of them with leprosy or some other horrific disease. They were dragging themselves around with their begging bowls, hundreds and hundreds of them. Each of them had a little pouch tied into his loincloth, or her sari, that held just enough coins to buy the wood for their funeral pyres.

Now, there I was in Banaras, walking through those streets. I'd just had a big meal at a nice, fancy, restaurant, with the ice cream parfait for dessert, and it probably cost more than these people had ever seen at one time in their whole lives. I had my traveler's checks in my pocket, and I was out to see the sights of Banaras. But the more I saw, the more uncomfortable I grew, because I was feeling such incredible pity for all those people around me. The thought that I was holding traveler's checks while they were there with not enough to eat—I couldn't stand it! I literally fled back to the hotel room and hid under the bed. It was just too much for me. It was, in a way, like the Buddha's encounters with the old, the sick, and the dying.

It was not so many months later that I went back to Banaras. But in the meantime, I had been with Maharajji, and so I had been opened to new possibilities about the nature of the game. And through that, I had begun to understand what Banaras was all about. I walked down by the burning ghats. The burning ghats are the places on the bank of the Ganges River where bodies are cremated, where the cremation fires have been going on since forever. I spent a whole night standing in the middle of the burning ghats, with the bodies burning all around me, smelling the smoke of the burning flesh, watching the skulls being cracked with a stick, and hearing Shiva whispering, "Rama, Rama, Rama."

And now when I looked at those people dragging themselves through the streets, I saw something totally new. I saw it from *their* point of view; and to my amazement, I suddenly saw that what they were feeling was great pity for *me*. Because they knew they had made it—and the chances of *my* ever making it were very slim, indeed. Look at me, rushing around, not knowing where I was going—the shoe was suddenly on the other foot. And with that new understanding of what was going on, what I saw was the deep joy in the scene. They were *happy*—they knew they were almost there!

At Maharajji's funeral pyre, there was one old devotee who sang and sang all night long at the top of his lungs, "Sri Ram, Jai Ram, Jai, Jai Ram! Sri Ram, Jai Ram, Jai, Jai Ram!" The next day, people asked him why he was singing that way, without any trace of sadness. He said, "When I looked at the funeral fire, I saw Maharajji sitting upright, laughing, and Ram standing next to him pouring ghee over his head so that he would burn faster. And all around overhead were the gods and goddesses, raining down flowers from above."

The body dies, but not the soul. That's what Maharajji was telling us. It's what Christ was trying to tell us as well. What Christ was saying to all of us was "Look, don't freak out. I'll show you how it's done. You're worried, so I'll run through it; then you won't be afraid anymore. I'll go through all the suffering, even the suffering of the final doubt: 'Father, Father, why have you forsaken me?' I'll take it all on, so you can see that it's really all OK. I'll even die, and I'll show you that that's no big deal, either, and then I'll drop back, just to let you know that it's all cool, that nothing much changes with death." I began to see the power of that teaching to liberate, once we get past the "poor Christ, hanging there on the cross" business. There's nothing to be afraid of—that was Christ's real teaching.

When Ramana Maharshi was dying of cancer, his devotees said, "Please, Baba, heal yourself!" He said, "No, no, this body is done."

They begged him, "Don't leave us! Don't leave us!" and they all started to weep. He looked at them with bewilderment and he said, "Leave you? Don't be silly. Where could I go?"[1] He was telling them, I'm here; that won't change. It's just the body that's leaving.

◎

Well, all those experiences — with psychedelics, with my mother, with Maharajji — began to add up for me, and to reshape the way I thought about death. They gave me a new perspective on things, and I began to see the way we, as a culture, were really doing a job on ourselves about the whole subject. We try very hard to pretend that if we hide death in the closet and never mention it in polite company, it won't exist. But the truth is, the more we try to hide from death, the scarier it gets. I saw that — and that led me to decide to start focusing more on death, to start talking about it more in my lectures and getting more involved with it in my work. And it seemed clear to me that one obvious way of getting involved would be to start hanging around with people who were dying.

Ginny Fiffer was a friend of Aldous and Laura Huxley, and when I met her she was dying of pelvic cancer. Ginny was an intellectual, part of the Ernest Hemingway crowd "way back when," and she didn't have much use for any kind of mysticism. She thought all that was some kind of bullshit. When I came to visit her the first time, she was still full of arguments. She asked me, "What do you think about all this dying business?" I told her what I thought, and she said, "I think that's a lot of crap!"

Some weeks later, I came back to visit her again. She was very weak by then — too weak to talk to me, and in great pain. The cancer was eating away at the nerves all through her stomach and thighs, and she was writhing in pain, just continuously writhing on the bed.

I came into Ginny's room. I sat down next to her bed, and I proceeded to meditate. But I didn't meditate by going away from her, into myself. I meditated with my eyes open, and I meditated on her decaying body. I used a Buddhist meditation, which the monks traditionally did in the charnel grounds, where corpses were left out in the fields to decay. The monks would go and meditate on the swollen corpse, on the festering corpse, on the corpse infested with worms, and finally on the skeleton. The value of the meditation was that it loosened one's attachment to the body. Some people are repelled by all that; they think the corpse meditation is very negative. But it's actually just counteracting all the denial and the Pollyannaish positiveness that we get so lost in.

Meditating there with Ginny, I saw the decaying body, and I saw the pain. But instead of being freaked by the emotions which that aroused, I let the feelings be present—and at the same time, I was the witness of it all. It was all right there: the awe-full beauty of the universe. It got very, very peaceful in the room, and very, very deep; the whole space filled with a kind of purplish glow. It was quite an extraordinary moment. After we had been in that space for maybe twenty minutes or so, Ginny turned to me and said, "I feel so much peace." Yet all the time, her body was writhing in pain. The pain was still there—it didn't go away. But Ginny had pulled herself out of the place where she was identified with being the person who was in pain. That was no longer who she was. She had connected with who she was *behind* that.

That experience with Ginny taught me a little bit about how we can work with pain. The toughest things about death are the pain and the fear. If we aren't prepared, if we aren't conscious, the pain and fear will create a lot of confusion; our minds will get lost in them. We need strategies for approaching them. When we meditate, and our legs hurt or our knees hurt, and we learn how to sit with that pain, to be open to it, we are beginning the long journey of learning to deal with whatever intense or unexpected pain might be connected with our dying. Ginny was a teacher for me, in showing me the need for that and in helping me see how to deal with such pain.

There was another lesson I learned by being around people who were dying, and that was how deficient our culture is in providing places for dying consciously. We don't have a Banaras here;

instead, we have hospitals. There was a friend of mine, Debbie Love, who was dying; she was married to Peter Mattheissen, who's written all those beautiful books about Nepal and the Himalayas. While she was dying, Debbie was a patient at Mount Sinai Hospital in New York City. Now, hospitals are very tricky places to die in; they are designed to keep people alive by whatever means possible, so when you die you represent a failure of the system.

Debbie was a member of a zendo in New York City, and all of her fellow Zen students decided that instead of meditating at the zendo every evening, they would come and meditate in her hospital room. So each evening they would converge on Mount Sinai Hospital, and pretty soon Debbie's room had been converted into a temple. There was a little puja shrine, and all the students, dressed in their black robes, would line the walls, doing zazen.

The first evening that the students met in Debbie's room, a gaggle of young resident doctors arrived in the middle of the meditation. They pushed open the door to the room and charged in, prepared with their hale and hearty "Well, and how are we doing tonight? Let's see your chart. Have you been a good girl? Did you eat all your dinner?" But they'd walked into this temple. They got as far as "Well, and how are we do—" and they stopped in their tracks.

By the third night, instead of barging in, they were gently opening the door, coming in, and standing quietly for a few minutes looking at the charts, and then leaving. They were doing their work, but they weren't dominating the scene. They were like the doctors for a football team; the doctors don't call the plays—they are merely there to help you if you break a leg. They are the servants of the system rather than its masters.

Debbie's experience showed me the possibility of creating a space for conscious dying right in the middle of the system. But, of course, it would be nice to have a space where that kind of environment for dying is not just accommodated, but supported and encouraged. What that has led to in my own thinking is a program I would like to call "Dial-a-Death." If you were dying, and wanted to die consciously, you'd dial us up. We would send somebody over who wanted to work on themselves through the process of being with someone—namely, you—who was trying to die consciously.

See, there are no professional die-ers, but there are many of us, myself included, who find it an incredibly powerful sadhana to work with someone who's dying. And there are plenty others of us who are dying, and who would like to have around them somebody who's done enough deep inner work to be really present with them in that space. So "Dial-a-Death" would be like a yenta, or a marriage bro-ker—somebody who arranges relationships between what we might call the die-ers and the guides.

Eventually, I would imagine that we *will* have Banarases in the West. We will have scenes where people can come and say, "This is where I want to die. I would like to die among people who aren't busy deny-ing death, or trying to cling to life." People coming to such a dying center will be able to decide which kind of doctor they want, and how much medication they need, and what sort of religious metaphor they would like to die in. They could die in a Christian metaphor, or a Mus-lim metaphor, or a Buddhist metaphor, or a Hindu metaphor, or what-ever. There would be people available from each tradition, and we would do all we could to have every tradition represented: Wiccan, Zoroastrian, Rastafarian, you name it. That is, we would do our best to arrange whatever setting the die-er felt would maximize her or his chance of being turned toward God at the moment of death. But although "Banaras West" is a nice vision for the future, at the moment we work with what we've got, and Debbie was a good teacher for me in how that could be done.

In any case, dying in an ideal environment presumes that we will have some time for preparation, and for a certain number of us, that won't be the case. For some of us, death will arrive very suddenly and unexpectedly. It can happen to anybody, at any moment. Within a period of one week at Naropa, for example, I dealt with a woman who had learned she had malignant cancer, with a boy who fell off a mountain and died, and with a woman who was in an automobile accident in which her companion was killed. All unexpected, all shattering.

Sudden death is in many ways more difficult to work with spiritually. There isn't time to arrange an external environment that turns us in the right direction. There isn't time to prepare ourselves—here it is! It becomes then a question of our inner environment at that moment, and once we realize that death can happen at *any* instant, we start paying more attention to the moment-by-moment content of our minds. We begin asking ourselves, "If I were to die in this moment, would my thoughts be turned toward God?"

That's where a practice like mantra can be so helpful. You carry a mala in your pocket, and as you're walking along you're turning your mala and chanting, "Krishna, Krishna, Krishna," or "Christ, Christ, Christ," or "Rama, Rama, Rama," or "Allah, Allah, Allah." If you've been filling your mind with the names of God all throughout your life, you've got a better chance of their being there at the moment when you're dying. Mahatma Gandhi was walking out into his garden, just another ordinary day, when he was shot three times by an assassin. He didn't say, "Aaargh!" or "I've been shot!" or "Long live India!" He just said, "Ram," and he died. He was so ready that even at the moment of the totally unexpected, he went right toward God. Just, Yeah—here I come. Wheeeee! Look ma, no hands. I'm free!

What we need most at the moment of death is incredible clarity of consciousness. Since dying is one of the most profound events of our lives, don't we owe it the respect of preparing for it, so that when it comes we can deal with it consciously? Confucius said, "One who sees the way in the morning can gladly die in the evening." Sadhana is the preparation, so that at any moment, no matter how unexpected that moment might be, we are able to let go of the thought of our own existence.

There was one more lesson that I learned from hanging out with people who were dying, and that was that I could be sucked in by all the melodramas surrounding death just as easily as the next guy. I learned firsthand about the depth of my own denial around the subject.

Wavy Gravy once introduced me to a young fellow who was dying of Hodgkin's disease. Wavy knew I was interested in being with people who were dying, and this fellow wanted to talk with me, so Wavy set things up. We met over at Tom Wolfe's house. I sat down next to the fellow and I said, "So, I hear you are going to die soon." He said, "Yeah." I asked, "Do you want to talk about it?"

He proceeded to tell me about how he was planning to die. He was in what's labeled stage 4B of the disease, which is the terminal stage. He had been through all the medical treatments, and he had decided that he wanted to go out on his own, in order to avoid the pain of the end stages of the illness. He was planning to take LSD, and then to overdose on heroin. I said, "That sounds reasonable to me. However, you ought to plan it very carefully and prepare yourself, so you won't get freaked out by the drugs. You should work with them in advance, so you will know how to stay conscious with them when the time comes." He said, "When I get too weak to move around, I think that's when I'll do it." I said, "Whatever you want—it's your death."

He went to light a cigarette at that point, and I noticed that his hands were shaking very badly. I thought, "Uh-oh, what am I doing? I've freaked him out by talking so casually about dying. Look how I've scared him." So I said to him, "Hey, man, am I freaking you? Because I don't want to do that." He said, "Oh, no—you don't understand! I have been looking and looking for the strength to die. You are the first person who's come along who isn't totally freaked in their vibration as soon as we get anywhere near the subject. You're giving me the strength I need. I am just absolutely overwhelmed by it."

He and I started to hang out together after that. We actually did a movie together, in which we talked about his dying. His hair had fallen out because of his medicine, but he always wore a long hippie wig. In the middle of the movie, I had him take off his wig; it really blew the audience apart.

It was an experience with that fellow that showed me just how easy it was for me to get sucked into the melodrama and denial around dying. One afternoon, he and I were driving along Highway 1 in California; if you've ever driven that highway, you know that it's a very narrow, curvy road with great, long drops straight down to the ocean. I was driving along; he was tilted back in the passenger's seat, and he and I were admiring the waves and the sky and the beauty of the day. At one point, we stopped for gas, and as we started to get back into the car the fellow said to me, "Hey—could I drive? It will probably be my last chance to do it." Now that's a pretty heavy one, right? Twenty-three-year-old guy, big investment in driving . . . So I said, "Sure, of course." He got behind the wheel, and we started off. As we approached the first curve, I suddenly realized that he was too weak to turn the steering wheel, and that we were aimed straight for the cliff. So I casually reached over, and (all the time making believe that I wasn't), I turned the wheel and steered us back onto the road. Then we careened off in another direction, and I very casually turned the wheel again.

I was sitting there, driving surreptitiously, when all of a sudden it dawned on me that I was involved in a vast conspiracy to deny the present moment. His anxiety was so deep, his clinging to who he thought he still was was so desperate, that he couldn't surrender into who, in fact, he *truly* was at that moment—which was somebody who was too weak to drive. And I had been sucked right in! I had gone right along with the whole charade. So I said to him, "Hey, man, you know what? We've gotten into a kind of conspiracy here, pretending you're still able to drive. At this point, you should be laying back and grooving, and I should be chauffeuring you around. We should just relax into what is, instead of trying to hold on to the past."

I told him the story from *Zen Flesh, Zen Bones* about the man and the strawberry.[2] Remember that one? A man was being chased by a tiger, and to escape he started to scramble over the edge of a cliff. But as he did so, he looked down and saw another tiger prowling around below him. So there he was, perched precariously on a tiny ledge of rock, a tiger above him and a tiger below. And as he clung there, between tiger and tiger, he noticed that growing right there in front of him was a wild strawberry plant, and that on it was one single red, ripe strawberry. The man plucked the strawberry and ate it. And the last line of the story is "How sweet it tasted!" So I said to the fellow, "Enjoy the strawberry of *this* moment."

That whole experience, of slipping into the melodrama and denying the truth of the moment, showed me just how seductive the conspiracy is, and how easy it is to get caught in the denial process when we're around someone who's dying. Denial is the first of Elisabeth Kübler-Ross's five stages of dying, and we can see why it would be the immediate reaction. Death is so inconsistent with who we think we are that we simply deny the possibility; you tell somebody they're going to die, and the first thing they'll say is, "No, not me. The diagnosis must be wrong." After the denial comes anger: "Who's done this to me?!" Then comes the third stage—bargaining to have it changed: "If I'm good and take my medicine, I'll get better." When it's clear that the bargaining isn't going to work, depression sets in. And finally, after the depression, comes acceptance.

However, I don't think Elisabeth goes far enough. Acceptance isn't the end point of the possibilities. Those five stages are all *psychological* states we go through when we're facing death, and that's still shy of a spiritual point of view. Acceptance can be merely saying, "Okay, I'm going to die. Right." And in that are still the subtle clingings attached to the thought, "*I* am going to die." A spiritual perspective takes us beyond acceptance. For someone on a spiritual path, death is a doorway, an opportunity, and all our practices are done to prepare us for that moment.

If we have adopted a reincarnational model for ourselves, we appreciate the fact that the thought we are thinking at the moment of death is a critical thought, because that thought influences what happens next. That is, whatever our desires at the moment of death, we go to the realms where those desires can be realized or fulfilled. It's

Sunrise after All-Night Chant: Guru Purnima, the full moon of
the guru, was celebrated with an evening slide show of Maharajji
photos, followed by an all-night chant. Chanting throughout the
night is a profound spiritual practice, and the deep inward
journey is reflected in the faces of Ram Dass and the other
participants as dawn arrives to end the ritual (see page 274).

summed up in that Gita passage I quoted earlier, where Krishna says,
"Those who pray to the gods, go to the gods." But the deva lokas and
the hell lokas, all the different realms, turn out to be just more incarnations, just more forms. They may seem more interesting than the
plane we've incarnated into this time, but they're still just more veils
between us and the Beloved.

If we want to avoid taking any more forms at all, the best thought
we can have at the moment of death is no thought. At the moment of
death, we all enter into the clear light—all of us. Each of us experiences Brahman, nirvana, the Void. But it takes a disciplined mind, a
spiritually prepared mind, to resist the intense pull of the karmic
forces—the powerful impulses of thoughts and feelings and perceptions that keep drawing us back into form. As soon as a strong-enough
desire happens by, we turn away from the light to follow it, and we
start to descend through the bardos, one by one, pulled by our karma,

until we come to the plane where that desire can manifest or be fulfilled. But someone who is without any desires at the moment of death—someone who can say, "This is life. This is dying. This is death. Yes!"—that person grabs for nothing, and pushes nothing away. And so, through dying, that person becomes free of the Wheel of Birth and Death. Dying, that one is born into God.

Conclusion

*T*his being the conclusion, custom calls for us to look back over the trip we've been taking together, and to try and figure out where it is we've come with it all. In service to that, it would seem appropriate for us to do a couple of things: The first is to bring together the various strands of thought we have been following, to tie up the loose ends so we can come to some feeling of closure about it all. The other is to reflect on what all this might conceivably have had to do with the Bhagavad Gita.

To take the last one first: I think we've found that the relationship between this book and the Gita is a little more subtle than we may at first have anticipated. Although this is supposed to be a book about the Gita, and although it has come out of many, many years of reading and studying the Gita, a lot of it hasn't been directly connected to the Gita in any technical sense. It clearly wasn't a scholarly discourse on the text, for example. It wasn't an interpretation of its slokas. I think what would be most accurate is to say that this book is a commentary on the foundation concepts on which the Gita is built, and a reflection on some ways we can bring the Gita's practices into our own spiritual lives. Those are the aspects of the Gita that we have been exploring.

As for creating closure and bringing it all together, I suspect that that will really have to wait until it happens, in its own time, in each of our hearts, as we bring the teachings into the light of our own experiences. But although we probably can't tie it all together in a neat package, what we can do instead is to trace the major threads that have run through this book.

Looking back, I think we can see that the underlying theme throughout all of this has had to do with the way the Bhagavad Gita provides us with a map for our own sadhana. The Gita sets out a system of practices, yogas, for bringing us into union with Brahman, with the One. And when those practices work, as they do in the case of Arjuna, then comes the Mystic Vision.

In the eleventh chapter of the Gita, we're given a taste of what that vision is like. Arjuna says to Krishna, "I have heard thy words of truth, but my soul is yearning to see thy form as God of this all." Then, because of the preparation Arjuna has had, Krishna gives him "divine sight," so he can see Krishna's *cosmic* form—which is Awe-ful: full of awe. Arjuna sees the whole universe there in front of him, all around him, with the radiance of a thousand suns—all of creation coming and going in Krishna.

That vision totally blows Arjuna's mind. He says, "I have seen what no man has seen before. I rejoice in exultation—and yet my heart trembles with fear. Have mercy upon me: show me again thine own human form." The mystic vision is too much for Arjuna's mind to take in; he's ready to go back to seeing Krishna in his human form again. But as a result of that experience, any remaining doubts Arjuna may have had are overridden, and he simply surrenders into doing his dharma. From that point on, Krishna starts to give him instruction in a much more direct way. The seduction is over, if you will.

Now the thing is when that experience comes to Arjuna, he's already leading a very *satvig* life, a spiritually pure existence. All the non-killing, non-stealing, non-lying, non-lusting, non-giving-and-receiving stuff is simply assumed in Krishna's dealings with Arjuna. The experience of the cosmic form comes after all that is already a given, and after a certain amount of wisdom—higher wisdom—has been developed in Arjuna through Krishna's teachings.

Preparation for the mystic vision is important. You recall that we've talked about the lower wisdom and the higher wisdom—that the lower wisdom is the stuff your ordinary intellect can manipulate, conceive of, play with, conceptualize, whereas the higher wisdom is the wisdom that comes to us only through initiation. The higher wisdom comes only through direct experience; you have to *become* it. And the Gita runs us through that whole process. The Gita presents the lower wisdom in the first few chapters, then follows with the purifications that are the groundwork for us to open to the higher wisdom, so that through the higher wisdom we can arrive at the possibility of having certain kinds of experiences which come with it—namely, the experiences that come to Arjuna in chapter 11.

Now, what happened to many of us, through our use of psychedelics, was that the sequence got inverted. We had the chapter 11 Experience before we'd read chapters 1 through 10. We were left with a mind-blowing vision without any structural understanding of it, or any degree of purification that would allow us to receive it. That was part of what all the "bad tripping" was about. But though sometimes in a fierce way, those visions ultimately did force us to go back and seek the purification, seek the higher wisdom, so that the launching pad for our mystical visions would start to be different. And so although the yoga that has been emerging in the United States may not be sequencing in exactly the way the Bhagavad Gita outlines, now that we have used the psychedelics, and blown ourselves out of our totally externalizing / worldly / philosophical-materialist mind-set, we are ready to hear what we need to hear in order to get on with it, so we can become the statement of the higher wisdom: a liberated being.

So we look to the Gita to tell us about all those practices we're ready to start doing. We do that, even though we know, as we said before, that in a way all practices are a hype. We do it because we feel a need for practices, because we feel intuitively drawn toward them. Something within us is simply nudging us. We see the dilemma in that, because we know that all our dramas, including the drama of "Getting Enlightened," are just more veils, and that veils keep us from seeing who we really are. So Getting Enlightened keeps us from getting enlightened. But then that becomes the incentive for deepening our practices still further, so they're coming from a purer place, and the cycle continues. From one level up, we see that the perfection *includes* our use of the methods. We realize that there is nothing at all to do, but in a state of total openness to all the possibilities in our lives, we're drawn to work on ourselves.

When we're ready to start doing practices, the Gita provides us with a curriculum of all the various yogas we can begin to include in our lives. A yoga is really any practice we undertake with the intention of coming closer to God. The key to it is the "intentional practice" part and so yogas can involve any and all parts of our lives. Martin Barber said, "There is no human act that cannot be hallowed into a path to God."

But although the Gita offers us a number of different yogas to work with, it's clear that the one it's mainly concerned with is the path of karma yoga. The Gita was, you will recall, meant in part as Hinduism's reply to Buddhism; it embraces a spiritual path of engagement in the world rather than withdrawal from it.

I see the Gita as basically a karma yoga manual, a guidebook for bringing spirit into action. I find the teachings of the Gita reflected in the lives of Gandhi and Martin Luther King. The Gita is a path of yoga that's designed for a life of action rather than a life of contemplation, and it tells us how to carry on our spiritual quest right in the midst of our lives in the world. It spells out the way we can do that: by offering all our actions to God, by acting without any attachment, and by acting without seeing ourselves as the actors.

Before we arrive at that place of pure, detached action, we will go through a lot of other levels first, and each one will contribute its own little piece to our sadhana. For instance, if we're still acting from the feeling "I *ought* to do karma yoga," our actions will come tarnished with guilt and anger, and to that extent, they aren't "pure" karma yoga. However, that very impurity will become the force that drives us to reflect more deeply about our actions; and then, as we do, and as our wisdom gets clearer, our motivation will get purer, and our karma yoga will change.

In earlier chapters, we talked about karma yoga and sacrifice as if they were separate practices. But the fact is that the highest statement of karma yoga is also a full expression of the act of sacrifice. In practicing true karma yoga, we sacrifice ourselves and our gratifications into selfless, dharmic action. The ritual of sacrifice satisfies some deep yearning in us to complete a cycle, to offer back for what we've been given. When Krishna agrees to come onto the physical plane as an avatar, it is *an act of sacrifice.* Can you imagine, being God and having to wear a people-suit? It's itchy, and it doesn't fit very well, and it's so constricting. But in order to reinstitute dharma on the physical plane, Krishna manifests in form. That sacrifice has come down to us as an offering. Then, to complete the circle, to close the ring, to make the whole thing sacred, we offer our lives back up in sacrifice. The whole movement of the formless into form into the formlessness becomes one huge *"Swaha!"*—one huge offering into the fire of ongoing transformation.

If all that seems too romantic to you, then work with sacrificing what you do every day to your higher consciousness. Sacrifice it all to your awakening—each thing you do, all day long. If you're driving a car, if you're getting gas, if you're making the bed, if you're brushing your teeth, if you're going to the toilet—whatever it is you're doing, make it grist for the mill of your awakening.

Any act we perform can be looked at in a worldly way, or it can be looked at from a different vantage point—a vantage point that redefines who we are and what it is we're doing here. Am I just "brushing my teeth"? Or am I "brushing my teeth as a way of going to God"? It's a choice, and that process of shifting our vantage point is profound. It's really a process of re-creating our perceptual field, re-creating our entire universe, act by act.

We can turn any part of our lives into a sacrifice, into an offering. We can turn our *feelings* into our sacrifice. If you're having trouble with someone, make them your practice. Add a picture of her or him to your altar. I take the people I'm having a really fierce time with, and I stick their pictures on my puja table. Maharajji said to me, "Whatever else you do with another human being, never put them out of your heart." And so now there's that being whom I'm angry with there on my puja table. I go to do my morning meditation; I look at the picture, and my heart closes to him or her. So I sit there with that picture, I sit there with that being, until I can let go of the anger, until

I can reperceive that being, until I am seeing her or him as God. I get as close to the fire of my feelings as I can—and believe me, it gets *hot!*

Sacrifice and renunciation are kindred practices. Sacrifice, in a way, ritualizes our acts of renunciation. There is a place for renunciation, *tapasyas,* or austerities, in our spiritual practice. It's useful to impose disciplines on ourselves, when we feel that's what we crave. If you crave it, it's good to fast, because it will let you see how attached you are to food. If you crave it, it's good to be brahmacharya, because you will see how captivated you are by your sexual desires. *Tapasyas* let us bring into consciousness the full extent of our attachments. If we can look at those attachments from the outside, from the place of the witness, we won't get quite so sucked in by our sense desires all the time. If our minds aren't always going outward so much, they'll be free to turn inward, back toward the Light.

That's what austerities are about. When they make us feel joyful, because we're releasing ourselves from something that's holding us back from God, that's a good indication that renunciation is the right practice at the moment. On the other hand, if we're gritting our teeth and doing it all in order to "be good," then maybe we should wait a while. When we start measuring "How *much* can I give up?—that's a pretty good indication that righteousness has crept in. "I've given up sex and I've given up meat and I've given up milk and I've given up . . . " What an ego trip that is! That's just being attached to being *non*attached, and you haven't even *begun* to renounce renouncing! The practice of renunciation is ultimately about renouncing our *suffering* over this or that, and when *that* happens, the whole melodramatic part of the renunciation trip starts to fade away. The game isn't to see how little food we can eat, or how little sex we can have, or how few clothes we can wear—that's nonsense. The point of the game is to be *free:* not attached to having, not attached to *not* having, but free.

Renunciation is a means to an end. Once we're free, renunciation is irrelevant. The minute we're free of attachment, we can use or not use anything in the universe. In fact, it all then *becomes* ours to use. All the energy of the universe is free energy, and once we're free, it's all there for us to use. But that's only *after* we are without attachments, because only then can we be trusted with the keys to the kingdom. When we are without desires, without attachments, we will act only when we are drawn by our dharma to act. There will be nothing we're looking to get from the situation that would take us away from our doing our karma yoga. Perfectly.

◎

Although it doesn't take center stage in the Gita the way karma yoga does, bhakti yoga is central to the Gita's message. In chapter 12, Krishna says that bhakti is the highest form of yoga. He tells Arjuna, "Those who set their hearts on me and ever in love worship me, these I hold as the best yogis." Bhakti yoga and karma yoga are woven together. Krishna tells Arjuna that those who serve him *with love* will be guided by him from within their hearts. It's the goal of the karma yogi to act out of pure dharma—that is, to have every action guided by God's will. And here Krishna is telling us that the way that's accomplished is simply by adding love to the equation.

So we add in the love, we engage in the bhakti practices, although at the same moment we recognize that there is a danger of getting lost in the object of our devotion and never moving past it. There is what we've called the lower bhakti and the higher bhakti, and the lower bhakti can be very dualistic—it's the worship of somebody or something "out there." Lower bhakti usually comes with a kind of needful, clinging attachment. There's nothing wrong with any of that; it's part of the way bhakti works. It's fine, so long as we understand what it's about and we keep developing our wisdom so we can move on.

I myself started out from a place of "lower bhakti," feeling incredible love on a very personal level for this being, Maharajji. Here was this guy who was loving me, taking care of me, feeding me, clothing me, patting me on the head, pulling my beard, and giving me great teachings. I had never been loved like that before! My heart opened to him at a very romantic level; I just loved "Big Daddy." However, through that love I opened myself to him, and so every teaching he was laying on me was just pouring straight into me, because my heart was so wide open. And in the course of that wide-openness, the teachings that came in from him kept redefining my existence and refining my understanding until my attachment to him as a form—that personal level of love for him—started to fall away, and something else came in its place. It became a love for that which he was showing me, that which lay beyond his form. At that point, my love for him had become the vehicle for my opening. That's the way the yoga of devotion does its work.

Chapter 9 of the Gita ends with Krishna telling Arjuna, Always think of me, always love me. "Give me your mind and your heart, and you'll come to me," he says. We can see a kind of daisy-chain of practices here: first karma yoga and bhakti yoga are linked—Krishna guides via the heart, the actions of his devotees. Now we see that bhakti yoga and jnana yoga are linked—to get to God, we have to give over both our hearts and our minds. We need wisdom to keep us from getting trapped in the lower bhakti; but the thinking mind needs to be balanced by the bhakti heart. When that combination of jnana and bhakti comes together, it's powerful! The devotion gets clearer and clearer, and the wisdom gets more and more subtle. The bhakti takes us through the emptiness, and into a *loving* dharma.

Papa Ramdas was a beautiful Indian holy man. He was born in 1884 and spent most of his life in Mangalore, India, at an ashram he had there with Mother Krishnabai. Papa Ramdas said that since all human beings have bodies, hearts, and intellects, they need to use all three in their spiritual development; otherwise, he said, it's like exercising one part of the body and ignoring all the rest. He said that the body is to be used for selfless service (karma yoga); that the heart is to be used for devotion (bhakti yoga); and that the mind is to be used for discernment (jnana yoga). That is, each yoga is a technique that uses some aspect of who we are, as human beings, in order to take us to a new perceptual vantage point on our lives.

All jnana yoga practices are ways of turning the mind back on itself. Papa Ramdas wrote, "Man should use the intellect for Vichara—i.e., he should discriminate between the real and the unreal so as to give up attachment to the unreal or perishable things of the world." He's telling us to switch our attention from the unreal—which is what we usually call "reality"—to the real. Working with a statement like that, with all its implications, with the writings and teachings of holy beings like Papa Ramdas: that's one form of jnana yoga. Then there are the forms of jnana in which we use the mind to beat the mind, practices like Zen koans or vichara atma. There are practices that focus the mind, like meditation or mantra. And there are practices that let us take a step back from the mind, like witnessing.

I think that the practice of witnessing can be a key spiritual exercise for us, because it lets us move outside the dramas of our lives. It shows us that there exists another plane from which to view our experiences. The danger of confusion in this practice is mistaking the judging voice inside our own minds for the spiritual witness. When we first begin to get some grasp of what the dance is all about, and we start to stand back a bit from our own trips, we frequently adopt a type of witnessing that is very judgmental. It's got a *standard*— you've got Buddha as your standard, or Christ as your standard, or Krishna as your standard, or Maharajji as your standard—and next to that standard you've got your own behavior and your own thoughts and your own feelings. You set those two things side by side, and then judge your own behavior against the standard. That's an extension of what is known as the superego, and it's a heavy emotional trip that only tends to lock you more tightly into your predicament. It certainly doesn't do much to free you.

The witness that's useful in our spiritual work has a totally different quality. It isn't judging—good, bad, it's all the same. This witness isn't trying to change anything—it's just seeing it all. It is the completely uncommitted; it's not committed to your enlightenment, it's not trying to get you ahead, it's simply witnessing, nothing else.

As we move into that perspective, however, we discover that in developing the witness, we sacrifice being the experiencer. That is, we sacrifice the thrill of the experience into the witness. Anytime we want to, we can become that part of ourselves that is the witness, which is just noticing it all, very calmly, very equanimously. It just takes a flick of our perspective—in fact, just the *intention* to be coming from that other place. That's all. But to do that, we have to be ready to let go of being the experiencer.

To develop that kind of witness, you have to have a little elbow room. That's why one of my first instructions for sadhana would be "Give yourself some space." Don't always be filling up your time and your mind with content; create a spacious environment for yourself, one that makes it easier to step back and notice your trip.

Then do just that. Notice it. Don't judge it, don't try to change it, don't do anything at all except to notice it. You will find that a lot of your stuff has only been able to survive *un*noticed; the minute you begin to bring it into the light of that "I" that is just looking at it all, it starts to change—without your ever having done a thing! All you did was to start identifying with a different part of your being, a part you could use to watch all the rest of it.

Say I'm sitting here, witnessing, and suddenly I move my hands. I'm witnessing, so I notice the movement. Now, I can say to myself, "Why are you moving your hands so much?" That's judging. Or I can say to myself, "Well, now that you've noticed that you're moving your hands, you'll stop." That's a program. But behind judgments and programs, there is just witnessing: hands moving, witness noticing, nothing more.

But even with this level of the witness, we're still operating within a dualistic framework: The witness is still witnessing *something*. Later on, there comes yet another kind of witnessing, a kind of pervasive perception of everything, which comes out of total nonattachment. When we come to *that* place, another transformation occurs: Then we are still the witness, but we are *also* the enjoyer. We are the experience, the experiencer, the total participant. There is no part of it we are not. And *that* is the witness Krishna is referring to when he says, "I am the Witness. I am the Knower of all the fields." That's not an ego witness; that's not a jnana-yogic exercise. That's Brahman. The practice has transcended itself; it has taken us to the place where we witness it all because we *are* it all, because we have merged. It is the

Oneness out of which the higher wisdom is born. It is the "beyond the Beyond."

So how does all of this add up? What does all of this mean in terms of our own sadhana? We are all at different places in our journey. Some of us feel we're right at the beginning of something new. Some of us feel like we've fallen off the path. Some of us are doing regular practices. Some of us don't know what to do next. For many of us, there is a lot of confusion about our sadhana: What should I do? Am I doing it right? Is some other path better for me than this one is?

In trying to figure out a way to approach our sadhana, there are a few strategies that I would suggest we keep in mind—and the first and most important one is *Relax!* It doesn't really matter *which* next thing you do, because whatever it is, it will become your next teaching. And it isn't the *thing* you do that matters, anyway—it's who it is that's doing it, where it's coming from in you. That means that all those choices and all those decisions that we agonize over aren't really quite so fraught and melodramatic as we like to make them out to be.

The second part of my strategy has to do with learning to listen within. It's about learning to trust the inner, intuitive sense of what it is you are about at any moment. Doing that may take you down some very unexpected avenues—in fact, it probably already has. For example, I'll bet that a large percentage of the people who are attending meditation retreats and monastic retreats these days wouldn't even have entertained the *possibility* of such a thing a few years ago. Can you imagine, wasting your vacation going someplace where you sit on a pillow for sixteen hours a day? But then suddenly it feels right on. It feels like the obvious next thing to do.

So instead of preprogramming how you *think* your spiritual journey is going to unfold, it's better to listen intuitively. That means you're going to have to keep being straight with yourself. Don't be afraid to change when your intuitive wisdom tells you to. You start a sadhana, and you go into it with total commitment, and you drink deeply of it. But then you begin to experience its limitations for you.

At that point, the tendency is either to deny your intuitive wisdom in order to stay on, or to start looking for things to criticize in the method so you can justify exiting. However, I think that a more sophisticated way of dealing with it is just to say, "I have no more work to do here right now." No judgments. It's not that *it* isn't beautiful, and it's not that *you* aren't beautiful—it's just saying, "We don't have any more work together at this time."

Now, you're going to have to trust your own heart in all that, because you're not likely to get much support for your decision from either your teacher or your fellow students. Your teacher is going to say, "You mustn't leave. If you leave, you're going to fall into the pits of hell." Don't worry about it, scary though it may be. You've got to keep trusting your intuitive heart. At some point, your heart drew you to the teacher, and if you trusted your heart then, trust it now when it says, "Go on." There is nothing wrong, either, with leaving a teacher and then coming back five years later and saying, "Well, I guess I made a mistake." Mistakes are an absolutely necessary part of the process.

Once you relax and trust your heart, you'll find that you will be drawn by exactly those forms and practices that are going to take you through. Work with whatever it is that's drawing you at the moment. At one moment, you'll sit by the river, and you'll look at a rock, and you'll feel its sacredness, and that will take you out of yourself. At another moment, nature won't do it for you, but something else will. Sometimes it will be just a word about Christ that will do it; your heart will open, and you will feel that spark of Spirit. Or there will come a moment when the intellect will be so clear and precise that you will see the whole panorama, the awesome nature of the design of it all, and that will take you beyond thought. Each of those is a different moment. At one moment, one form feels comfortable, right, useful; at another moment, another form. Just keep flowing in and out of the forms. Use them and then drop them—the forms aren't "it." The point isn't to cling to one practice or another, one teacher or another; the point is to use whatever can in *this* moment open you to living spirit.

If you have any doubts about whether you should be doing a practice, stop doing it. If you have any misgivings about doing sadhana, if there is any question in your mind as to why you are doing it, stop. Go back and live your life just the way you lived it before you ever heard the word "sadhana," before you ever turned on, before you ever meditated or prayed, before you ever knew anything about all of this nonsense. Go and live exactly as you did, and forget this whole meshuga business. And then watch what happens. Watch the way you are drawn by some inner thread to open a spiritual book and read a few passages, or to sit quietly and watch a candle flame.

If we can just quiet down all the oughts and shoulds in ourselves, if we can be finished with that whole Protestant ethic trip we've been on, we will see that we are really already further out than we give ourselves credit for being. We keep thinking we have to get behind ourselves and push, when all the time we are actually being propelled full speed ahead. When we see that, we recognize that sadhana isn't something we do to get ourselves somewhere; it's something we do to get ourselves out of the way, so we can stop being obstacles to the process.

When we try to quiet down and listen for what to do, we often find that there's a lot of emotional stuff standing in our way. We find that before we can get on with it, we have to get rid of all our accumulated personality stuff, and cleaning up our stuff means we first have to look at it. We all have things we keep closeted away in our minds—thoughts about who we think we are; thoughts that are so gross, so personal, so humiliating, so awkward, so . . . yick!—that we would never want to let another person see them. You can run your own personal laundry list of what those things for you—but whatever they are, they make us feel so uncomfortable about ourselves that all we want to do is hide from them. We seal them off in some dark corner of our minds and never look at them.

When I work with people, there's a practice I sometimes use to help them get their stuff out on the table, where they can look at it. I'll sit across from a person and say, "Let's focus our eyes on each other's ajna" (that's the third-eye point—it's on the forehead, between, and just above, the eyebrows). Then I'll say to the person, "If there's anything at all that you can bring to mind that would be too uncomfortable, embarrassing, disgusting, obnoxious, scary, or wild to share with another human being, share it with me. Go ahead." Saying that is like saying, "Don't think of a rhinoceros." What immediately comes to mind is whatever it is you most want to hide: "When I'm alone, I pick my nose." Or "I'd like to have sex with my mother." Or whatever it is that you've been hiding. If the person can bring herself or himself to be really honest, to tell me what comes to mind, that brings it out into the light, which is the first step in letting go of it.

That exercise also lets us see that we aren't as vulnerable as we thought we were. I'll start to do that exercise with somebody, and that person will say, "Oh, no—I can't tell you *that!*" Then he'll wrestle with it for a while, and finally he'll say, "Well, all right, I'll tell you. I masturbate thinking of my father's penis, and I tie my legs together first." Then he waits for some kind of reaction from me—he waits for me to gasp, or draw back, or look askance or something. But I'm just sitting there with my mala, chanting, "Ram, Ram, Ram . . ." He could have said *anything!* Whatever it is, it's just another thing. Yeah, right, so what else is new? What stuff could you possibly have that's unique? Do you really think you've got stuff that's so *special?* I've been doing this exercise with people for years now, and I haven't heard anything new so far. Little permutations on this and that, but nothing really new. And furthermore, I haven't found one thing yet that has freaked me out. From where I'm sitting, in the middle of my mantra, it's all just stuff, stuff, and more stuff passing by.

So you let it all come out, and you look it all in the eye. But then once you've brought all the stuff to the surface, once you've looked at it in the daylight, the next question is, how quickly can you let go of it? That's the critical next step. You don't keep dwelling on it— haven't you had enough of all those melodramas yet? Let them go;— it's OK. So you are lewd, lascivious, lazy, disgusting, disgraceful, perverse, greedy, passionate, hateful, vengeful, and despicable. Right. And here we are. See? "And here we are"—in other words, it's the human condition! We're all part of it—what can we do? So, finally, you just let go of all your stuff. You let go of it, inside your head. You just release it—that's all. There's such a sense of lightness and freedom that comes with that.

After you've been working with bringing all the terrible stuff out into the light, it's a good idea to balance it by flipping the exercise around, and examining your own beauty and your own divinity. Let yourself experience—*deeply* experience—the incredible beauty of your own being, without allowing any sense of unworthiness to hold you back. Feel the radiance of your own inner heart, touch the depth of your own inner wisdom. Sit with that, until it deeply permeates your being. An exercise like that helps offset the whole negative core-ego trip that we seem to be stuck with.

Another way to experience your divinity is to identify yourself with a Being of Light, like Christ, or Quan Yin, or Rama, or the Buddha. Start by visualizing her or him "out there," in front of you, external to yourself. Then gradually begin drawing that Being into yourself. You can use your breath to help: with every in-breath, you draw the Being into yourself more deeply. With every out-breath, you feel that presence filling you. Draw that Being into your heart, into the center of your own being. Let that presence expand and expand, until it fills you, until it becomes who you are. Let yourself become that Being of Light and Love. Then afterward ask yourself, "During the time I was being that Being, what happened to all those 'negative' things in me? Where were they then?"

So my suggestions thus far are that we relax, trust our hearts, and to do whatever cleaning-up operations present themselves. My final suggestion for a strategy of sadhana is this: Trust the dharma. Trust it, even if you feel at some ego level that you're shucking yourself a bit. It's very helpful to our sadhana if we can start looking at the laws working around us and upon us as benevolent. Notice that I don't mean benevolent as "nice," in the sense of something that's trying to keep our egos happy or even trying to keep us alive. I mean something that's benevolently guiding us through our karma—that is, something that's benevolent because it's helping us to *awaken*.

My understanding of the dharma is that it's a system designed to help us on our evolutionary journey. We are all part of an evolutionary journey, and every experience happening to us at every moment is a gift, a teaching we're being given. All we need is the perceptual stance that allows us to appreciate it for what it is. This moment, right now: Do you see what a gift it is to your awakening? It's perfectly designed to help you break out of the shell of your ego, to dissolve the separation between yourself and the Beloved.

As I understand the law of it all, we are all dwelling in Grace all the time. The only thing that ever falls out of Grace is our own thinking mind: We fall because we *think* we fell. The minute we give up our thoughts—just our *thoughts!*—there we are. God is always exactly one thought away—and the minute we quiet that thought, here we are again.

Well, the issue of the law and its workings brings us back to those still unanswered questions about free will and determinism, about karma and responsibility. I was in a dialogue with Trungpa once, in Vermont, and he said to me, "What do you do about sorcerers?" I said, "What sorcerers, Trungpa? I don't see any sorcerers, and besides, I wouldn't do anything about them, anyway. My guru takes care of me; that's his business. I just love God." And Rinpoche replied, "You're copping out." He said, "These are critical times, Ram Dass, and we must assume responsibility." I thought about that for a moment, and I decided that he must be putting me on, so I said to him, "All times are critical, Rinpoche, and God has all the responsibility." He said, "No, you don't understand. *You* must take responsibility."

I've come to believe that Trungpa was right, in a certain way, and that I *was* copping out. If I deny the "sorcerers"—that is, if I deny this physical plane with its individual differences of good and evil—then I am caught. I am caught in denial, out of *fear* of this plane, with all its stuff. I am no less hung up than if I had been totally preoccupied with the individual distinctions and failed to appreciate the One that lies behind it all.

So I've worked with that concept of "responsibility" over the years, and what has emerged is a deeper and deeper understanding of the whole question of free will and determinism, and of the paradox: that they are both simultaneously true. It's like there are *levels* of free will and determinism, almost like a free-will sandwich, with determinism in between. Before we start awakening to who we really are, we're living within the laws of karma, and it's all just running off mechanically. But within that mechanical runoff, we *think* we're making choices, and so we have to make them. We have to exercise our "free will." Then we begin to become a little more aware, and we see that we *have* no free will, that it's all just law upon unfolding law. We see that everything is just lawfully running through us, including our apparent "choices." So we say, "I have no responsibility—I'm just my karma running off." But then, as we keep going further still and transcend the gunas, we come into the Brahmanic state—and there our will is truly, totally, absolutely free. We can do whatever we want to do.

The only hitch is that by then there is absolutely no desire left within us. In a state of total bliss, what would you desire? From that place, the only acts we end up doing with our "free will" are the things we are drawn to do by the workings of the dharma. That is, we end up acting only to fulfill the law, because there is nothing else we would conceivably do. We exercise our free will by surrendering into being the pure instruments of the dharma. All those desires that preoccupied us for so long? We could fulfill them with a thought—except that the desires themselves are long since gone. There is no longer any personal trip whatsoever that would motivate us to act, so although we're entirely free, we act only to fulfill our role in the way of things.

So do I have responsibility, or don't I? Well, I do *and* I don't. It all depends on where I'm standing. These days, I try to stay aware of both levels—to surrender it all to my guru, and at the same moment to assume responsibility for my dance. As far as I'm concerned, it is all being done by Maharajji—and yet I do my best to play my part as impeccably and as responsibly as I can. I am trying to learn to keep both of those perspectives going at the same time. At first, back before I met Maharajji, I thought I was making all the decisions. Then I was caught in rejecting the responsibility, and saying, "Maharajji's doing it." Now, more and more, I'm appreciating that it's a both / and situation, and I am living with all the richness of that paradox.

⊚

And so it goes. We try to learn to live with all these complicated, multilayered dimensions of who we truly are. We see the trip we are on, and we see where it's taking us. We see that it's all an inevitable unfolding, and we open ourselves more and more to the process. In the meantime, we are all just lawfully running off our stuff. We are all each other's karma, and it's all the guru's game. It's all God's lila: us and our lives, our melodramas and our sadhanas, it's all just God at play.

Krishna describes the various ways in which the divine manifests in the universe: as that which creates form, as the forms that it has created, and as the essence within each of those forms. Krishna says, "I am also Brahman. I am the formless, timeless, spaceless, beginningless, endless Brahman. In each individual, the spark of that Brahman, the Atman, is me." So Krishna produced each individual; Krishna is each individual; Krishna is within each individual. We are all Krishna. We are all God. And through the experiences of incarnation after incarnation, our souls will shed the veils that separate us from the Beloved.

Slowly, slowly, we begin to appreciate the awesome nature of the design of it all. Just think: All of this—*all* of it!—is a totally preprogrammed trip we are on, a trip that is taking us through this dance of incarnations, through all the myriad roles and forms, all to bring us back to God, back into the One.

Every now and then we get a glimpse behind the scenes, and we see our own lives as stories running their course. All of the choices and decisions and crises: most of the time we're seeing them all as: "What should I do next??!" But then we turn the page—and all of it was already written. It's like a murder mystery, where you are the butler walking toward the pantry on page 42. But you are also the person who is reading the story—and who's read it all before, it seems, so that somehow you already know what's going to happen when the butler reaches the pantry. And finally, when you're ready and when the moment is ripe, you recognize that you are the author as well.

And behind the butler and the reader and the author, behind the Brahman and the prakriti, behind the formless and the forms, behind every polarity and every distinction—I am. Formlessness to form, form to formlessness—all one. *Sub ek*. And in recognizing that dance of the formless and the forms, we recognize the sacredness of every-thing. *Every thing*. So we begin to acknowledge that recognition, and we begin to respect that sacredness: by reinvesting our lives with Spirit; by rediscovering ways of honoring the sacred; by offering our-selves and our incarnations into the fire, as our sacrifice to God. And it all gets lighter and lighter, it all starts to become more and more transparent. We are still *doing* our dance, but our egos are less and less intrusive all the time. We are dancing more lightly. We are learning we can walk without touching the ground.

The Course Syllabus for
The Yogas of the Bhagavad Gita

$\mathcal{I}$n addition to the lectures, this course includes a number of exercises designed to provide experiences which can evolve into a complete <u>sadhana</u> (program for spiritual practices) based upon the *Gita*. The exercises include:

This syllabus is reproduced from the original and contains some variations in typography and usage from the rest of this book.

तस्मा ज्जन्मप्राय

प्रधानोपसर्जनभ

एकप्रघट्टकेनमरणंप्रसा

जन्मकरोनि न्चुजन्मनेनेकेनकर्म

स्मिन्नापुषिते नेवकर्मणाभोगः सं

पोज्जन्यायुभागह्नुत्वात्रिविपाके

कनविकः कर्मोंग्रायाउक्तइति

वपाकारंभीभोगमात्रइत्युक्ता

हेतुत्वान्नीदोष्वन्वह

A. KEEPING A JOURNAL

During this five-week journey, beginning as soon as possible, keep a journal in which you record the insights and experiences that arise from going deeply into the *Gita*. Like the other exercises, writing will be used as a vehicle for becoming more conscious, for becoming an open book. Journals have a way of reminding us that we are constantly changing, that we are constantly changing, that there is no immutable, fixed self. "I seem to be a verb," says Buckminster Fuller in his journal.

The first entry should concern the personalizing for you of Arjuna's predicament as defined in chapter 1. His despair, confusion, inner struggle, depression, loss of savour of experiences, desire to cling to old habits, etc., are to be recognized as part of the journey. What specific anecdotes or immediate states <u>from your own "personal history"</u> can you bring to mind which are a foundation for your empathy with Arjuna's situation.

Subsequent entries will include your reactions to each of the various exercises in the course as well as to points in the text or lectures from which you experience a profound affect. Entries can be as brief or extensive as you wish to make them.

The entries can be in any form, whatever form feels right for the transmission. Some might be in discursive diary form; others might be less linear, more poetic. You may want to include quotes from other beings who are connected to your spiritual growth, or pictures, or anything that fits between the pages. Don't write for an audience or reader. It should should be your honest experience, a record of your own journey through these paths of consciousness, simple comments on what you are seeing about yourself, your world, and your relation to the teachings of the *Gita*.

It is helpful to meditate before writing, to get closer to the source of the Word. If you can clear your mind, if you can create an open space where there is no thinking, no trying, the words will arise spontaneously and you will only have to transfer them to paper.

At the beginning of the fifth week those of you who wish formal course credit will be asked to submit your journal. In general, they will be scanned for the administrative purpose of determining a "pass" or "not pass" for the course. Any sincere journal effort will, of course, get a "pass."

Because of the number of students registered in the course and the time limitations, it will be impossible to read more than a page or two of any journal. If there are one or two specific pages which you wish the staff to read or comment upon—please note and clearly mark the page numbers on the cover. If there are specific pages you do not wish to have read, also clearly make note of these. The journals will be returned to you.

B. CONTEMPLATION

*The characteristic of intellectuals is that they like what they
cannot understand. If they do not understand it they will say,
"Very good, very good." If it is something they can easily
understand, they say, "Nothing new, nothing special."*

In true spiritual work, intellectual achievement *per se* is inadequate.
The mind must carry out its conclusions in the heart, the seat of the
emotions. The emotions, in turn, must effect actual deeds.

Scriptural study can bring to us both exhilaration and humility. The
sublimity of the words of truth will bring delight and inspiration to
our minds and hearts. We will be stimulated to continue our study.
Humility will come as we realize the inherent limitations in the intellect's attempt to fully integrate and understand the Nature of Truth.
The Word may be a taste, but we humbly realize that the "word" is not
the thing. Our minds are continually inspired, humbled and blown as
we advance in our studies.

When we concentrate, we always concentrate on an object produced by our own mind. However, when a person is calm enough and
pure enough, the act of concentration may, as Aldous Huxley says,
merge into "the state of openness and alert passivity in which true
contemplation becomes possible." True contemplation is true prayer,
a state of union with the divine. Contemplation in its lower forms is
discursive thought. <u>Don't get lost in the lower forms.</u>

EXERCISE

Begin this exercise early in the day, preferably after your morning
centering practices. Choose a verse or a portion of a verse from the
Bhagavad Gita which seems particularly meaningful to you right
now, which touches some place inside of you. Read the verse several
times. Try to understand the meaning of the verse with your rational

mind. Now read it again and take the meaning inside. Just sit with it—not using the mind to understand. Take it as deeply within your heart as it wants to go. If you wish, do this last step again. Let the verse take you where it will, but witness the distractions and images that are brought up in your mind along the way.

During the remainder of the day, when you find yourself becoming anxious, speedy, bored, or just in need of centering, remember the *Gita* verse and let it take you inside once more.

If you truly desire freedom, and you understand and believe that living the truth of the *Gita* will actually set you free, you will find that the *Gita* becomes more and more an integral part of your daily actions.

Optimally this exercise with the *Gita* would be done daily during the entire five weeks of the course.

In addition, select from time to time other objects of contemplation, such as:

1. A holy picture (you will find later that any picture can become holy through contemplation).
2. A flower, leaf, rock, tree, etc. Sitting by a stream and contemplating the water is a very powerful exercise.
3. A divine quality such as loving-kindness for all beings, compassion, equanimity, etc.
4. The marketplace as you sit on a bench at a bus stop, etc.
5. Anything else (e.g., relationships, etc.) which brings you to a place of deeper understanding.
6. Time.

The body is always in time, the spirit is always timeless and the psyche is an amphibious creature, compelled by the laws of man's being to associate itself to some extent with its body, but capable, if it so desires, of experiencing and identifying itself with its spirit."

—A. Huxley

Time is what keeps the light from reaching us. There is no greater obstacle to God than time.

—*Eckehart*

Our true future is our own growth in Now, not in the tomorrow of passing time.

—*Nicoll*

In order to open the doors to a feeling of what time is and how our lives function in relationship to it, it is useful to experiment with the following:

EXERCISE

Do each of the following for 10 minutes, one after another:

1. Watch your breath—follow it as it enters the body and as it leaves.
2. Eat your favorite food.
3. Watch TV or listen to the radio with your eyes closed.
4. Sit around and do nothing.

Notice how your perception of time changes in each activity.

EXERCISE

Sit quietly for 20 minutes. Divide a page of your journal into two columns: <u>Past</u> and <u>Future.</u> List simply your thoughts under the headings. Reflect on how much of your thought comes under these two categories.

EXERCISE

Conceive of a world of only two dimensions—all surface (length and breadth), but with a small extension into the third dimension (thickness), like a piece of paper. Imagine beings living in this paper world, cognizant of nothing else but their world and what lies in it. Now if a pencil is pushed through the paper, they would know only a cross section of the pencil because that would be all of the pencil in their world.

Envision our relationship with time as limited in the same way. For us, the pencil exists in its entirety—the beginning and the end. For them, only the cross section in the paper exists. The cross section in their world corresponds to the measure of time called "present moment." What the paper beings knew with their two-dimensional senses, we would know to be only relatively real—only a part of the pencil. Reflect on the possibility that our sense of "passing time" may also be only relatively real.

If one of us could descend into the paper world, learn the two-dimensional views and habits of thought, and explain that this world is only a limited expression of an infinitely larger and different world, what would they say? Examine your views of time in this light.

In your journal keep a list of the objects of contemplation you work with and diary notes if you wish. If you are not able to "grok" or fully incorporate one or more of them initially, perhaps you will want to work with them again later.

C. MEDITATION

The quieting of the mind is perhaps the single most important foundation for all other yogic practices. Naropa has provided meditation halls for us. If you are not in the habit of meditating regularly, it would be useful for you to attend a regular sitting each day at one of these halls. The presence of other meditators and a meditation master helps. Later, as you prefer, you can meditate in any quiet place where you will not be disturbed during the period of practice.

Each week throughout the course, during a lecture period, a meditation teacher of Satipatthana Vipassana from the Theravadin Buddhist tradition will introduce one of a series of formal meditation exercises. He and other members of the staff will be available during office hours to advise you about any difficulties you may encounter.

If you are already an adept in another form of meditation, or are simultaneously receiving meditation instructions in another course at Naropa, feel free to pursue these other practices if you prefer.

D. THE WITNESS

"Suddenly I remembered that I had forgotten to remember myself!"

—*Ouspensky*

The method of developing the witness is useful practice on the path although <u>it must be eventually left behind with other methods.</u> The blossom must go as the fruit will grow. It is a voluntary creation of the intellect, a place of detached watching of phenomenal activity, where no judging or comparing takes place. ("If you wish to see the truth / then hold no opinions for or against anything.") Just see what is. The witness dwells in the cool space between the heat of one's imagined self and one's projections. It is an aspect of ego used to extricate yourself from unconscious attachments to other aspects of ego.

Moments of consciousness are brief compared to the vast intervals of unconscious, mechanical, conditioned ways of being. We are continuously losing the thread of attention, seeing who we are, losing it again, finding it again, being pulled this way and that by the forces around us.

The witness, however, does not come into existence by desire or decision alone. It must be developed by specific techniques and exercises. Certain meditation practices of mindfulness may be used as well as exercises that take us out of our normal patterns. Many of the exercises in this course will allow us to observe our beings through new lenses. Special mindfulness meditations will also be taught during the course to help in establishing the witness.

Situations that take us out of our normal patterns often allow us to observe our workings more clearly. Time of silence and fasting are examples of this. Yet all our daily actions are available to the witness, particularly if we slow them down enough to see the precise quality inherent in them. Opening a door, eating a salad, washing a dish—all are potential exercises in mindfulness. Any of our usually "thrown away" actions can have the clarity of the tea ceremony.

The witness is not evaluative. It does not judge your actions. It merely notes them. Thus, if you perform an act because of desire, such as eating something that is not helpful to your sadhana, and then you put yourself down for having eaten it . . . the witness—when it finally appears—would merely note: (a) he is eating such-and-such, and (b) he is putting himself down for eating such-and-such. Thus the witness has noted a "you" of desires and a super-ego you . . . two "you's."

This point is important. Most of the time the inner voices of most people are continually evaluative. "I'm good for doing this" or "I'm bad for doing that." You must make that evaluative role an object of contemplation as well. Keep in mind that the witness does not care whether you become enlightened or not. It merely notes how it all is.

Appearance of the Witness

At first the witness is adopted because of an intellectual understanding of the need to separate the Self from the Doer. You probably remember your witness only now and then, when you are in a calm dispassionate state of mind. The moment you get distracted you lose the witness. Later you "come to" and remember that you forgot.

For example, you are walking down a street witnessing yourself walking down a street. You feel happy and witness feeling happy . . . and so it goes. Then you meet someone or see something that irritates you. Immediately you get irritated and forget all about the witness. The adrenaline pumps through you and you think angry thoughts. At this point "angry me" is who you are. Only <u>much</u> later do you remember that you were attempting to witness.

At that point you promise yourself that you won't forget again. Ah, how little you know about the subtleties of the seductions of the other "you's." Again you are walking and again witnessing walking and so forth. This time you meet with another situation which irritates you. Again you lose your witness (or <u>center</u> as it is called sometimes) and again your endocrine glands secrete and you think angry thoughts. But this time right in the middle of the entire drama you "wake up" . . . that is, you realize your predicament. But at this point it is difficult to get free of the angry you because you are already getting much gratification. (It's like trying to stop in the midst of a sexual act.) And so you use some rationalization such as "I know I should be witnessing but after all he deserves to be punished" and with that you climb back into the "angry you" role with a certain amount of self-righteousness. And so it goes through thousands of such experiences.

After a time (however long is necessary) you notice that although you still lose the witness (fall asleep) as often as before, you are starting to "remember" sooner. That is, you are getting to the point where the actual falling asleep is starting to "wake" you. This is a big step forward.

Again, after some time, it all gets much more subtle. Now you are walking down the street and again you witness it all . . . and again an "irritant" presents itself. This time—as you are about to get angry—the witness says, "Ah, about to get angry, I see." This often short-circuits the energy the "angry you" was fueling up with, and it falls away. So now the lapse between being awake and being asleep is getting much smaller. Simultaneously, you begin to note that you don't fall asleep (i.e., fall out of the witness) nearly as often. Throughout the day you are remaining centered in the witness watching the drama of life unfold.

Later, when you are established in the witness, it will begin to disappear as a conscious stance and you will be left with a feeling of spacious, timeless presence surrounding each act.

E. GIVING AND RECEIVING

"Neither give nor receive."

—*Patanjali*

"Not as the world gives do I give."

—*Jesus*

"Saints and birds don't collect."

—*Neem Karoli Baba*

True giving and receiving are just part of the energy flow of the constantly changing universe in which we are all one and everything belongs to all of us . . . all the food and all the books and all the houses and cars and clothes and all the energy of the universe. Maharajji, who owned nothing but a blanket, and he periodically gave that away, said, "Why give me money? All the money in the universe is mine." (Then he laughed.) We all share in it—it belongs to all of us and none of us. "Neither give nor receive," warned Patanjali. Don't be a giver or a receiver, just a void channel for the ever-changing energy. True giving is dwelling in a state of spontaneous compassion, dwelling in the open heartspace. True receiving is the same. From that space you perceive a need in someone and you fill it if you can. No ego motives. Pure action.

That's one level. At another level, most of us own things and desire to own more things. When we give, there is usually some feeling that "This is mine. I'm giving it to you, then it will be yours. And you should thank me and think that I am a generous person and love me a little more than if I hadn't given it to you." Often our gifts are Greek horses in Troy—they are filled with soldiers of the mind. They are given to fulfill our desires for power over others.

In Hindi there is no commonly used word for "Thank you." One rarely hears it expressed. The Indian tradition holds that giving is part of doing your <u>dharma</u>. One gives what is appropriate and pre-scribed for him to give and "why should I be thanked for doing what is my duty?"

Most of our giving and receiving habits are based on the ego-created sense of separateness. They keep us from experiencing true giving and receiving, which is simply dwelling in the heartspace, the center, and letting the energy flow through. When we are being still within that space, compassion—unconditioned love—arises sponta-neously. For many of us, the most direct path to the center is medi-tation. When you're there, you know openness. You know you are not the doer, the giver, the receiver.

To work with these exercises is to try to give and receive from within that consciousness and to witness yourself doing it. Choose two of the following exercises—one that seems difficult to you (it will show you where you're deeply attached) and one that seems easy (it will allow you to be more gentle with yourself, go more slowly, spend more time witnessing your attachment). After doing each of the exercises, write about it in your journal.

GIVING EXERCISES

1. Give away fruit on the street. Take enough to last a few hours so that you'll experience a wide range of responses from peo-ple. Offer it to passersby. You might try doing it at two loca-tions: one where many people are hungry (industrial and campus lunchtime) and then one where they're probably not (middle-class shopping area in mid-afternoon). Watch the dif-ference in your inner and outer behavior in the two places. Don't be attached to the fruits.
2. Give away some of your possessions.
3. Give away something you don't care about and then give away something that is precious to you.
4. Give something to someone you like and then something to someone you don't know or are not quite straight with.
5. Give two gifts—buy one and make the other.

6. Give something to your parents or your children.

7. Give away money anonymously.

8. Give fruit or sweets at an institution—a mental hospital or orphanage or old-age home.

9. Give something to a child and then something to an adult.

10. Give time. Offer an hour or a day in service to a friend or institution.

11. Give it all away! (Except for your journal.) Because the administrators of the course have not done this particular exercise, we are offering it as useful based on hearsay.

RECEIVING EXERCISES

1. For one day eat only what is offered to you by others. (Don't tell anyone what you are doing until the day is over.) Many yogis in India practice this tapasya. It helps you realize that you are not the Prime Doer and awakens you to the level at which it is being done for you.

2. Reflect on recent things that have been given to you and your reactions to these gifts.

"Satisfied with whatever comes unasked . . . even acting he is not bound."

—Gita 4,22

"Tukaram, a saint in India and a poor man, was once given ten sticks of sugarcane as a gift. On his way home, he gave away nine of the sticks to beggars, saving one for himself. When he arrived home and told his wife, she beat him with the remaining stick."

—Story told by Maharajji

F. SILENCE

"The whole world is tormented by words
And there is no one who does without words.
But only insofar as one is free from words
Does one really understand words."
                              —Saraha (early Tantric Buddhist)

Select a day when you can arrange to go deeply into silence. Choose a time with the least obligation for speaking, having previously taken care of business matters and concerns for physical maintenance. It is probably best to tell your friends about the exercise so they will understand. Don't speak to anyone during the day, though at least part of the day should be spent among people. Use brief written notes when necessary. Be compassionate in your silence; don't make other people uptight in your presence. If you are becoming too fierce in your resolve, and your living situation is becoming awkward or uncomfortable, stop and wait for a day when you can handle it better.

This day of silence is part of the continuing exercise of developing the witness and its reflection in your journal. Silence gives us the space to listen to the many voices we are. Journal entries might include some of this inner dialogue as well as other teachings of the silence, such as an awareness of how others around you use conversation.

When the impulse to speak arises, this energy might be channeled into a spiritual affirmation or mantra, the Prayer of the Heart, the Triple Refuge, or whatever method is right for you.

Sometime during the day, reserve at least one hour for the silence of body, speech, and mind. Find a comfortable position for the body, keeping the spine erect, and determine to sit for an hour <u>without moving at all</u>. At the same time, practice the silence of the mind through meditation or prayer. ("The inner silence is self-surrender— living without the sense of ego."—Ramana Maharshi) You will already be practicing the silence of speech. These three silences—of body, speech, and mind—are known as the Noble Silence.

Some inspirational words on the unspoken:

"I realized in this place that people feared silence more than anything else, that our tendency to talk arises from self-defense and is always based upon a reluctance to see something, a reluctance to confess something to oneself.

Directly a person is quiet himself, that is, awakes a little, he hears the different intonations and begins to distinguish other people's lies."

—*Ouspensky*

"Quietness is master of the deed."

—*Tao Te Ching*

"My life is a listening—
His is a speaking.
My salvation is to hear and respond.
For this, my life must be silent.
Hence my silence is my salvation."

—*Thomas Merton*

"Silence provides economy of psychic energy and increased power of concentration."
—*Meher Baba (silent for the last 40 years of his life)*

"Silence is the language of God—
It is also the language of the heart."

—*Swami Sivananda*

"Be still and know that I am God."

—Psalm XLVI

"Silence is the mother of truth."

—Thomas Merton

"Only that which can be expressed in words is being said."

—Ananda Mai Ma

G. TAPASYA

"When in recollection he withdraws all his senses from the attractions of the pleasures of sense, even as a tortoise withdraws all its limbs, then his is a serene wisdom."
—*Bhagavad Gita, 4—58*

Tapasya or religious austerity is the most direct way of dealing with attachment. Fasting, silence, and sexual continence are widely practiced tapasyas.

Fasting as a spiritual practice not only cleanses your body, but alters your consciousness just enough to allow you to hear the inner voices a little more clearly than usual. Fasting also gives those voices something to struggle with. If you can dwell in the witness place, you'll be able to hear arguments from the grossest to the most subtle.

Try jumping into the fire. Completely stop eating for a prescribed period of time. This gives you the space in which to witness the desire (probably over and over again)—space in which to see that you are not the desire; space in which to see how the desire rises and then falls away. And from this inner struggle comes the fire which will eventually consume your impurities.

Resolve firmly to fast for a full day (24 hours). You might make the resolve just before sleep or just after your morning meditation, when you'll hear it in the deeper places. Then, in the middle of the morning, when one of the many voices of the ego announces, "Tomorrow would really be better—I have so much to do today," or "Small bites don't count," you can refer that voice to your resolve and get on with the business of fasting.

Decide before you begin whether you will take juices, or fruit, or just water during the day. Some say the purest fast is to take just water; Maharajji said, "Always take a little something." Whatever you do, it is important to take plenty of liquids (water, unsweetened herbal tea, etc.) to prevent dehydration. If you have to decide during the day what you will take, you may become confused about whether you are really keeping the fast. The simplest practices are best—decide on the rules for the day and then just remind yourself every time you are tempted. "Pleasures of the senses, but not desires, disappear from the austere soul." *Gita,* 4–59

It is best to do this fast on a relatively quiet day—if you're concentrated on busy-ness all day, you may not even realize that you are fasting—you'll be aware only of a gnawing hunger. You should try to stay quiet enough to hear the workings of the ego.

Austerities are an act of will and will can be used to strengthen the ego as well as to subjugate it. Be aware of any spiritual pride, self-pity, or feelings of competition that may develop. But if you undertake this exercise as an offering to the one Divine Being, there will be little room for these ego manifestations to arise.

Make your journal entries either during the fast or just when it is over. Such insights are elusive.

Re-enter the food realm gently, respectfully. "From food creatures come into being." Take juice or fruit as your first meal and be careful not to overeat the day after your fast—your digestive system may not be able to handle it. Continue to witness your relation to food. Watch to see how not eating has made the habits of eating a little more conscious.

> *"Offer unto Me that which is very dear to thee—*
> *which thou holdest most covetable.*
> *Infinite are the results of such an offering."*
> —Srimad Bhagavatam

H. HATHA YOGA ASANAS AND PRANAYAM

During the course it would be useful for you to become tuned to your body as the temple in which you dwell; as the most immediate environment in which you reside. An unhealthy or tense body can be a major impediment to one's effort to open one's heart and concentrate one's mind. While it is true that the changing of mental and emotional tendencies will in itself cool out and harmonize your body, conversely, purifying of the physical will help in harmonizing the mind and heart.

The traditional Hindu method for tuning, calming, and vitalizing the body is Hatha Yoga, which involves consciously assuming a set of meditative postures or "asanas" and controlling the breath (pranayam). Certain of the asanas, in addition, are primarily concerned with liberating or transmuting energy from one form to another or from one part of the body to another, and with purification of the blood and "nadis" (spiritual nerves).

Intensive hatha yoga practiced for five weeks would rather dramatically change:

1. Your ability to sit quietly in meditation without being preoccupied with your body.
2. Your desires with regard to certain foods, tobacco, drugs, by sensitizing you to your subtle body reactions.
3. Your general body tone and sense of well being.

However, even twenty minutes a day would be a useful start.

Many of you already know a set of asanas and pranayamic exercies. For those of you who do not and wish to receive an instruction manual and guidance, please see one of the teaching fellows.

Here we offer one composite exercise known as Soorya Namaskaram—the Sun Worship. It should be done four to six times on a level space in a quiet place. Clothing should be light and flexible. It should not be done within two hours after eating.

EXERCISE
Soorya Namaskaram: The Sun Worship

Traditionally this is done early in the morning, facing the sun, with an attitude of worship. It is a good way to begin any asana session.

Exhale 1) Stand erect with palms touching opposite the middle of chest, fingers upward.

Inhale 2) Raise arms over head, locking thumbs. Bend backward, looking up, with feet firmly planted.

Exhale 3) Bend forward, separate hands, keeping the knees straight, but not locked; keeping head between arms, placing palms flat on the floor if possible.

Inhale 4) Stretch the left leg back, bringing the left knee to the floor. The right foot remains between the hands. Look up and back. Stretch and curve spine.

Exhale 5) The right leg is brought back to meet the left foot. The body is forming an arch.

Inhale 6) Bring your knees to the floor, then the chest and chin, in a flowing motion. The palms should be beneath the shoulders.

Hold breath 7) Lower the pelvis and stretch up the head, neck, and chest, looking up and back.

Exhale 8) Bring the head between the arms, raising the body once again to an arch.

Inhale 9) Thrust the left leg forward between the hands, with the left knee touching the chin. Look up.

Exhale 10) Bring the right leg forward, straighten out the knees. Return to position 3.

Inhale 11) Stretch up and back into position 7.

Exhale 12) Bring arms down, palms together, as in position 1.

Note: To quiet a restless mind, do slowly. To bring alertness to a dull mind, do rapidly.

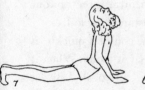

Sun Salutation: This was an illustration from the original
Course Syllabus. It shows the twelve poses of Soorya Namaskaram,
the sequence of yoga postures known as the Salutation to the Sun.

I. JAPA YOGA

The "Word" is one of the most powerful devices for transforming your perceptions of daily life experiences. Repeating a word or phrase which is associated with your ever-deepening spiritual awareness can become a moment-to-moment way of "remembering." Repetition of the name, such as RAM and KRISHNA, which have come to represent the various aspects of God, work in this way. Or a mantra such as the Tibetan OM MANI PADMA HUM, which reminds us of the jewel on the lotus which is manifest in our heart, is used in a similar fashion.

To help keep your mantric word or phrase going, it is often useful to work with a kinesthetic reminder such as beads (called a <u>mala</u> or rosary). We will provide you with a small mala which you can use for this purpose.

In beginning to work with mantra it is advisable to set aside an extensive period of time for doing <u>only</u> the mantra: three or four hours at least, preferably longer. This is the investment period.

Then, each morning, as you start to awaken, come as quickly as you can "remember" into the mantra. At first, say it aloud. When it feels right, let the mantric repetition become sub-vocal. Later it becomes mental and finally continues to sound only in your heart. If the mental repetition falls away and all that is left is the feeling, just keep "listening" to this feeling of the mantra.

During the remainder of the day keep the mantra going as much as possible. If the mantra is on your lips but not in your heart, don't worry. The sound itself will eventually find its way to the cave of your heart if you persist.

Co-ordinate the mantra with your steps as you walk. Realize the vibration of the mantra in each person you meet, even their (and your own) impurities. Notice that when your mind is calm, the mantra is as delicate and subtle as you will allow; when you are floundering, the mantra is also there, as strong and as gross as you need. Notice which desires, which situations, separate you from the mantra. And then gently come back to it. No blame.

One of the most beautiful stories of the use of mantra is *The Way of the Pilgrim,* translated by R. M. French. In this tale, a simple man transforms his life, and the lives of those around him, through the use of "the Jesus prayer."

> "I go about now and ceaselessly repeat the prayer of Jesus, which is more precious and sweet to me than anything in the world. At times I do as much as forty-three or -four miles a day and do not feel that I am walking at all. I am aware only of the fact that I am saying my prayer. When the bitter cold pierces me, I begin to say my prayer more earnestly, and I quickly get warm all over . . . and doing this I am filled with joy. God knows what is happening to me."

> *"The power and the effect of a mantra depend on the spiritual attitude, the knowledge and the responsiveness of the individual. The <u>sabda</u> or sound of the mantra is not a physical sound (though it may be accompanied by such a one), but a spiritual one. It cannot be heard by the ears but only by the heart."*
>
> *—Lama Govinda*

> *"Place the name of RAMA as a jeweled lamp at the door of your lips and there will be light, as you will, both inside and out."*
>
> *—Tulsi Das*

J. GOING TO CHURCH OR TEMPLE

"If even two come together in my name, I am there."

—*Jesus*

"He who worships me comes to me."

—*Krishna*

"Christ and Krishna are one."

—*Maharajji*

The yoga of worship is America's chosen path. Much American energy has gone into institutionalizing worship as a path. In most cities there are dozens of temples and churches. To most people in America, spiritual paths other than church worship (such as meditation, renunciation, contemplation, and service) seem alien. Unfortunately, often the church rituals have lost much of the spiritual powers with which they were initially invested.

So many people came to church to "get something" that many churches have little spirit remaining. Yet the rituals often were designed "in the Spirit" and need only a re-investment or re-consecration in order to once again become forms for sharing the Light.

By attending church with the devotional stance of the *Gita,* which can allow you to see the living Spirit in existing rituals, you can participate in this process of re-investing the Spirit. Through the interaction of the devotional heart you bring and the form of the service, you will realize again the Living God.

As our witness develops, we can begin to strip away the many veils between us and the place where we really dwell with the divine energy.

EXERCISE

Go to two different churches or temples. Do it on the same or different days. First attend a service at a place of worship different from the one you were raised in, then go to the one you went to as a child (if you did). Participate as fully as you can in the service, finding a shared space while at the same time maintaining a witness. Watch the ways you hold back from participating, the ways you judge the congregation and the clergy, and so on. Open your heart to the prayers, hymns, fellow beings, images, sense of Presence.

This experience allows you to share an intimate space with beings you probably are otherwise unlikely to be with. Witness the ways in which this special context changes your perceptions (projections) of the other participants (fellow pilgrims on the path) and allows a sense of either communion or separation to manifest. See if the form of structured worship allows you to surrender to the Divine—through prayer or singing or merely being in the presence of group worship. Enter whatever you learn from the experience in your journal.

K. KIRTAN

Kirtan is the chanting of the names of God—a devotional yogic technique which has the power to purify and open our hearts. Just as devotion has many levels, kirtan can be done from any state of mind or level of evolution and it will lead to deeper levels of opening and understanding.

Kirtan uses music as a vehicle of communication, but is not concerned with musical ability. Singing beautifully is not important; what is important is singing from the heart. In devotional singing in India, many times it was the old man who sang last, with no teeth, raspy broken voice, and hacking cough, who would totally blow everyone out because he knew what and to whom he was singing, and the beauty of this communication with God was moving and powerful.

To practice kirtan, the instruction is always to do it in a disinterested spirit. Give up wanting to "get off" and give up a judgmental, evaluating attitude. Go into it with an open mind, allowing yourself to make the effort necessary to experience the way in which this method works. It isn't necessary to be "feeling devotional" to sing kirtan; let thoughts and moods pass through making space for new things to come from within. If you're blissful, be blissful and singing; if bored, be bored and singing. Just keep offering it all into the fire of the name. The more you can give up, the more your attention will orbit around the mantra.

If someone is leading the chanting (call and response), listening is as important as singing and will help keep the monkey-mind from wandering.

During the night from about 9:30 p.m. of July 3rd until 8:00 a.m. of July 4th, we will share a traditional Hindu "yagya" (fire ceremony) and the singing of a chant.

For the all-night chant, bring a blanket or pillow to sit or sleep on. If you need to nap, do it right there—you may find yourself dreaming the mantra. It's an informal experience of sharing space for the night, so bring whatever you need to keep the physical plane together (juice to drink, etc.), but keep it simple.

The deeper you go, the less you know, the more you are. You may wonder at times whether you're chanting the mantra or the mantra is chanting you. Or you may find that you've stepped back far enough so that while you are chanting, the whole process and all thoughts are being witnessed from a deep calm space within, and that with each repetition of the mantra this place gets deeper and more "here."

<u>Kirtan</u> is a devotional yogic technique. For the lovers of God, the very sound of His name brings joy. It's said that "in its highest aspect, divine love is nothing less than the immortal bliss of liberation."

> *"Taking the name of God, dive deep, O mind*
> *Into the heart's fathomless depths,*
> *Where many precious gems (of love) lie hid.*
> *Never believe that the bed of the ocean is bare,*
> *If in the first few dives, you fail.*
> *With firm resolve and self control*
> *Dive deep and make your way into God's realm."*
>
> —*Ramakrishna*

> *"God is not different from His name."*
>
> —*Old saying*

> *"When hearing the name once, you shed tears and your hair stands on end, then you may know for certain that you do not have to perform devotional rituals any more. It will be enough just to repeat the name."*
>
> —*Ramakrishna*

> *"However huge may be the stock of our accumulated sins, the whole of it gets burnt as fuel, is burnt by fire, as soon as the name of God is uttered with a sincere heart."*
>
> —*H. P. Poddar*

L. SATSANG COLLABORATION

Sharing your inner work with another person who is also on the path can be useful: helping each other. There are many ways in which such a collaborative contract to become conscious through one another can be carried out.

EXERCISE

One possibility is to silently sit opposite one another about two feet apart.

Focus on the point between the eyes of the other individual so that you can see both eyes and the face. Relax. Sit this way for a half hour. During this period, or at separate sessions, you can:

1. Study the other person as a being in an incarnation.
2. Be aware of being studied and reflect on who you may be appearing to be in the eyes of the other person. Notice your feelings at being studied and where judgment creeps in.
3. Let your models of who the other person is keep changing. Each one you fix on, notice, and then let it go.
4. Don't dwell on any particular thoughts, images, or sensations (positive or negative). Just allow flow.
5. Look for the deeper places in yourself and the other person behind body and personality where you can meet.
6. Just sit focusing on the point between the eyes.

Note the experiences in your journal. In order that your mind be free to range unhampered by social anxiety, agree in advance not to share what you see in each other. It is all right to share what you experienced in yourself if you choose.

EXERCISE

Another possibility would be to hang out with another person for several hours taking turns in the role of a witness-reporter who is attempting to dispassionately study nature in the form of the processes of the "other." As the witness, remain quiet inside and just notice how another being works. As the one witnessed, experience your life as it is appearing to a dispassionate observer. Avoid judgments.

Keep a note of the experience in your journal.

M. PUJA TABLE

In developing an inner Center, a meditative stance, or connecting with your heart cave, it is most useful to create an external quiet space where you can hook up for refueling.

When setting up the puja table, choose a quiet place, a place that can be a refuge. You come home feeling speedy, you're angry at someone—whatever—sit down in front of the puja table and Remember.

Typically, pictures of holy beings, statues, flowers, fruit, beautiful stones or shells, or things which you associate with the highest place in yourself, are put on a puja table. Here you may worship God with form in any way that opens your heart. You can sing, meditate, offer food, perform ritualistic worship with bells, candles and mantras, incense, or you may just want to hang out in the space that you and the puja table create together.

You may want only one picture on the table. Buddha, say, is your connection, your refuge, and one statue or picture of Buddha is all you want or need on the altar. Or there may be many manifestations of the One that brings you to that place.

A puja table is a good place to do conscious work on yourself as well as a place to worship. For example, you feel great love for Christ and His picture is there, right in the middle. But Shiva is an energy that you would rather not think about—too fierce. Put His picture or a symbolic Shiva lingam (or a picture of someone with whom you have real difficulty being conscious) next to the picture of Christ. In the supportive, quiet atmosphere you are in while in front of your puja table, your relationship with Shiva can be more deeply established and the relationship between and the identity of Christ and Shiva can be realized. Possibly you're preoccupied with sex. Then work with a picture of Mary the Mother of Christ or of Anandamayi Ma and perhaps a pornographic photo, too (if you are a male this time around), and later in the day try to feel the divine essence in all women that you meet. Perhaps putting a picture of your parents right between Christ and Buddha would be meaningful work for you right now.

The statue of Buddha is not just a symbol of Buddha, it is Buddha. The picture of Lord Rama is not just a piece of paper, but a manifestation of the true spirit of Rama. Realize this and later wherever you are becomes your puja table, a place to open your heart and feel the presence of the One Supreme Being.

> *"Not by the Vedas, or an austere life, or gifts to the poor or ritual offerings can I be seen as thou hast seen me. Only by love can men see me, and know me, and come to me."*
> —Bhagavad Gita XI, 53, 54

N. KARMA YOGA

"Do whatever you do, but consecrate the fruit
of your actions to me."

—Krishna in the Gita

"He who sees the inaction that is in action,
and the action that is in inaction, is wise
indeed. Even when he is engaged in action he
remains poised in the tranquility of the Atman."

—Gita

Actions done as a sacrifice or offering or in a disinterested fashion are the central component of the *Bhagavad Gita*. We consider this yoga at length in the lectures.

In order to experience the process of this yoga, you will have to look around you for opportunities to serve as an offering to God. Of course, ultimately you will experience every act (including the taking of this course) as an exercise in karma yoga. However, until you become familiar with the stance of a karma yogi, it would be well to carry out some specific exercises. Try to do at least one specific karma yogic exercise a week during the duration of the course. By keeping notes in your journal you will be able to see changes in your approach and appreciation of the subtlety of this method in even the short time we are together.

EXERCISE

(possible examples)

1. Clean litter from the highways surrounding Boulder.
2. Volunteer at local hospitals and/or old age homes (Boulder or Denver) by offering to help and hanging out with the patients. Perhaps read to the blind or elderly.
3. Get involved in some local volunteer organization for a day (recycling center, child care).

Try to choose a project where you don't immediately fall into your old role as the doer, i.e., do something that is not usually part of your daily activities. If you are primarily an intellectual person and choose a project which is manual in nature, it will probably be easier to remember to keep remembering to offer your actions.

Also take a few activities you regularly do each day and attempt to do them in the spirit of karma yoga. Choose one activity you usually "enjoy" and another which you usually "dislike." Notice the relation of the karma yogic stance to these emotional concomitants of the action.

The Supplemental Syllabus

तस्मा ...जन्मप्राय
प्रधानोपसर्जनभ
एकमध्यह्रकेनमरणंप्रसा
जन्मवकरोनि तच्जन्मनेनेकेनकर्मो
स्मिन्नापुबिनेनेवकर्मणाभोगः संप
तापोजन्मायुभोगइेतुस्त्रात्रिविपाको
एकभविकः कर्मोग्रामाउक्तइति
विपाकारंभीभोगमात्रइेतुत्ात्
हेतुस्त्रात्रं दोष्वननङ्

A. VIPASSANA MEDITATION

Being with the universe, just the way it is. Sounds, sensations in the body, just allowing each sensation to be, to be just the way it is. Sometimes the awareness is drawn to the sound of a bird, sometimes to coldness in the body, sometimes to pain, and other times to thought. Just notice your awareness skipping from sensation to sensation, from thought to thought. If you experience discomfort, just move your body very gently, noticing the intention to move, and then the moving.

Notice that the awareness is like a flashlight, and the beam focuses now in one place, now in another. Sometimes it's focused on a sensation on the surface of the body, and other times on a fleeting memory or a plan. At other times it's drawn to a sound, when the beam focuses on the sound. Each thought and sensation arises and draws your awareness to it, and then soon your awareness passes on to something else.

Let the awareness move—from thing to thing to thing. Notice that the sensation of a moment ago is now gone. The thought you might have been having two minutes ago—where is it now? The awareness has gone on to something else.

Now one of the processes in meditation is concentration, which means, very simply, bringing that flashlight beam of awareness to one point, and letting it rest on that one point; and each time it moves away from the point, very gently bringing it back again. We're able to use most any point for concentration; sometimes it's a candle flame, or a point on the forehead. In this case, we'll use one of the traditional points of focus: the breath. But the whole breath would be too much to follow, so you pick a very tiny component, a small sensation that goes along with each breath. There are two places where you can do that. The first is to focus at the tip of the nose, just inside the nostril. You will notice that with each in-breath, there is

This meditation is transcribed from Ram Dass's audiotape "Vipassana Meditation." It is an example of a session of concentration meditation, in which the attention is focused on a primary object, in this case the breath.

the feeling of air against the inside of the tip of the nostril, and that with each out-breath there is again the feeling of air passing by the inside of the nostril. So you can focus at that point, and with each in-breath, notice it as "breathing in," and with each out-breath, notice it as "breathing out."

The alternative point of focus is in the abdomen; within the abdomen is a muscle, which you can feel rising with each in-breath and falling with each out-breath. As it rises, you note "rising," and as it falls, you note "falling." After you've experimented for a few moments with these two options, pick one of them, and for the remainder of this meditation, stay with that particular choice—either the "breathing in / breathing out" at the tip of the nostril, or the "rising / falling" in the abdomen.

This point is now called your primary object. It becomes like the center of a flower: you let your awareness rest in the center, at the tip of the nose or in the abdomen; and each time your mind, your awareness, is drawn away from the primary object—to a thought or to a sensation—notice that it has been drawn away, and very gently return your awareness to the primary object.

Meditation is a very sweet art. You'll find the primary object becomes like a home, like a cave, and after a while you are content just to stay with the breath, and give the awareness a rest from all of its wandering and jumping, here and there.

It helps in the early stages to silently note "breathing in" and "breathing out," or silently note "rising" and "falling." Each time the awareness moves away, as soon as you notice it, in a very soft and gentle way draw it back to the rising / falling or to the breathing in / breathing out.

If you're just beginning in meditation, you will notice how resistant the mind is to staying on one point. It's had years of freedom to roam here and there. It's a very slow and patient process, to train the awareness to stay with the primary object. You must be very gentle with yourself.

If your awareness is drawn away by pain, note "pain," and then return to the primary object. If the pain persists, then you may want to make the pain itself your primary object, and just notice the pain as precisely as you can. To keep the mind from wandering, keep it right with the pain. When the pain dissolves, then you turn once again to the breath.

If you experience sleepiness, you may want to take a few intentional deep breaths, noticing them very attentively as "rising / falling" or as "breathing in / breathing out," and then let the breath return once again to its natural rhythm.

Thoughts that arise about the meditation or about your ability to do the meditation are just judgments, just thoughts that are drawing your awareness away; note them, and then once again return to the "breathing in, breathing out" or to the "rising, falling."

Examine the breath at your point of choice very precisely. In the "breathing in" or in the "rising," note the beginning, the middle, and the end of it. Note the space after the in-breath, before the out-breath begins. Then in the "breathing out" or in the "falling," note the entire exhalation—the beginning, the middle, and the end of it. Notice the space between the exhalation and the next inhalation.

During these few minutes of meditation, you have no other business than just to stay with the breath. You're free not to have to plan, or to remember, or to collect sensations. Just come home to the breath. Sounds, sensations, thoughts—each like a flower petal that draws your awareness away from the center. Notice it, and return again to the center.

<hr>

At the conclusion of each meditation, it's good to take whatever quietness you have achieved, and allow that opening to make you a conduit, to bring messages of peace and light out into the universe. You may want to offer this "Metta Meditation," or blessing, to do that:

> *May all beings be free from danger*
> *May all beings be free from mental suffering*
> *May all beings be free from physical suffering*
> *May all beings know peace.*
> *Om*

B. MINDFULNESS MEDITATION ON FOOD

by Joseph Goldstein

One way to stay grounded on the experiential level rather than on the thought or conceptual level is to develop a very strong mindfulness of all the processes involved in eating. A lot is revealed about our own minds and bodies when we learn to eat with awareness, to eat mindfully. First, we begin to see that point at which desire arises. We then become mindful of desire and our subsequent actions. As we observe the processes involved, there can be a deep and penetrating insight into the fact that it is all impersonal phenomena happening. There is no self, or I, or me, or mine in the food, there is no self or I in the eating of it, or in the awareness of the eating. It is all an empty, impersonal process going on.

Eating meditatively is a profound practice, in that one can attain high states of samadhi and even enlightenment in the very process of eating. There have been many cases, in meditation centers or where people are practicing to a very high degree, where in the very process of lifting the hand, someone may go into samadhi, and their hand just stays there, halfway to their mouths, for as long as they stay in samadhi. Or they may experience the moment of nirvana while eating, experiencing a moment of enlightenment. It's a very good practice to cultivate.

What we're going to do now is to learn how to observe eating with a silent mind, to experience all the different mental and physical processes involved. For this exercise, you might use a few raisins. The first thing that happens is the intention to look at the food. So that intention should be noted: "intending," "intending." Then the head turns, so that it can see the food. The turning of the head should be done mindfully, noting the whole process that's involved: "turning," "turning," "turning."

As a result of the turning of the head, the color of the food, comes into contact with the eye, and seeing-consciousness arises. There should be a mental note, a state of mindfulness with regard to the fact that we are seeing: "seeing," "seeing." Notice that all the eye sees is color—the eye does not see "food." Food is a concept. In this practice of mindfulness we want to stay on the *experiential* level of the process. So we note "seeing," "seeing."

Because of seeing, the intention arises to move the hand to take the food. The noting of the mental intention before the act should be done carefully: "intending," "intending." Then the movement of the hand should be done mindfully: "moving," "moving." Just experience the sensations of movement—no "arm," which is a concept, no I, no self, no me, no mine. There is simply the impersonal, material process of moving, and the process of knowing the movement, all done very meditatively, very mindfully. "Moving," "moving."

Then there is touching of the food. The experience of the touch sensation. The intention to lift the arm—the mental intention—should be noted before the movement is begun: "intending," "intending." That mental intention becomes the cause of the arm being raised. The cause and effect relationship should be seen very clearly.

Then "raising," "raising"—experience the whole movement of the arm. No I, no me, no mine, no self, simply movement and the awareness of movement. The arm is brought up. Intention to open the mouth: "intending," "intending." Opening of the mouth: "opening," "opening." Very aware, very mindful of all the physical processes involved, and the knowing of them.

Opening the mouth, then the intention to put the food into the mouth: "intending," "intending." Putting the food into the mouth, placing the food. The feeling of touch of the food on the tongue—just touch sensations and the awareness of them. No self, no I, no me, no mine, simply the awareness of sensation.

The intention to close the mouth: "intending," then the subsequent closing. Not chewing yet, unless you want to eat your meal with your arm up in the air. So—intending to lower the arm, noting the mental intention, then the moving of the arm, making the movement the object of mindfulness. Then the intention to begin chewing, and the subsequent chewing process, watching the movement of the mouth, of the jaws, of the teeth. The awareness of taste—the tasting that comes in the process of chewing.

Just at this point, there is a very interesting thing which happens: generally after the first couple of chews, taste begins to arise—and then it disappears! The food is still in the mouth, but it's rather tasteless. At this point, because of our desire for more pleasant taste sensations, we often find the hand again reaching for more food. Food is still in the mouth, and we're still chewing it, but the hand is moving and taking food and putting it into the mouth. Become mindful of the arising and passing away of the taste and the whole subsequent process, of the food being mashed up, then the intention to swallow and the swallowing. Again, the intention arising to take more food. Notice the intention, and then the reaching for the food again, following the whole process through the taking of the food, the intending to move the arm and the moving of the arm, the intention to open the mouth and the opening, the placing of the food, the closing of the mouth, the replacing of the arm, the chewing, the tasting, the swallowing—all very distinct, impersonal processes happening.

By cultivating this kind of mindfulness of process, not only do we become aware of how our desire for food arises, and watch that desire mindfully without identifying with it, we also begin to penetrate into the very basic nature of the entire mind-body process. And done very mindfully, it's a deep and penetrating meditation.

As a general suggestion to those of you who are cultivating awareness or mindfulness around food, a useful exercise might be to eat one meal a day (or even just a piece of fruit) in silence, mindful and very attentive to the entire process involved. The entire exercise becomes meditation. And in this way we gradually expand the state of mindfulness to include the entire experience of all our activities, and we begin to live in a very meditative space. It's valuable to cultivate this kind of penetrating awareness.

C. BUDDHIST MEALTIME MEDITATIONS

by Jack Kornfield

The techniques that I'm going to share with you, which come from my teachers and from the Buddhist tradition, are all designed for the same purpose: for breaking the illusion of separateness between you and the food, or breaking the attachment or desire. For it's not what it is that you eat that makes you wise and leads to the development of insight, but the process of *how* you eat that will lead to that. And the Buddhist emphasis is always on the attitude, on the cultivation of certain mind-states, on letting go of the attachment to sense desires.

The first meditation that's done in the Buddhist tradition is a meditation on loving kindness and compassion, on the Boddhisattva nature, on the sharing of our food with all the beings in existence. I'll share with you one Buddhist chant, a Pali chant, that's often used to offer food: *Sabe lokami ye satah, Jivanta hara he tukamanunang, oh jinungsabe labante mamaje tasah.* "May all sentient beings share this meal with me, and by the power of merit, may all beings live in health and happiness." Then throughout the meal you keep to this mind-state of loving kindness, of compassion, of sharing whatever there is with all the beings in the universe.

Another technique to use in eating is to consider the food as broken down into its elements. The purpose of this is to develop detachment and wisdom into the emptiness of self, or into the Brahmanic nature of all that you're doing. So you take your piece of food, and you hold it up and look at it, and you recognize in it the aspects of the earth element—of solidity, of hardness or softness; of the element of fire—the heat or cold of it; of the air or vibratory element—the element of distension that keeps it in that shape; and of the element of cohesion that keeps it together, the water element. You see that in the food, and you feel it, and you examine it. And then you look at your own body and you say, "Wow! There's the element of hardness, of solidity . . . the element of heat and cold . . . the element of vibration, distension . . . the element of cohesion." So all I'm doing when I'm eating is taking the elements and putting the elements into elements. And you notice that when you chew the elements, they change. The cohesion increases and the hardness disappears somewhat. You can watch the process of the transformation of the elements from the food as you chew them and swallow them.

Another way to approach eating is to do a meditation on the emptiness, again related to the Brahmanic meditation that was spoken of, where you take a piece of food, and you see that the food is not self, that there's no one there, just food. You see your body reaching for the food and holding it, and you look at your arm and the rest of your body and realize that that's not you—that's just the body. And you look at the mind that knows, that's watching all that, and you see that that's not you either—that's just awareness of the fact of the body or awareness of the food. And then as one very famous Buddhist teacher said, "Eating is like putting nothing into nothing."

Another technique to use, to break down the illusion of self, the illusion of separateness, the illusion of permanence, is to look at the whole process of eating in terms of change, in the change of form and also in the change of feeling when you're doing the eating. Imagine the whole sequence. Imagine the genesis, of the food that grew from the earth, of the green shoot and the ripe stalk or fruit, then the picking of it, the cleaning of it, the bringing of it to your table . . . now seeing the food there before you, and continuing the process—in your mind first, before you start to eat—of considering the change in the food, the eating of it, the tasting and swallowing, the change of that food into elements, into nutriments for your body, into excrement, back into the earth, and the whole cycle beginning again of the regeneration of food. So you see everything in terms of a flow, in terms of a process, and you see that it's all changing. That's another way to look at eating as a meditation.

Still another way is to be mindful of sensation and touch. Sensation and mindfulness of sensation are the basis for a lot of vipassana, or "insight," meditation practices, because they're something you can see very clearly changing from moment to moment: the arising and ceasing of sensation. So in eating, you can be aware first of the sensation of yourself sitting there . . . you can be aware of the sensations in yourself—of hunger, or desire, the feelings in your body. When you reach for the fork, you can be aware of the sensation of your hands touching the utensil, feeling that in your fingers; you can be aware of the sensation of the movement of your arm, bringing the food up to your mouth, and of the sensation of the touch of the food on your lips. Be aware of the sensation on your tongue and your teeth, as you chew the food . . . be aware of the sensation as you swallow, feeling the food go all the way down into your stomach. By paying close attention to the sensation, you cut off the discrimination of your mind. You don't allow yourself to say, "Ooo—wow! That was delicious!" Or "Ugh. That was awful." You're just mindful of the process of each sensation arising and ceasing as you eat, and so you're able to cut the desires.

A way that's very commonly taught in monasteries, and especially talked about among the bhikus or the monks in the Buddhist tradition, is to look at food just in terms of its sustenance: the contemplation of food for sustenance. The body is simply a vehicle to be cared for and not to be pampered, and food is simply a means of sustaining life to continue your spiritual practice. You're not eating because you enjoy eating, but you're eating as a way to sustain your energy to continue your practice on the spiritual path.

There's a story that's told about the kind of attitude that eventually needs to be developed in this meditation on food for sustenance: There was a couple and a young child who were crossing a vast desert. They brought very little food with them, and they had run out of food and just about run out of water, and they still had a long way to go. And they were quite sure in fact that they would die. Well, from the heat of the day and the desert, in fact the child did die. And the two parents decided that in order to continue the crossing of the desert in their journey, so they would not die, they would eat the body of the child. And that's the attitude of taking food not out of pleasure, not out of desire or out of attachment, but simply for sustenance, just as those parents ate the flesh of their own child. That's a very powerful attitude, one that breaks through the greed and the attachment to the sense pleasures of eating, and it is another kind of meditation.

When you've developed that attitude, you don't eat more than you need. All of these different meditations are merely techniques, devices for developing balance in the mind. Because the whole of the dhamma is just a question of balance, really. Here you have to balance your greed and your habitual patterns of enjoyment and attachment with a meditation, to get you to a point where you're no longer attached.

When I was first in the monastery in Laos, it was an ascetic monastery, and I'd been there a few weeks and was really checking it out, to make sure that the teacher looked like he was enlightened and that all the monks were practicing right. And I saw some things I didn't like. Monks were a little sloppy eating, or they'd get their food and they'd say their chant and then they'd start to eat very fast. And even the teacher I wondered about; he would say very contradictory things at times to different people. I went to him; I was very disturbed, and I even thought of leaving and going to find another teacher, a better guru to fit my model of what a teacher should be like. And I said, "I feel really uncomfortable. Why do you say one thing to one person and one to another about how we should eat or how we should act?" And his answer to me was this: "The way I teach is very simple," he said. "It's like someone walking down a path or a road at night, and sometimes they get off a little bit onto the right side and I see them and I say, 'Go left.' And sometimes they almost fall in the ditch on the left side and I see them and I say, 'Go right, go right.' That's all I do. And all of the meditations are techniques to use to develop a balance of mind and mental factors."

So I asked him further. I said, "Well, I'm still disturbed. Some of the monks are eating quickly, and even you sometimes seem to be sloppy." It was very hard to say—I thought a lightning bolt might strike me! Nothing happened. He just laughed and he said, "You have to be thankful for the appearance of imperfections in your teacher— the things that make him look like he's not enlightened." I said, "Oh, yeah?" And he said, "Because if it were not for these imperfections, you might be deceived into thinking that the Buddha was somewhere outside of yourself."

The balance of mind is the key. When there's a very strong imbalance, you need strong medicine to balance it. Some of us really get into food trips—Thanksgiving dinner, or going to the refrigerator and the pickles and olives and cheesecake and all those wonderful things. And in order to balance that, one other meditation that's used is to contemplate on the true repulsiveness of food. Think about it: the benefits of the meditation on the repulsiveness of food are that you really begin to know the nature of food and of the process. Your mindfulness grows. You understand the lust in yourself, and you are able to let go of it. The meditation on the repulsiveness of food begins with contemplation on the procurement. So you think, if you still eat meat, of the animals and their carcasses, and of the flesh and blood and fat, and of the disgusting juices that run out when the animals are cut open. Or if you don't eat meat, think of the food from the earth, and even of the dirt of the earth itself, of the shit from the cows and the horses, the dirt of all kinds. And in this society, they're trying to keep your food clean, so they put in preservatives. But just let the food stand out in the sun for a short time and it turns rancid and moldy, or rotten and foul and oozing and fermenting.

And the meditation for the monks as it's given in the scriptures is this: he's eating his food, he's dipped his hand into the bowl and is squeezing the food in his fingers, "and the sweat trickling down from his five fingers wets any crisp food that there may be and makes it sodden, and when its good appearance has been spoiled by his squeezing it up and it's been made into a ball and put into his mouth, then the lower teeth function as a mortar and the upper teeth as pestle and the tongue as a hand, and it gets pounded there with the pestle of the teeth, like a dog's dinner in a dog's trough, while he turns it over and over with his tongue. And then the thick spittle at the tip of the tongue smears it, and the filth from the teeth in the parts where the toothbrush cannot reach smear it. When thus mashed up and besmeared, this peculiar compound, now destitute of its original color and smell, is reduced to a condition as utterly nauseating as a dog's vomit in a dog's trough. Yet notwithstanding that it is like this, it can still be swallowed because it can no longer be seen by the eyes. And where does it go? It is swallowed by one who is twenty-five years old, or thirty years old; it finds itself in a place like a cesspit, unwashed for those twenty-five years or thirty years." That's strong medicine, but it's a very effective balance for the passions and desires that go with the delicious taste of food and with all the food trips in our culture.

So food isn't what it appears. The very highest practice, the place where this initial balance developed, is the practice of vipassana mindfulness. This is the mindful observation of all of the mind and body processes that are involved in eating, as they change from moment to moment to moment: the thoughts, perceptions, feelings, and sensations in the form. To quote the Buddha, "The merit made in serving one thousand meals to the whole order of monks with the Buddha at its head cannot compare to him who develops clear insight into the arising and vanishing of phenomena for just one moment."

D. SATSANG MEDITATION

Satsang means a coming together in Truth. The beauty of having sat-sang is that you are sharing a contract with another person that you will help one another go to God. That means that you are both consciously working at seeing one another as souls.

The best way to see another person as a soul is just to sit down and do it. It's something to be experienced, not talked about. It's the place where our individual differences look like background and not like a figure anymore. If you have spiritual friends to hang out with, here is a little satsang collaboration you might want to try together. It's like a joint meditation exercise.

Sit down opposite somebody. Get comfortable; take a couple of slow breaths. Don't talk to each other—this isn't a social thing. Don't "talk" with your expressions, either—forget about the smiling and the nodding and all those facial gestures. Just sit and look at the other person.

Focus at a point right between one another's eyes, so you're able to see both of their eyes at once. Now just sit with one another like that, with the eyes as the focal point for, say, a thirty-minute meditation. Relax, sit there, and let it all happen to you. Let yourself see all the things that arise in the other person, let yourself experience all the feelings you have as you are being looked at intensely by another person. Keep looking and looking.

Pretty soon, you will see the other person's face begin to change. Sometimes it will become incredibly beautiful, and sometimes incredibly horrible. Either way, don't let it create a reaction in you. Don't let it suck you in—just stay right with the eyes and say, "And this too. And this too." Look at your ten thousand horrible visions and your ten thousand beautiful visions, and let them all go by. Just keep looking and looking and looking.

After a while, you will discover that the "stuff" of it all starts to change. It starts to become ground rather than figure. The good, the bad, the beautiful, the ugly, all just passing show, and you see deeper and deeper and deeper until you are just looking at another being who's looking back at you. You are soul acknowledging soul.

Those are the kind of games you can play when you have satsang as your playmates.

E. HOW TO USE A MALA

A mala is a string of beads, used to chant the names of God. It's the same thing as prayer beads, or a rosary. A Hindu mala typically has either 108 beads (108 being considered a sacred number in Hinduism) or 27 beads (which is one-fourth of 108). In addition to the 108 or 27 "counting beads," a mala generally has an additional bead, called the "guru bead," which hangs perpendicular to the circle of counting beads. The illustration on page 300 gives instructions for making one—all you need are some beads and a string.

A Hindu mala is usually worked with by using the right hand. The mala is held resting over the third finger of the right hand, and the beads are brought toward you, one by one, using the thumb. Each bead counts one repetition of the mantra. When you get around to the guru bead, you don't count it, and you don't pass it; you stop there, mentally bow to the guru, flip the mala around, and start going back the other way. Each time you come to the guru bead you awaken once more, then you turn around and go back the way you came.

Now for those of you who are left-handed (as I am): In India, you would be inclined to use the right hand anyway, because of certain cultural traditions. The Tibetans, on the other hand, have no such rules; they use their malas in either hand, and with any finger. In the Hindu tradition, you can use any finger of the right hand to hold the beads, except for the first finger, which is the pointing or "accusing" finger; you don't use that one. The reason most people use the third finger is that there is a nerve on the inside of that finger which is connected to your spine in such a way that you're getting a little added benefit from the practice. It's similar to an acupressure point, and it adds a little extra energy rush to the process.

Doing a mantra doesn't require using a mala; the mala is just there to add another dimension to the practice. Besides speaking the mantra, and hearing the mantra as you speak it, the process becomes tactile as well. If you want a psychological analysis of the use of a mala, you could say that it is a "kinesthetic cue device." Without it, you could be doing the mantra and get lost in doing it mechanically. But if you suddenly feel the bead between your fingers, it wakes you up again. Bead by bead—it's like the steps of a ladder, walking you straight into the Brahman.

1. Put 36 beads on string and knot so that they can move slightly
2. Put string ends thru large Guru Bead.
3. Tie a double or triple knot around the piece of blanket.
4. Melt string ends so they dont unravel.

Instructions were given on how to make a mala and each student received a bag containing 36 small wooden beads, one larger wooden bead, a white nylon cord, and a thread from Neem Karoli Baba's blanket with which they could make their own mala.

F. THE CHAKRAS

The chakra system works within the energy framework of our bodies; although the chakras themselves are operating at the astral level, they express themselves through our bodies' energy patterns. Traditionally there are said to be seven chakras, starting with the muladhara at the base of the spine, and ending with the sahasrara at the crown of the head. The chakras aren't physical forms; they're more like foci of energy, and they're located along the sushumna, which is a kind of astral-level spinal cord. The sushumna is said to run down the center of the spinal column, but it isn't something you would find on an X-ray. In the same way, the "ida" and the "pingala" are the "nerves" of the system, running alongside the sushumna, but they aren't "nerves" you could dissect in an anatomy class. These are all astral entities.

The energy which moves through the sushumna is known as "kundalini," which literally means "she who is coiled." Kundalini energy is visualized as a coiled serpent, which resides at the base of the spine, until something—something in our practices, or something in the course of our evolution—causes it to begin to uncoil and to rise up the sushumna. As it does, it encounters each of the chakras.

The first chakra, the muladhara (which is at the base of the spine, halfway between the anal sphincter and the genitals) is primarily connected with survival functions. The second chakra, svadishtana, is the sexual chakra. The third chakra, which is called manipura, is located in the area around the mid-section, at the solar plexus; it's thought to be connected with expressions of ego-power. The fourth chakra is called the anahata, or the heart chakra, and it's related to compassion. The fifth chakra, the visuddha, located in the throat, is connected with turning inward toward God, and therefore with the development of the "true voice," the divine sound speaking through us. The sixth chakra, which is the ajna, is located in the center of the forehead; it is usually called the third-eye chakra, and it is connected with the inner guru and the higher wisdom. And finally the seventh chakra, the sahas-

rara, at the crown of the head, is the thousand-petaled lotus, enlightenment, the merging into Brahman.

As the kundalini energy uncoils itself up the spine, it passes through
each of those chakras in turn, through the focus of each form of
energy. The kundalini radiates out from the sushumna at each chakra
level, and it energizes, or activates, each of those physical / psychological energy fields. But if, as the kundalini begins to rise, it comes
to a center which is blocked, the energy will emerge as some form of
behavior. It's like water going up a tube; if it gets to a crimp in the
tube, it can't go up any further. Say the energy gets to the second
chakra; the name for the second chakra, which is the sexual chakra,
translates as "her favorite resort"—referring to the kundalini. It's sort
of like the Riviera of the chakra-world; the kundalini gets there and
decides to hang out and vacation for a while. Or maybe it manages to
dodge that shoal, but then it gets to the third chakra, and it gets
grabbed by all the ego's power needs and it can't go any further.

In the real world, the process isn't as neat and orderly as all that
makes it sound, however. It's not like you finish with the first chakra,
now you go on to the second . . . you finish with the second and go
on to the third, and so on. Everybody's got a little of everything going
all the time, more blocked in this chakra, less blocked in that one. As
you get more sophisticated about the chakra systems, you begin to
assess your own predicament in terms of the movement of the kundalini—you'll say: "Well, a lot of my energy is still tied up in my second chakra, but my fourth chakra is beginning to open."

I've worked some with the energies of the chakra system, and
sometimes when I'm sitting and talking to somebody, suddenly what
I see is a living chakra chart, right there in front of me. I see the various chakras, all sending out energy: "Bzzt, bzzt, bzzt"—like "lust,
lust, lust," or "power, power, power," or "compassion, compassion,
compassion." Or maybe I'll see that nothing's coming through the
heart chakra, but the third eye is like a headlight beam.

The kundalini gets awakened in many different ways. Swami Muktananda had the capacity to give shaktipat, a direct hit of energy that

would awaken the kundalini. It would have the strangest effects on people. Suddenly somebody would get up and start to dance—somebody you'd *never* have expected to behave that way: a rotund gentleman in a conservative blue serge suit, for example, who got up and started to do an incredible Indian dance. And the man sitting next to him, who looked like a professor, with his tweed jacket and the pipe in his mouth, who suddenly started to do mudras—complex, exquisite, perfect mudras—but the look on his face was one of total perplexity. Somebody else would be doing automatic breathing and bouncing across the floor like a beach ball. The whole place would begin to look like the back ward of a mental hospital.

All the while, Swami Muktananda would just be sitting up there, with his eyes closed, playing his ektara. But his presence was like a beam of energy, activating the kundalini, the energy centers, in all the people around him. The shaktipat—his giving of shakti—caused the kundalini to begin to uncoil, and depending on where the chakras were blocked, the energy came out in different behavioral manifestations. Block a little of it here and some more of it there, and that combination will make you get up and dance. Some other combination will cause automatic breathing. If you understand the system, you can keep score of who's got which chakra-thing going.

If you're drawn toward working with energy systems, you might decide to explore working with these chakra energies. There are different ways to do it. You can try doing it through meditation, for example—you can visualize bringing the energies up through each of the chakras, and out through the crown of your head. Or you might want to work with another type of visualization exercise, like a mandala from Tibetan traditions. In some other traditions you might be given a specific mantra, a "bij" or seed-sound, for opening a certain chakra. You can use pranayam, a method which works with breath control to move the energy from chakra to chakra. Each of those is a technique that works in a specific way to awaken the kundalini energy. You can try them out, experiment with them; you can see how they affect the chakra energies, and how that jibes with your other spiritual practices.

G. THE YOGA OF PSYCHEDELICS

First off, I want to say that I would never recommend to anyone that they use psychedelics as a means to alter their consciousness. But if someone comes to me and says, "I'm going to take this," then I say to them, "I think you should study and understand something about the method you're about to use, so you can enter it in the spirit of its being a yoga for you, a path toward union."

The predicament we face at the moment is that most psychedelic substances are currently illegal. When people ask me what I think about government policy toward psychedelics, I always respond that the most reasonable thing to do about substances which alter human consciousness is to educate people, not to police them. It makes very good sense to prepare people for a psychedelic experience, maybe even to license them, the way you do before you let someone drive a vehicle. But you shouldn't *prohibit* anyone from using whatever substances they choose. You respect the right of other beings to alter and to explore their own consciousness in their own way. That ought to be a basic human freedom.

At the moment, however, it isn't. And so if we use psychedelics, it will be in an atmosphere in which we can't really fulfill Maharajji's criterion of "feeling much peace." In our minds there will be the inevitable paranoia that comes from working with something that is illegal; that means there is always a certain little part of our consciousness which has to be held down to "watch out for the fuzz," to put it in the vernacular. That's why if we are using psychedelics, it's good to have someone available to take care of the scene on the physical plane, so we can relax and concentrate on doing our inner work.

In thinking about psychedelics, the first thing to understand is that there is a whole range of substances which share that name, and that they are of very different strengths. Some are mild; most marijuana, for example, falls in that category. Mild psychedelics open up the possibilities, but they don't override the personality. Stronger psychedelics, on the other hand—things like mescaline, or psilocybin, or LSD—are likely to override our existing thought patterns in a very powerful way. If we aren't prepared for that, it can get pretty hairy. If we don't have a sufficiently deep jnana practice, some understanding of what's happening to us, we freak when the entire structure of our existence starts to fall away. That's why it's important to do some reading and studying and contemplating in advance, so we'll have some foothold in the experiences as they start to happen to us.

Those of us who have experienced psychedelic trips know that there are two points in the session where problems can arise. The first is going up, when we find the world and ourselves in it dissolving all around us. That's the Kansas motel trip I described (see page 191): "Help, I'm dying!"

The other point that can be freaky is the re-entry, when we start to come back and we see what a schlock scene we're returning to. That can send us into a tailspin, as we try to run away from our lives and hang on to the high. Usually, however, once we come down, those are exactly the experiences that motivate us to clean up our act. It's just part of the process of seeing the horror show we have created for ourselves, out of our ignorance, and it becomes the inducement for doing the practices of purification and all the rest of it. Then we can be a little more open the next time around.

It's extremely useful, especially with a first session, to have someone on hand who is very experienced, someone quiet and calm, someone with whom you feel loving and safe. If that's not possible, try to have something else, like some music that you love and can surrender into, something that is familiar and comfortable. And always take a psychedelic in a place where there's minimal paranoia and where you can trust that you won't be disturbed.

Be open in your heart to each moment, and only do what feels totally right. Let's say you and some friends have a psychedelic session planned for Saturday night; everybody's all ready, but there's a feeling inside you that says, "No—for some reason, this isn't right." Trust that feeling. Wait. Wait until the moment feels absolutely "right on." Listen carefully to your own heart; if you feel that using psychedelics seems to be part of your practice, then use them, but use them very consciously.

Notes

Backward and Foreword

1. This and other quoted information about the workshop was taken from a copy of the program for the Naropa 1974 Summer Session, generously provided by Richard Chamberlain of the Communications Department at Naropa University.

Introduction

1. Jakob Böhme, *The Confessions of Jakob Böhme,* edited by W. S. Palmer (1954).

2. Kabir, *Songs of Kabir,* translated by Rabindranath Tagore (1915).

3. Thomas Merton, *A Search for Wisdom and Spirit: Thomas Merton's Theology of the Self,* edited by Anne E. Carr (1989).

4. Peter Ouspensky, *The Psychology of Man's Possible Evolution* (1945).

Chapter 2: Karma and Reincarnation

1. Rumi, *The Pocket Rumi Reader,* edited by Kabir Helminski (2001).

2. Jack London, *Star-Rover* (1915).

3. Lama Anagarika Govinda, quoted in the foreword to *The Tibetan Book of the Dead,* by W. Y. Evans-Wentz (foreword by Donald Lopez) (2000).

4. The Buddha, *The Words of the Buddha (An Outline of the Teachings of the Buddha in the Words of the Pali Canon),* compiled by Nyanatiloka (undated).

Chapter 3: Karma Yoga

1. Plotinus, *The Six Enneads,* translated by Stephen Mackenna and B. S. Page (1991).

2. Meister Eckehart, *The Essential Sermons, Commentaries, Treatises and Defense,* translated and edited by Bernard McGinn and Edmund College (1981).

3. Mohandas Gandhi, *The Gospel of Selfless Action, or The Gita According to Gandhi* (1946–2000).

4. Carlos Castaneda, *Journey to Ixtlan: The Lessons of Don Juan* (1972).

5. *The Book of Tao,* translated by R. B. Blakney (1955).

6. Meher Baba, *Is That So?* (1978).

Chapter 4: Jnana Yoga

1. Gurdjieff quoted in P. D. Ouspensky, *In Search of the Miraculous: Fragments of an Unknown Teaching* (1974).

2. Ramana Maharshi, in his poem "Reality in 40 Verses (and Supplement)" in *The Collected Works of Ramana Maharshi,* edited by Arthur Osborne (1972).

Chapter 5: Brahman

1. Janeshwar, *Janeshwari* (a thirteenth-century commentary on the Gita), quoted at www.sscnet.ucla.edu/southasia/Religions/texts/Janesh.html.

2. Rumi, quoted at www.iranonline.com/literature/Articles/Persian-literature/Rumi.

3. Ramana Maharshi, *The Collected Works of Ramana Maharshi,* edited by Arthur Osborne (1972).

4. Franklin Merrill Wolfe, *Consciousness Without an Object* (1973).

Chapter 6: Sacrifice and Mantra

1. P. D. Ouspensky, *In Search of the Miraculous: Fragments of an Unknown Teaching* (1974).

2. *The Way of a Pilgrim and The Pilgrim Continues His Way,* translated by Helen Bacovcin (1985).

Chapter 7: Renunciation and Purification

1. Mohandas Gandhi, *Epigrams from Gandhiji,* compiled by S. R. Tikekar.

2. Mohandas Gandhi, "The Gita According to Gandhi," in a translation which appeared in the columns of *Young India* on June 8, 1931.

Chapter 8: Devotion and the Guru

1. Hafiz of Shiraz, *Divan-y-Hafiz,* edited by Mirza Mohammad Qazvini and Dr. Qasem Ghani (1941).

2. *For Love of the Dark One: Songs of Mirabai,* translated by Andrew Schelling (1993).

3. Ramana Maharshi, *Spiritual Instruction of Bhagavan Sri Ramana Maharshi* (1974).

4. Swami Muktananda, *Play of Consciousness: A Spiritual Autobiography* (1978).

Chapter 10: Dying

1. Ramana Maharshi, *The Collected Works of Ramana Maharshi,* edited by Arthur Osborne (1972).

2. *Zen Flesh, Zen Bones,* compiled by Paul Reps and Nyogen Senzaki (1994).

Glossary

Abhidhamma The section of Theravadan Buddhist scripture concerned with philosophical, cosmological, and psychological analysis.

adharma / adharmic Unrighteous conduct. Failure to perform spiritual duty or to act from the Truth within one's heart.

Ahamkara The false belief in individuality. This I-ness or I-maker is the source of egoism, the root cause of dualism.

Ahimsa Non-harming in deeds, words, and thoughts. One who does not have compassion for others, including all life-forms, is in some way harming them. One of the *yamas*.

ananda Absolute bliss.

aparigraha Non-covetousness, non-acquiring, non-attachment. To accept only that which is absolutely necessary in deed, word, and thought. One of the *yamas*.

arti A ritual performed to show reverence to a deity. A holy person moves clockwise around an image of the deity while chanting and carrying a tray containing a lamp / candle, camphor, and other items such as sacred ash, Tulasi leaves, flowers.

arti lamp The flame carried during an *arti* ceremony. The flame symbolizes both the embodiment of the deity and the deity's transcendence of bodily form.

asana(s) Literally "seat." A posture that is stable and comfortable. One of the eight limbs of *ashtanga yoga*.

ashram(a) A spiritually based residence or retreat site where *yoga* is lived and taught; Often, an ashram is founded in honor of a particular spiritual master. Also, a stage of life; human life has four "ashramas: student, householder, spiritual seeker, ascetic.

ashtanga yoga A physical discipline to synchronize the breath with postures to balance the body and calm the mind. The "eight-limbed" yoga: *yama, niyama, asana, pranayama, pratyahara, dharana, dhyana,* and *samadhi*.

asteya   Non-stealing. Not taking what does not belong to oneself. One of the *yamas.*

atman   The spark or breath of the Divine in all beings.

Avadhuta   An incarnate being who lives in a state beyond body consciousness. An ascetic who enjoys liberation and supernatural powers.

avatar   The highest form an entity can attain and still incarnate. The incarnation of a deity, such as Rama, Krishna, Christ, Zoroaster, or Buddha.

bardo   Literally "island." The state between death and rebirth.

bhakti   The *yoga* of devotion. ("The way bhakti works—you just love until you and the Beloved become one."—*Ram Dass*)

bhikhu   An individual devoted to the task of following the path by renunciation of the distractions of worldly affairs.

Bhuta Yagya   Offering food to birds and animals as a spiritual practice.

Brahma Yagya   Surrendering oneself to the Divine, especially through the study of religious texts and ideas.

brahmacharya   The practice of chastity. The spiritual student who is practicing impeccable behavior, including chastity. One of the *yamas.*

Brahman   The inconceivable, the inexpressable, the indescribable. The principle of illumination by which all phenomena, without exception, emanate and to which all return. Ultimate reality.

buddhi   The reasoning and discriminating faculty of the mind. Functions independent of the senses, and therefore is able to clarify and control them.

chakra(s)   One of seven energy vortices or nerve plexuses along the astral spinal column. Each chakra has a physical and emotional counterpart.

chit   Absolute knowledge.

darshan   Receiving a glimpse of Truth from being in the presence of a holy person, sacred idol, or sacred place.

dharana   Concentration on a single object.

dharma/dharmic   The bases of all universal order, social and moral. Conformity to natural righteousness or spiritual duty.

dhyana   Meditation or contemplation.

dokusan   In the Zen Buddhist tradition, a private interview with one's teacher.

dorje   The thunderbolt in art and ritual that symbolizes the method of using something invincible that can cut through anything.

entheogens   From the Greek, *entheos,* meaning "God within." Often called psychedelics. Use of these substances (e.g., peyote, ayahuasca, cannabis, etc.) permits temporary freedom from the perception of reality created by the rational mind.

ghee   Clarified butter. It represents abundance and fertility, often used as a ritual offering.

guna(s)   In Hindu philosophy, literally, "threads or strands." The three inherent characteristics or qualities of nature: *sattva* (truth/purity), *rajas* (energy/passion), and *tamas* (inertia/illusion).

gyan(a)   The *yoga* of intellectual introspection and discernment. The goal is toward mind control.

hatha yoga   The path of body control and discipline. Includes the breath and postures.

ida   The left nadi (stream of energy) that runs along the *sushumna* (the astral spinal column that carries the kundalini energy). It is feminine, watery in nature, cool, and soothing. See *pingala.*

indrias   The powers of the senses (hear, feel, see, taste, smell) and the powers of action (voice, hand, foot, organ of excretion, organ of generation).

Ishta Dev   A "chosen deity" or personal God who protects and assists the devotee on the Path. ("Hanuman is Maharjji's Ishta Dev, his route through."—*Ram Dass*)

japa   Devotional repetition of a *mantra,* a prayer, or names of God.

Jiva/Jivatman   The incarnate individualized Self. The soul identifies with its manifested or incarnate state.

jnana yoga   The path of knowledge and wisdom arrived at through inquiry and discrimination.

kalpa   In Hindu chronology, 4,320,000,000 years. The length of a day and night of *Brahman.*

karma   Literally, "action." This includes not only one's actions this lifetime, but throughout all lifetimes. It is the fuel of *samsara.* The karmic principle of cause and effect is not a system of reward and punishment outside ourselves, rather it is a natural law maintaining the balance of the universe.

karma yoga The path of action. The practice of consciously using one's daily life and work as a spiritual path while relinquishing attachment to the fruits of the actions.

Kaya A form or body. The body of *dharma* is the dharmakaya.

koan An unsolvable riddle used as a meditation practice in some schools of Zen Buddhism. ("The mind using itself to beat itself."—*Ram Dass*)

kshatria One of the four social classes of Aryan clans in India: Brahmin (learned), *kshatria* (warrior), valshya (merchant), and sudra (laborer). *Kshatria* is the fighter of the senses and protector of people. Arjuna is a *kshatria*.

lila Divine play; reality seen as God-at-play.

loka Other realms or dimensions than the physical world.

manas The lower mind. The rational faculty of the mind which has a dual role as a sense organ and an organ of action. Through manas, impressions from the external world are received (sense) and conscious and creative responses are given (action).

mantra Rhythmic repetition of words or phrases that support an individual's inner journey. A method of silencing the mind. Om is the supreme mantra.

mauna Spiritual silence.

mauni A *sadhu* who uses silence as an *upaya*.

maya Literally, "illusion." The flux that underlies everything that is created and dissolved (the phenomenal world). That which diverts humans from Spirit (Reality) to matter (unreality).

murti The manifestation of sacred power or a deity in the form of an icon, often a statue.

namaste A verbal greeting, often with palms held together at the heart center, meaning I honor the divinity in you. ("I honor the place in you where, when you are resting in yours and I am resting in mine, there is only one of us."—*Ram Dass*)

nibbana / nirvana Liberation from material existence. The transcendental freedom that stands as the final goal of the Buddha's teachings. Unconditional wisdom, unlimited awareness.

nivritti To flow back. Involution, away from activity. Opposed to *pravritti,* evolution.

niyama(s) The internal disciplines of ashtanga yoga: *saucha* (purity of mind and body), *santosha* (contentment), *tapas* (self-discipline), *svadhyaya* (devotion and spiritual study), and *hvara pranidhara* (surrender, union with the Divine).

Nri Yagya   Offerings to guests or to the needy (such as food to the hungry) given as a spiritual act or practice.

pingala   The right nadi (stream of energy) that runs along the *sushumna* (the astral spinal column which carries the kundalini energy). It is masculine, fiery in nature, hot, and stimulating. See *ida*.

Pitri Yagya   Offering oblations, usually of water and rice, to the dead, especially ancestors.

prakriti   Nature; phenomenal world. Oneness manifests as *purusha* (spirit) and prakriti. Prakriti is part of the Divine Being, not subordinate to it.

pralaya   Periodic cosmic dissolution marking the end of an age. When all forms merge into one indiscriminable whole.

pranam   To bow down to show respect, especially to a *sadhu*.

pranayama   Regulation of the breath to control prana, or the life force of the body. Used in *yoga* and meditation for cleansing the body and concentrating the mind.

pratyahara   Withdrawal of senses from objects to still the mind. One of the eight limbs of *ashtanga yoga*.

pravritti   To flow forth. Evolution, toward sense stimulus. Opposed to *nivritti,* involution.

psychotropic   A substance that can influence human consciousness, changing the functioning of the mind.

punya   Right understanding. To act mindfully.

purusha   Spirit. Pure consciousness. Oneness manifests as purusha and *prakriti* (phenomenal world).

raja yoga   The "royal" path. The mind becomes the instrument of the soul.

rajas/rajasic   Energy. Action, stimulation of desires. One of the *gunas*.

Ram Nam Satya Hey   The Hindu *mantra* that accompanies bringing the body of a deceased person to the Ganges River during funeral rites. Often heard in Banaras (Varanasi).

Ramayana   Literally, the vehicle of Rama. Composed by the sage Valmiki, the Ramayana is the oldest known Sanskrit epic poem of India. The adventures of the *avatar* Rama and his consort Sita with the demon Ravana. The Ramayana brings to life the eternal struggle between the impersonal laws of nature and *dharma*.

Rinpoche   Literally, "precious One." A title of honor given to *Tulkus* and others of high spiritual attainment.

rohatsu dai sesshin   A Zen tradition of intense meditation practice. For the first eight days of December, continuous meditation with breaks for sutras, eating, and sleeping.

sadhak   A spiritual aspirant of God or Truth doing *sadhana.*

sadhana(s)   From the verb root *sadh,* meaning "to go straight to the goal." Spiritual way or spiritual disciplines that ultimately create evolutionary energy for all beings.

sadhu   A holy person, saint, or sage.

samadhi   Concentration, absorption, unification. The person and the object of meditation merge. Total absorption of body, mind, soul, and spirit into the One Reality. Oneness, ecstasy.

samsara   Literally, "to circle." The bondage of the repetitious cycle of birth, death, and rebirth initiated by one's *karma* (actions in each lifetime).

sankhya   A Hindu school of philosophy focusing study on the human body and soul.

sat   Truth Absolute Being. Beyond duality.

satori   In the Zen Buddhist tradition, "direct perception." This experience may vary from a flash of intuitive awareness to *nirvana.* It is the beginning and not the end of Zen training.

sattva/sattvic   Ritually pure. Being in a state of tranquility or purity. One of the *gunas.*

satya   Truthfulness.

sesshin   A period of intense meditation practice.

seva   Service without attachment to the fruits of one's labor. ("God serving God—puts it into a loving space."—*Ram Dass*)

shabhd yoga   The *yoga* of working with the inner sound.

shakti   The feminine principle of Divine energy or power. Recognition of one's own inner power.

siddhi   From *sidh,* "to attain." Supernatural or hidden powers inherent in the human spirit attained through *mantra,* meditation, and other yogic practices.

siddhi baba   A perfected yogi who has mastered the eight *siddhis:* the power to become infinitely small (anima), infinitely large (mahima), light (laghima), heavy (garima), to create (ishatwa), command (vashitwa), reach anywhere (prapti), and gratify any wish (prakamya).

sila Purification, morality, virtue.

skandas The causal and impermanent elements inherent in all forms of life. There are five elements (skandas) creating the personality and temporal nature of humans: rupa (form), vedana (sensation), sanna (perception), sankhara (reactions), and vinnana (consciousness).

stupa Literally, "crest, top, summit." The monument built over the ashes or relics of a spiritual master.

sunnyas A renunciate. One who has renounced the world for a life of solitude and meditation.

sushumna The astral spinal column, where the *chakras* ascend and where the kundalini energy is carried.

swaha Invocation used during offerings to spiritual deities. Has the intent of "So be it!"

Svayamvara The Indian ceremony when the princess chooses her own husband.

tapasya/tapas Self-discipline and austerity to achieve progress in spiritual growth.

Theravadan Buddhism: Literally, "the Way of the Elders." A council of five hundred elders committed the Buddha's teachings from oral tradition to written form. From this text, the Pali Canon, Theravadan Buddhism draws its spiritual inspiration. It is the predominant school of Buddhism in Southeast Asia, and is often referred to as Southern Buddhism. Since the nineteenth century it has spread across Europe and North America.

tucket A low bed or platform made from planks used by some of the holy beings in India.

Tulku(s) A sage who has chosen to reincarnate, rather than accept *nirvana,* to be available to spiritual seekers.

Upanishads Literally, "to be close-by devotedly." One of the most important Hindu spiritual texts. The Upanishads, along with the Aranyakas and Brahmanas, are the principal commentaries on the *Vedas* and on Hindu scriptural ideas. The central teaching is that the Self is the *same* as *Brahman.*

upaya   A way or path. Any means or method used to achieve spiritual awareness.

vasana(s)   Self-limitation caused from memories (habits or conditioning) that can prevent enlightenment. Awareness of these memories can be used to progress.

Vedas   Literally, "wisdom." The ancient sacred writings of India which form the heart of Hindu scripture. The Vedas were composed beginning in 2000 B.C. The four Vedas (also called the Samhitas) are the Rig-Veda, the Sama-Veda, the Yajur-Veda, and the Atharva-Veda.

Vichara Atma   "Who am I?" A practice of self-inquiry, taught and practiced by Ramana Maharshi.

Visuddhimagga   A fifth-century work on *Theravadan Buddhist* doctrine. Translated into English by Bhikku Nanamoli. Visuddhimagga, the title, is also a phrase meaning "the Path of Purification."

yama(s)   One of the external disciplines: *ahimsa* (non-harming), *satya* (truthfulness), *asteya* (non-stealing), *brahmacharya* (chastity), and *aparigraha* (non-covetousness).

yoga(s)   Literally, to yoke or join. The way to or the union of the soul with the Ultimate Reality. Includes meditation, breath control, postures, right behavior, devotion, etc.

yuga   An age in Hindu chronology lasting 432,000 years. There are four yugas in each cycle of creation: *Satya* or Krita Yuga (Truth or Golden Age), with emphasis on meditation; Treta Yuga (Silver Age), sacrifices; Dvapara Yuga (Bronze Age), worship of deities; and the present Kali Yuga (Dark or Iron Age), chanting of Holy Names. The Kali age began in 3102 B.C. and is the fourth yuga of this cycle.

zazen   "Just sitting" method of meditation in Zen Buddhism.

zendo   In the Zen Buddhist tradition, a place used to practice *zazen*.

Resources

An extensive resources guide has been compiled to help you get started with practices that have been introduced in this book. The guide is too long to include here, but it is available online at www.RamDassTapes.org. It is a compendium of information about books, tapes, CDs, videos, and websites, relating not only to the teachers and teachings that have been mentioned, but to Hinduism and Hindu philosophy in general. Please visit the site and make use of the wealth of information it offers.

Here are a few of the more important resources directly related to the Gita.

Books

The Bhagavad Gita. Introduction and translation by Juan Mascaro, Penguin Group, 1962.

Bhagavad Gita. Translated by Swami Prabhavananda and Christopher Isherwood, Barnes & Noble Books, 1995.

The Bhagavad Gita: A New Translation. Stephen Mitchell, Three Rivers Press, 2002.

The Bhagavad Gita. Translation and introduction by Eliot Deutsch, Holt, Rinehart and Winston, 1968.

Jnaneshwari. Interpretation and commentary of the Bhagavad Gita by the thirteenth-century poet-saint Jnaneshwar, George Allen and Unwin Publishers.

Illuminations from the Bhagavad Gita. Kim and Chris Murray, Mandala Publishing Group, 1998.

Ethics of the Bhagavad Gita. Swami Sivananda. Why the Gita was taught on a battlefield and more, Divine Life Society, 1995.

The Gita Vision. Swami Chidananda. Pithy exposition on the first three chapters of the Bhagavad Gita, Divine Life Society.

The Song Celestial. Ramana Maharshi's selected verses from the Bhagavad Gita. Sri Niranjanananda Swami, 1951.

Spiritual Heritage of India. Swami Prabhavananda. Comprehensive history
   of India's philosophy and religions; discusses the Vedas, the Upanishads, the Gita, the six systems of Indian philosophy. Sri
   Ramakrishna Math.

Electronic

http://eawc.evansville.edu/inpage.htm. A wealth of information on the
   historical context of the Gita and the Gita's relation to Indian
   religious thought.
www.geocities.com/somsram. A valuable site on the Gita, with dis-
   courses, interpretation, and verses and chanting of slokas in
   audio.
www.onlinedarshan.com. Entire text can be read online: Ramayana,
   Vedas, Upanishads, Puranas, and the Bhagavad Gita. Also,
   Goswami Tulsidas's life story and teachings.

Organizations

International/American Gita Society. Offers free distribution of the Gita
   to hospitals, libraries, and other public entities; entire Gita for
   online reading; support and guidance in establishing Gita discussion groups; free correspondence courses. www.gita-
   society.com, or 511 Lowell Place, Fremont, CA 94536.

NOTE: CDs and cassette tape recordings of the "Yogas of the
Bhagavad Gita" lectures from which this book was drawn are
available from the Ram Dass Tape Library Foundation
(www.RamDassTapes.org).

Index

About the Author

Ram Dass has served on the faculty at Stanford and Harvard Universities. Since 1968, he has pursued a variety of spiritual practices, including guru kripa, devotional yoga, meditation, and Sufi and Jewish studies.

Also by Ram Dass

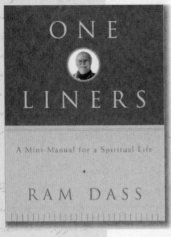

One-Liners offers more than two hundred observations and spiritual instructions on topics such as Love and Devotion, Suffering, Aging, Planes of Consciousness, Death and Dying, Service and Compassion, Psychedelics, Social Awareness, and Liberation.

One-Liners
978-1-4000-4623-2
$14.14 HARDCOVER (CANADA: $17.17)

Be Here Now is the timeless classic that tells the story of Ram Dass' own journey to India, his meeting guru Neem Karoli Baba, and his ultimate spiritual transformation.

Be Here Now
978-0-517-54305-4
$15.15 PAPER (CANADA: $20.20)